The Writers' Game

JIMMY CANNON. *The Sporting News*

RING LARDNER. *The Sporting News*

DAVID HALBERSTAM. *The Bettmann Archive*

HEYWOOD BROUN. *The Bettmann Archive*

RED SMITH. *The Sporting News*

RICHARD ORODENKER

The Writers' Game

Baseball Writing in America

TWAYNE PUBLISHERS
An Imprint of Simon & Schuster Macmillan
NEW YORK

PRENTICE HALL INTERNATIONAL
LONDON MEXICO CITY NEW DELHI SINGAPORE SYDNEY TORONTO

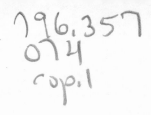

Twayne's United States Authors Series No. 663
Frank Day, General Editor

The Writers' Game: Baseball Writing in America
Richard Orodenker

Library of Congress Cataloging-in-Publication Data

Orodenker, Richard.
    The writers' game / Richard Orodenker.
        p. cm. — (Twayne's United States authors series ; 663)
    Includes bibliographical references and index.
    ISBN 0-8057-3998-X (cloth : alk. paper)
    1. American literature—History and criticism. 2. Baseball stories, American—
History and criticism. 3. Sports stories, American—History and criticism. 4. Baseball in
literature. I. Title. II. Series: Twayne's United States authors series ; TUSAS 663.
PS169.B36076 1996
810.9'355—dc20   95-4582
                                                                                         CIP

The paper used in this publication meets the minimum requirements of American
National Standard for Information Sciences—Permanence of Paper for Printed Library
Materials. ANSI Z39.48–1984. ∞

10 9 8 7 6 5 4 3 2 1 (hc)

Printed in the United States of America

For Robyn

Contents

Acknowledgments

Many thanks to Bill Deane, formerly of the National Baseball Library in Cooperstown, for tracking down some items for me. Thanks also to Bill Wood of Community College of Philadelphia for digging up the Charles Dryden sources on microfilm at the Free Library of Philadelphia, to Harold Rosenthal, Arnold Hano, and Ray Robinson for sharing their wealth of experiences, and to Jack Kavanagh for sending me his "Keepers of the Flame" file on American sportswriters. A tip of the Hatlo hat to Eric Drake for making me computer-literate in a hurry, to Frank Day, Mark Zadrozny, Cindy Buck, and Dawn Lawson for their wise editorial assistance, and to Mike Csensich of Peirce College for talking some of the baseball that went into this book. Thanks most of all to my wife, Robyn, without whose love and support this book would not have been possible.

Introduction

Thomas Boswell, speaking for the baby boom generation, writes, "I was a baseball boy, one of the last. I look at myself in the mirror now and see a dying breed. I grew up without a uniform. The streets and alleys of Capitol Hill were my diamonds and stadiums."

My own baseball experiences happened on the streets of Philadelphia in the early sixties, and my diamonds and stadia took the shape of brick walls, telephone wires, front stoops, garage doors, and cement driveways. I spent many afternoons throwing a small rubber ball (called a "pinky" because of its bubble-gum color) against the wall of my house and playing an imaginary game in which I faced real-life ballplayers who occupied the "Murderers' Row" of my mind. The space between two windows served as the infield *and* batter's box; the top of the wall, near an air conditioner, where birds nested the way pigeons once roosted in the steel supports of Connie Mack Stadium, was the outfield grass. I threw the ball to any one of a number of spots on the wall; if I failed to catch it, the ball would land for a double, triple, or Texas-league single. (In time I got to know every angle on the wall. Like Carl Furillo, the great Brooklyn right fielder, "I'd take that sight line and know just where [the ball] would go.") Balls thrown against the bottom of the house were ground balls back to the pitcher—or singles up the middle when they whizzed by me. If I hit the lip of the wall, the ball would carom high over my head and onto my neighbor's house: a home run.

Fifty years earlier, James T. Farrell recalled a variant game two boys could play "in the back yard with a ten-cent soft ball":

> They each represented a big-league team and batted according to that team's lineup, hitting right-handed or left-handed just as the real players in the lineup did. They played swift pitching and called balls and strikes. The home base was near the back fence so they didn't have to chase pitched balls that weren't batted at. The whole yard was plotted out and the game was played according to a complicated set of rules devised to make hits hard to get and to keep the score tight. Foul balls that went over the back fence or up on the greenhouses to the right were outs. Over the whole yard, there were only certain places where batted balls were scored as base hits. Over the back fence was a home run.

In a more idyllic America, before television and Nintendo—before unsafe streets and random violence—most American boys were outside playing baseball or one of its folk variations. As a boy, Stanley Coveleski, a great Cleveland right-hander in the teens and twenties, worked in the anthracite mines of western Pennsylvania for 72 hours a week and learned to pitch not by playing baseball but by throwing stones at tin cans in the evenings after work. "Whatever the gap between these games of truncated baseball and the real thing," wrote Harold Seymour, "boys bridged it on the wings of their imagination."

Baseball's literariness grew out of the zeitgeist that characterized mid-nineteenth-century America. The rise of baseball, not coincidentally, occurred during a period in American letters that F. O. Matthiessen called the American Renaissance, a time when writers came to believe "that there should be no split between art and the other functions of the community, that there should be an organic union between labor and culture." Baseball often defines the spirit of the age, and all baseball writing can be brought together by exploring certain recurrent themes and myths, which are themselves functions of literature.

That my own experiences mirror those of Boswell and Farrell and countless others demonstrates A. Bartlett Giamatti's theory that, "if baseball is narrative, it is like the others—a work of imagination whose deeper structures and patterns of repetition force a tale, oft-told, to fresh and hitherto-unforeseen meaning."

For Giamatti, the tale speaks of leaving home and returning home; Philip Roth saw it conversely for Alexander Portnoy: "Oh, how unlike my home it is to be in center field, where no one will appropriate unto himself anything that I say is *mine*!" For others, the baseball narrative means something different, perhaps the theme of fathers playing catch with their sons (and daughters). "Baseball is fathers and sons playing catch," wrote Donald Hall, "lazy and murderous, wild and controlled, the profound archaic song of birth, growth, age, and death." "You play baseball with love," wrote Roger Kahn, "and you play baseball to win and you play baseball with terror, but always against that backdrop, fathers and sons." In his memoir about his birth as a fan, Roger Angell noted "how often its trail circled back to my father." His story and his father's "are so different yet feel intertwined and continuous." Roy Blount, Jr., parodies this familial notion in "Baseball in My Blood" when he states that "people assume of every American male that (a) what is wrong with him and (b) why he cares so much about baseball is that his father played catch with him and then made him figure out everything else himself." When her father died, wrote Doris Kearns Goodwin, "suddenly my feelings for baseball seemed an aspect of my departing youth, along with my childhood freckles and my favorite childhood haunts." Charles Krauthammer dismisses the sentiment entirely: "Am I the only child of immigrants who did not commune with his father through box scores? My father could not tell a fungo bat from a polo mallet. I was crazy for baseball. We got along splendidly."

The subject of this book is that body of baseball narratives that have appeared outside the realm of fiction—in journalism, nonfiction books, and, most significantly, essays. Why the essay and not fiction? Two reasons, foremost, come to mind. First, baseball has always been about real events, real places, real people, and real life. As a result, nonfiction— from newspapers at the turn of the century to the satyric musings of Jim Bouton in *Ball Four* (1970)—has been the best place to find the most representative baseball writings.

Second, as Jerry Klinkowitz points out in his postmodern anthology *Writing Baseball* (1991), baseball prose is largely self-referential; the best baseball writers are those who "write baseball" rather than "about baseball," so that "both journalists and fictionists have shared an appreciation for baseball as a thing in itself." The great American game has yet to produce a great American novel—"the baseball novel," Roger Kahn quotes one editor as saying, "Thomas Wolfe would have written if Thomas Wolfe had written a baseball novel." "No contemporary novelist," adds Roger Angell, "would dare a supporting cast of characters with Dickensian names like those that have stuck with me ever since I deciphered my first box scores and began peopling the lively landscape of baseball in my mind."

Instead, baseball novelists have turned to mythology, fantasy, satire, magical realism, or nonsense, while realists have used baseball to express more universal themes ("The clubhouse is a place of mortal ache and higher woe, life is short, dismissal imminent, the rivalries brutal, and we are all anxiety," wrote Mark Harris about his novel *The Southpaw* [1953]). Invariably, the baseball novelist borrows material from the lives of real baseball people (Roy Hobbs wields a bat called "Wonderboy" in Bernard Malamud's *The Natural* [1952]; Joe Jackson used a 48-ouncer he named "Black Betsy"; and when Hobbs is shot by an obssessed female fan, Malamud recreates the Eddie Waitkus incident of 1947), while insisting upon verisimilitude in describing the action on the field. I do not mean to discredit the place of fiction in a study of baseball literature. Ring Lardner's journalism led him to his baseball short stories, and the Nebraska Crane passages in Thomas Wolfe's *You Can't Go Home Again* (1940) (the title an oft-used pun) has influenced many a writer who turned to baseball "with a feeling of sadness and wonder in his heart."

The nonfiction field is a vast and uneven one, to be sure. To narrow that field, each piece I have chosen for this study exerts, in William Zinsser's words, "a strong hold over us because it not only summons back the past but makes us think about the present." And all these pieces are by "writers who come bearing information, who explain what they know clearly, and who make an arrangement of it that raises their craft to an art."

The information the baseball writer comes bearing, writes David Sanders, can "be summoned up by collector's cards, table games, statistics, halls of fame, and burnished memories." Memory is baseball's muse, but statistics are its prosody. Thomas McGuane considers the baseball card as good a model of sports writing as anything else. Baseball cards and their grown-up counterparts—entries in the "Big Mac"—bespeak the game's intrinsic numerology, its *Gematriya*; but they also provide important facts. Writes Luke Salisbury, author of a "serious" book of baseball trivia, "My love of the written baseball word did not come from a book or a newspaper, but Joe Reichler's 1957 Baseball Records."

Of some 60,000 box scores that had been compiled by 1950, the *New York Times*'s Arthur Daley figured there were but a few "striking instances the box score never did tell the full story." Among only ten such instances he could remember and write about—most of them legendary—were Johnny Vander Meer's two back-to-back no-hitters; old Grover Cleveland Alexander's strikeout of "Poosh 'em Up" Tony Lazzeri; and Babe Ruth's "called-shot" home run—all of them the kind of game, in novelist T. C. Boyle's phrase, that "goes on forever."

That is reason enough to believe that numbers—despite the current prominence of statistically driven writers in the genre, especially those scholars belonging to SABR (Society for American Baseball Research)—do not tell the whole story. Baseball may be the one sport you do not have to know all that well to write well about. "After the Civil War," writes Tristram P. Coffin in his excellent study of baseball in folklore and fiction, "America needed a national game, as well as national heroes, legends, and literature, to shore up its pride, soothe its self-consciousness, and explain its attitudes to established European and Asian cultures," a need that explains why more than a century later Joe DiMaggio, in Robert Creamer's words, took "on something of the aura of George Washington in Grant Wood's painting *Parson Weems' Fable*," and why writers from Ring Lardner to Jim Bouton have lampooned the game. Literature, to be literature at all, needs its mythmakers, although baseball prose is certainly well served by writers, like David Halberstam, who understand that it "is not so much that Joe DiMaggio has gone away, and that America is thereby diminished; it is more that in the end he was a great center fielder and a great hitter, which is at once far more than enough, and yet a great deal less than myth." Nonetheless, if writers hope to set the statistical record straight, or to interpret statistics in a new light, they have to contend with lore. As the well-traveled pitching ace Bobo Newsom once said, while arguing about the number of wins he may or may not have had one season, "Who you gonna believe, the record books or the guy that done it?"

Without dismissing seminal texts, from the early baseball guides and dime novels to the "as told to" books, ghostwritten accounts, and histories and oral histories, I am more inclined to discuss the familiar essay, the in-depth personal profile, and the memoir or autobiography whose description of baseball strikes us, as Roger Kahn observes, in a way that "we remember certain ballgames, certain players, certain plays on vanished fields." Every baseball writer is dependent upon the whole of baseball literature. Baseball has its own version of the "great conversation" in which (with apologies to Robert M. Hutchins), "one book naturally leads to another book both forward and backward in the time-sequence [and] each book also leads to many others that deal with the same subject or have some affinity in style and treatment."

This point suggests another reason the essay is more suited to baseball's literary landscape. As John Gross's brief description of the essay makes clear, "Essays come in all shapes and sizes. There are essays on Human Understanding, and essays on What I Did in the Holidays; essays on Truth, and essays on potato crisps . . . ; essays that start out as book reviews, and essays that end up as sermons. Even more than most literary forms, the essay defies strict definition. It can shade into character sketch, the travel sketch, the memoir, the *jeu d'esprit*." True, contemporary baseball journalism, with its emphasis on idle chitchat and "instant comment," has provided "less time and scope for the essay proper." This was not the case, however, for baseball writers in the first half of the century, and it is also not true of essayists influenced by the *New Yorker* writers of the thirties and forties—Joseph Mitchell, James Thurber, Dorothy Parker, E. B. White, John Hersey, and, most important, A. J. Liebling, who Americanized Pierce Egan but very likely was indebted to W. O. McGeehan.

Liebling caught "the musical sigh" of a boxer's vernacular and brought it up a notch without pandering to elites or sounding like a hack: "Sometimes when I boxing with a fellow that hit me right on the button, and I know he ain't got no right to hit me on the button, and I boxing with him again and he hit me on the button again, then I going to quit." Of course, the baseball enthusiast coming to the literature for something other than its style sometimes does prefer the hack. The goal of the essayist is to make the difficult accessible or the ordinary extraordinary; by that standard, baseball has produced essays worthy of consideration alongside the best American essays.

While we can read equally good essays about any subject, including other sports (John McPhee's stylistic account of the Arthur Ashe–Clark Graebner tennis match at Forest Hills, Norman Mailer's meta-analysis of the Ali-Frazier fight), few events besides baseball can be as satisfyingly and comprehensively read about as they are watched or experienced. Baseball, wrote Charles Einstein in the preface to his *Fireside Book of Baseball* (1956), "is a game of infinite range," a sport not "limited in any total sense by boundary lines."

The baseball essayist can provide the simple pleasures of the written word by demonstrating, according to Halberstam, "an unerring instinct for exactly what the fans want . . . to know each day," while finding ways, as Donald Hall notes, to "take the popular and find the universal in it, take the boys' game and find in it ambition and failure, success and aging." It was just such a moment in "Box Scores," when Roger Angell elicits "from a box score the same joy, the same hallucinatory reality, that prickles the scalp of a musician when he glances at a page of his score of *Don Giovanni* and actually hears bassos and sopranos, woodwinds and violins," that led me to similar works of baseball prose.

Finally, I think that baseball may prove to be a twentieth-century phenomenon only. What has changed baseball more than labor-management strife, television, World Series night games, expansion, franchise shifts, or artificial turf (all of which have been subjects of baseball literature) is the modern mind's restless capacity for constant change and variety. As C. S. Lewis's old devil Screwtape said, "Children, until we have taught them better, will be perfectly happy with a seasonal round of games in which conkers succeed hopscotch as regularly as autumn follows summer. Only by our incessant efforts is the demand for infinite, or unrhythmical, change kept up." American children also once experienced happiness through the baseball seasons.

What is missing from baseball more and more these days—as it is missing from American culture in general—is a sense of tradition, and that is precisely what makes writing about baseball so unlike writing about any other sport. "You have to fill out the game you're watching with your own thoughts and memories," writes Wilfrid Sheed, "and place it in the rich context of a season and a tradition, in order to appreciate just how much you can do with a stick and a ball." As Stephen Jay Gould, a "card-carrying liberal," added: "Most fans are deeply conservative in this jewel-like world where legacy is so precious . . . and where you do die when age drops you from the realm of true and appropriate laissez-faire."

But were the game to disappear, it might still rise again soon from the dust (or grass), for every time a child picks up a stick and a ball he is starting all over again "this rage for play," as Longfellow described the game. In lamenting the demise of the big bands, Gene Lees asks a question apropos of baseball: "Why? Why does this sound haunt our culture?" It is because the crack of the bat, like the strains of swing music, still manages to create "a general excitement and . . . the sense of an event."

CHAPTER 1

The Great Conversation

In *Spring Training* (1989), his in-depth look at one team's experiences during baseball's short preseason, William Zinsser considers whether a rookie pitcher will make the team: "I told the man next to me that the young pitcher reminded me of Warren Spahn. The man said he thought he looked like Preacher Roe. His wife said the kid was a ringer for Harvey Haddix. An old codger mentioned Lefty Grove. A young codger mentioned Vida Blue. We were typical springtime fools, seeing what we wanted to see." A small publication called *Baseball: Our Way* advertised for contributors this way: "We're interested in seeing any type, form or variety of baseball talk. Picture, if you will, a nation-wide network of sports buffs spouting off, discussing, arguing, concurring, and generally dispensing information unique to each contributor." When he first began writing about baseball, Roger Angell was content to sit in the stands and view the happenings from there; eventually he "summoned up the nerve to talk to some ballplayers face-to-face." "The baseball reporter," Stanley Woodward once wrote, "is writing for an informed readership which has a morbid desire to catch him in the wrong. If he makes a mistake he and his boss will get a dozen letters the next day telling about it." Baseball has always liked the sound of its own voice.

Talk forms all about the field, from the bench jockey to the bleacher bug, who, Ring Lardner wrote, will "talk unhesitantly, as if he had all the facts and never stammer or back up when his assertions are questioned." "Baseball is a game of talk and meetings," writes Roger Kahn. "Managers meet with teams. Catchers meet with pitchers. Pitchers meet with coaches. And then, completing the cycle, the manager meets with the team." Not all of it is "talk" in the narrowest sense of the word, for baseball has its own sign language in the form of signals and unwritten rules (taking a runner out at second, brushing a batter back), as once it had a "gentleman's agreement" and "collusion."

Baseball talk reaches beyond the field to the broadcast booth, where Red Barber introduced "the catbird seat" and "the pea patch," and to the press box, where, Tom Clark noted, Damon Runyon once worked into his columns "items snatched from the running conversations of [Bozeman] Bulger, [Irvin S.] Cobb, and other talkative scribes." Thomas Boswell refers to baseball as "this garrulous game," filled like a newspaper not just with exploits of what happens on the field but with columns of gossip, editorials, opinions, and stories about almost anything. Ballplayers are "tale tellers who have polished their malarky and winnowed their wisdom for years."

Writers (and fans) of any generation may "talk baseball" of any other era with a degree of familiarity. They devise "all-time lists" and speak with authority about Christy Mathewson's three shutouts for John McGraw's New York Giants in the 1905 World Series as though they had been there themselves. And they may further ponder Connie Mack's reluctance to pitch even once in the series the great, though usually inebriated, Rube Waddell for the Athletics. Their authority is prompted by statistics, which, as Bill James observes, may also "have acquired the powers of language." Statistics and the ritual of the hot-stove league (literally, baseball talk during the cold winter months) color baseball's great conversation. Notes Lee Allen, "No one knows when baseball followers first began to gather around the hot stove of a barber shop or country store. Obviously there has been talk about baseball as long as the game has existed."

The hot-stove league turns up in speculative and argumentative essays in the current pages of the *Baseball Research Journal* ("Who Would Be the Highest-Paid Baseball Player?" or, "Another Look at Hypothetical Cy Young Award Winners") much as it did a century ago in the off-season baseball columns of sportswriters and half a century ago in the essays of writers like Tom Meany: "Baseball Needs Three Big Leagues to Survive," "Where Are Baseball's .300 Hitters?" and "Why So Many Home Runs?"

Hot-stovers argue over fine points of history. The biographer Jack Kavanaugh complains that "Shirley Povich is particularly guilty of negligent research. His book *The Washington Senators* has Bill Donovan, not Joe Cantillion, as the manager who brought Johnson to the Senators. His account is a re-hash of all the bad guesses, elaborations, etc. about Johnson's discovery as a phenom." "Don't Believe Everything You Read," Warren Brown, the editor of the *Chicago Herald and Examiner*, titled one 1954 essay, reminding us that Tinker-to-Evers-to-Chance "accounted for just 54 double plays in the four seasons when they caused Franklin P. Adams to start twanging his lyre."

In 1951 a *New York Times* writer dug into the archives to find a 1908 article on the famous Merkle "boner." " 'Blunder Costs Giants Victory' wrote the headline hunter on a remarkably complete account. Correct. And the reporter, after describing the play on the field, concludes: 'And then begins the argument which will keep us in talk for the rest of the season.' Correct again, except as to the 'season.' The forty-third since the 'blunder' was made is rolling on and the 'argument' is still going on." The numerous quotation marks are indicative of the hot-stove league, baseball's ritual sounding-off, its annual venting of the spleen—it is the art of being vindicated, or eating crow.

Three Pitches

If the essay form gives baseball prose its best structure, the great conversation—the whole of baseball talk, or "talking baseball"—lends it its style. In her review of George Plimpton's *Out of My League* (1961), Marianne Moore singled out three main qualities of baseball prose: vernacular, simile, and verisimilitude. Since verisimilitude goes without saying (Professor—turned pitcher incognito—Vernon Simpson in the novel and film *It Happens Every Spring* [1949] discovers a tonic that makes wood repel a baseball, but he still must get three strikes to strike a batter out), we can add anecdote to the list.

All three are essential ingredients of good writing in general, but they take on greater significance in any analysis of baseball writing. A writer uses metaphor the way a ballplayer uses cant (which, in many cases, the writer has been responsible for recording in the first place). Casey Stengel's "Mister, that boy couldn't hit the ground if he fell out of an airplane" or Satchel Paige's take on Cool Papa Bell ("That man was so fast he could turn out the light and jump in bed before the room got dark") are not far removed from this description of Lefty Grove: "He could throw a lamb chop past a wolf," a line so good it has been attributed to two sportswriters, Westbrook Pegler and "Bugs" Baer. The statelier metaphors of a Grantland Rice seem almost comical today ("Trailing by three runs at the end of the seventh inning of the world's series game, with Art Nehf in supreme command of their waning destinies [the Yankees] came through shadows as black as the heart of Stygia to find for the first time the radiant sunlight of a championship"), but as Donald Hall writes, "with a subject ostensibly light" like baseball, "writers feel free to play, to vary tone, to lose themselves happily to metaphor, to laugh, and even to lament." Metaphor reminds us that baseball, after all, is still only a game, still fun.

The use of metaphor often begins in a baseball writer's futile (and often pretentious) search for the noun or phrase that best completes the sentence "Baseball is. . . ." Marvin Cohen's metaphysical *Baseball the Beautiful* (1974) embraces them all. "Baseball is a thing of dignity," "Baseball is eminently *fair*," "Baseball is our great national myth," "Baseball is bigger than us all," "Baseball is a game of inches," "Baseball is monumental," "Baseball is an open world," and so forth. "Baseball is a country all to itself," writes Donald Hall. Among other qualities, writes Bruce Catton, "baseball is plebeian, down-to-earth, and robustious." "Baseball, in short," Merritt Clifton offers, "is a fertility rite." Or it is, in the radio announcer Ernie Harwell's view, "cigar smoke, hot-roasted peanuts, *The Sporting News*," and 27 other things.

Baseball is like a poker game, like church, like life, like a novel, like a ballet. It is "a game," thinks Garrison Keillor, "but it's more than a game, baseball is people dammit, and if you are around people you can't help but get involved in their lives and care about them." Baseball, W. P. Kinsella writes in *Shoeless Joe* (1982), "is stable and permanent, steady as a grandfather dozing in a wicker chair on a veranda." Baseball is "like life itself," says the Hall of Famer Bob Feller, in that "every day is a new opportunity"—or, no, it is not like life, a character in Eric Rolfe Greenberg's novel *The Celebrant* (1983) observes, because it "is all clean lines and clear decisions. . . . Oh, for a life like that."

For Michael Oriard, baseball is a text. "One has only to compare football and baseball to their closest equivalents in European sport, soccer and cricket, to recognize that what is most distinctive about the American games—in structure, organization, and presentation—contributes to a heightened quality of narrative."

> Fanaticism? No. Writing is exciting
> and baseball is like writing. You can never tell with either
> how it will go
> or what you will do,

a Marianne Moore poem begins, while Max Apple thinks that "pitching really is like writing. How your arm feels. Change that to imagination and you have writing." Without metaphor, baseball would be a potter's field.

Other writers, like Zinsser, do not "have any patience with the idea of baseball as metaphor. Baseball is baseball. . . . A metaphor reminds you of something else." Wilfrid Sheed told a television interviewer, "Baseball doesn't remind me of anything else. It is not representational art." For George Will, metaphors describe mostly "silly and sentimental things." Stephen Jay Gould adds, "The silliest and most tendentious of baseball writing tries to wrest profundity from the spectacle of grown men hitting a ball with a stick by suggesting linkages between the sport and deep issues of morality, parenthood, history, lost innocence, gentleness, and so on *ad infinitum*." The title of Thomas Boswell's first book is *How Life Imitates the World Series* (1982), not the other way around.

Writers who feel that baseball is its own best complement do not necessarily eschew metaphor in other circumstances. Gould calls the *Baseball Encyclopedia* "that *vade mecum* for all serious fans," and Will reminds us that "getting a fastball past [Hank] Aaron was . . . like sneaking the sun past a rooster." Too often though, as Donald Hall notes, such writing can be "terrible by being tired, ordinary, trite, and false. Old clichés revisited acquire charm, but in day to day reading they deaden the mind." The use of the comic simile in sports writing can be traced back to the innovative Chicago school (see chapter 4) at the end of the nineteenth century, but despite the decrease in flowery and figurative language over the decades, metaphor remains a strong part of baseball prose. Since metaphor (along with aphorism, witticism, truism, and so on) is essential to the player vernacular, it appears likely to stick around, for better or worse.

Some writers open up the possibilities of language gleaned from baseball talk. Zinsser satirized Aesculapian jargon (and baseball nicknames) in a 1966 essay for the *Saturday Evening Post* called "Ben Casey at the Bat," in which an orthopedic surgeon takes the helm of a major league ball club. "You give me a pain in my posterior lalapalooza," he says, and "I'll go with Bone Chips at first base . . . and at second I'll stick with Floating Cartilage. . . . At third I'd like to stay with Slipped Disc, if he's ready." Other writers stay close to the great conversation even when it seems far removed from the fields of play. In *Blue Highways: A Journey into America* (1982), William Least Heat Moon comes upon baseball in the backwater town of Grand Forks, North Dakota. In a bar, men are watching a ball game on television, which had "cast a cool light like a phosphorescent fungus." An older man, who misses "the old clichés," cannot understand the new jabber of sports announcers, or the fact that the "ninety-three point four miles per hour" recorded by a radar gun has come to supplant "smoke, hummer, and the high hard one." Describing the decline of baseball talk on the airwaves, the man calls it "nothing but beans and hot air."

Anecdotes, on and off the field, on the other hand, fuel the story of baseball and help give it continuity and closure. "I have found through the years," the comedic duo Bob and Ray used to say, "that baseball anecdotes go down through the years. If it happened to Abner Doubleday in 1890, it's sure gonna happen to Walt Dropo in 1955." Baseball is a forward-looking game *and* a traditional one. George Will, for example, frequently retells familiar anecdotes, some of which help explain baseball tradition: "Eight decades ago (or so the story is) an extremely fat man, finding his seat at the park confining, heaved himself to his feet to stretch. It was the seventh inning. Because the 300-pound fellow was the President of the United States, everyone around him stood up respectfully. William Howard Taft thereby started a useful tradition, which is more than can be said for many presidents." As Joseph Epstein notes, in professions (like baseball) "where temperament is given relatively free rein . . . where egoism runs rampant and adulation is handed out in triple scoops, the incidence of memorable anecdote is especially high." *Anecdote* derives from a Greek term meaning "unpublished." Though numerous baseball anecdotes have come to be published or standardized in one way or another, in their purest form they demonstrate baseball's most folklorish quality, since so many stories were originally passed down by word of mouth (before sportswriters recorded them). It is commonly accepted, for instance, that the Waner brothers, Paul and Lloyd, got their nicknames "Big Poison" and "Little Poison" from a corruption of the word *person* when, as Lee Allen told it, "a baseball writer overheard an Ebbets Field fan continually say, in Brooklynese, as the Waners came to bat, 'Here comes that big poison' or 'Here comes that little poison.'" That particular anecdote aptly provides occasion for baseball metaphor and vernacular as well. Like baseball itself, anecdotes may be apocryphal.

Even in their published versions, anecdotes get retold again and again, often embellished or renewed, whether or not they happen to be true. As with the Doubleday myth, lore is persistent. Thus, there are many tellings of the story of the sparrow under Casey Stengel's hat. John Lardner, the son of Ring Lardner, insists that the wonderful Babe Herman "never tripled into a triple play, but once doubled into a double play, which is the next best thing." The Black Sox legend has it that Joe Jackson answered the boy who asked him, "Say it ain't true." The facts claim that Jackson kept stone-silent. One is reminded of the classic line from the director John Ford's *The Man Who Shot Liberty Valance*: "When the legend becomes fact, print the legend."

In the era of the sound bite, baseball vernacular—the native tongue of what Donald Hall calls "the country of baseball"—has become so familiar (and predictable) that sportswriters now print "quotes of the week" in spite of the fact that, as Robert Lipsyte observes, "baseball argot changes as soon as it becomes public knowledge." Paul Dickson's book of baseball quotations expands a nomenclature that began with "Stengelese" to include "Deanisms," "Yogisms," "Gomez Zingers," "Reggiespeak," "Veecksations," and "Quisinberries."

Baseball vernacular arose out of baseball's Americanization, which was not a pastoral process but an urban one—the game began in the streets and towns, mostly in and about New York—and not strictly an American one either: the game evolved from British rounders and cricket. Despite its beginnings as an amateur gentleman's game, baseball soon gave way simultaneously to professionalism and proletarianism (and eventually rowdyism). "The language of the street is always strong," Emerson wrote in 1840. "I confess to some pleasure from the stinging rhetoric of a rattling oath in the mouths of truckmen and teamsters." Though he did not know it at the time, Emerson was talking about baseball. The vernacular allows Ring Lardner's Jack Keefe in *You Know Me Al* (1916), as his biographer Donald Elder saw it, to become "characterized primarily by his language (rather than his feats)—vain and boastful of his athletic prowess . . . a champion liar and flourisher . . . [yet] curiously sympathetic and not unlikable." Other types of vernacular become absorbed into the stronger baseball idiom, as when Catfish Hunter used to say upon a loss, "The sun don't shine on the same dog's ass all the time."

The vernacular produces baseball's many oral histories and "as told to" books and essays, such as the Chicago sportswriter John P. Carmichael's long-running series "My Biggest Day in Baseball." The contemporary baseball oral history was begun by Lawrence Ritter, who had the foresight, perseverance, and good fortune to track down aged ballplayers, most of them stars—Rube Marquard, Fred Snodgrass, Harry Hooper, and 19 others—who had played at the turn of the century. *The Glory of Their Times* (1966), which may have had a model in William Riordan's classic *Plunkett of Tammany Hall* (1905) ("I seen my opportunities and I took 'em!"), remains for readers like Louis D. Rubin, Jr., "simply the greatest baseball book ever written—the distilled essence of the game." Ritter's subjects talked generously "not only about what it was like to be a baseball player in the early days, but also about what it was like just to be alive then; about how they got started, and about how they felt when, at the age of thirty-five or so, they found they were too old to continue playing; about what their contemporaries were like as ballplayers, and what they were like as human beings—all with a sense of drama and urgency that could not have been surpassed had it been about this morning's headlines." Occasionally the vernacular itself, as Dickson notes, comes "close to being the game itself." "Goad[ing] the Dodgers to a pennant" in 1934 was Bill Terry's quip, "Is Brooklyn still in the league?" The Cardinal bench jockeys never let Schoolboy Rowe forget his casual radio remark to his wife, "How'm I doin', Edna?" during the 1934 World Series. And the pitcher Billy Loes defined the 1962 Mets when he said, "The Mets is a very good thing. They give everybody a job. Just like the WPA." Marianne Moore's famous line, "When a thing has been said so well that it could not be said better, why paraphrase it," seems to apply to much of baseball writing.

Good writers choose their metaphors and anecdotes wisely, of course. Baseball writers seem able to accelerate them, along with vernacular, through the body of their narratives. The great conversation comprises many different voices and points of view, and the baseball essay seeks out language that best suits the moment.

CHAPTER 2

Matties and Rubes

Baseball writers have used the style derived from the great conversation in a number of ways. We might call one group of stylists the "Matties," after Christy Mathewson ("the Christian Gentleman"), the great New York Giants' pitcher noted for his class and refinement—"all bone and muscle and princely poise," as the historian Lloyd Lewis described him in a 1943 *Chicago Daily News* article—the sort of pitcher who would study a batter "as a scientist contemplates a beetle." Matties are graceful, polished writers, baseball's elegant phrasemakers. John Kieran, who wrote for the *New York Herald Tribune* and later the *New York Times*, was one of the finest columnists in the Matty tradition. The lead of one of his 1923 pieces shows the limits to which the style could reach, as well as the (usually understated) humor that often accompanied it: "By dog sled, portage, and courier service, confidential messages have been received here at Yankee headquarters that Nicodemus Culopp, whose right-handed services have just been purchased by the Ruppert Rifles, is a curly wolf of the wild outdoors, a hole-in-one golfer, a socking soccerite, a dashing sprinter, a drawing card at poker, and a man worth a basketful of ordinary basketballers. Now, if he can only pitch a little bit, everything will be all right."

James Crusinberry, one of the stalwart sportswriters of the early part of the century, covered the famous nine-inning no-hit duel of 2 May 1917 between Fred Toney and Jim Vaughn in characteristic Matty fashion by relying on several quaint alliterations and hushed tones to catch the mood of the game: "Toney walked two batsmen, but those two were the only men to reach first base. He was given perfect support by his mates, not a bobble being made behind him. The duel was so desperate

9

that when the ninth inning was over and the honors were even, the crowd cheered both men."

Grantland Rice came to dominate the style. "Were he writing today," writes his biographer Charles Fountain, "his florid style and unfailingly upbeat assessment of all that he witnessed would doom him to deserved obscurity at some weekly newspaper buried deep in the bowels of the heartland." Like most popular writing, Rice's style, which he had patented early, was formulaic. Still, his signature "Four Horsemen" story contributed something to American literature. Few writers could deliver a lead with his flair for drama and color. In 1924, the day the Washington Senators behind Walter Johnson became world champions for the first and last time, Rice began: "Destiny, waiting for the final curtain, stepped from the wings to-day and handed the king his crown. In the most dramatic of baseball's sixty years of history the wall-eyed goddess known as Fate, after waiting eighteen years, led Walter Johnson to the pot of shining gold that waits at the rainbow's end."

Rice's purely individual style was soon widely imitated by epigones who, wrote Stanley Walker, composed "maudlin balderdash, an esoteric jargon which did not even have the authentic ring of American slang." An unsigned *New York Times* article describes Mathewson himself during a 1905 World Series game: "He bestrode the field like a Colossus, and the Athletics peeped about the diamond like pigmies who struggled gallantly for their lives, but in vain." The Matties would gradually pave the way for what Donald Hall calls "the High Belletristic Tradition" of John Updike, Roger Angell, and literary journalists like Gay Talese and W. C. Heinz.

Another type of stylist might be called a "Rube," after Rube Waddell, the Athletics' bizarre left-handed genius, Matty's contemporary and arguably his equal on the mound (he struck out 349 batters in 1904), but his antithesis in character and demeanor. A farmer's son, he hailed, appropriately enough, from Punxsutawney, Pennsylvania, the town that invented Groundhog Day. What distinguishes him are the many anecdotes that proliferated about him and his odd behavior (wrestling alligators in the off-season, turning cartwheels on the mound). Like the legendary Mose, the Bowery B'hoy of American folklore, Rube was known to chase fire engines whenever he heard them, even jumping off the bench during a game to do so. The players disliked him, and he gave his manager, Connie Mack, fits; but the fans adored him. The Rubes rarely share Waddell's flippancy or his lack of professionalism but rather an attraction to colorful stories that, "like their progenitor,"

Donald Honig writes, "had a character uniquely their own, a zany charm, an impetuousness, a quality foreshadowing self-destruction."

Arthur "Bugs" Baer wrote in a Rube style for the Hearst syndicate for more than five decades. In a story about the day in 1912 when the Detroit Tigers, protesting Ty Cobb's suspension, were forced to field a pickup team against the Philadelphia Athletics (to whom they lost 24–2), Baer assumes the voice of one of the men who rode the bench for twenty-five "smackers" and recounts the travails of one player in a way that combines fact and fiction in absurdist fashion: "The fellow who got the toughest break was the semipro picked to play Ty Cobb's spot in center. His moniker was too wide for the printers and it came out in the Sunday papers this way, 'L'n'h's'.' Today nobody knows whether his name was Loopenhouser or Lagenhassinger and I bet his wife still calls him a liar when he says he once played on the Detroits."

The Rubes were the first true baseball essayists and aphorists. They understood that the essence of baseball writing is talk and that what happens off the field sometimes matters as much as what happens on it. As W. O. McGeehan wrote, "Baseball is a circus, and as is the case with many a circus, the clowns and the side shows frequently are more interesting than the big stuff in the main tent." Most of the Rubes were humorists as well as sportswriters.

"Aw Nuts" and "Gee Whiz"

The differences between Matties and Rubes later gave way to the now-familiar "aw nuts" and "gee whiz" schools of sportswriting. However, those later, and not always clear, distinctions were ones of tone rather than style. Marianne Moore, for instance, was a Matty, but she had a great fondness for Rubes.

The "gee whiz" writers (who might include in their ranks a Rube like Damon Runyon) were generally optimists, mythmakers, and sentimentalists. The "aw nuts" writers (Ring Lardner in particular) were mostly skeptics, cynics, and curmudgeons. McGeehan, thought by some to be the father of the "aw nuts" group, could also be a sentimental writer— not because he wrote like one but because he preferred, as did most of the "aw nuts" writers, pure, even raw, unadorned sport. On "The Passing of Matty" (1925) he said, "There is nothing that makes me angrier than the perpetuation of the legend that he was a young man of the Sanford and Merton type, and in fact a sort of prig. He was the opposite of that." But McGeehan also believed that "if baseball will hold to the ideals and examples of Christy Mathewson, gentleman, sportsman, and soldier, our national game will keep the younger generation clean and courageous and the future of the nation secure." "Aw nuts" writers welcomed few changes. Even the possibility of television in 1925 worried McGeehan. Gate receipts would drop, he thought, and Babe Ruth "would be forced to depend entirely upon literature for his livelihood, and literary work at best is a precarious existence."

Poor play, not to mention the Black Sox scandal, turned the foremost "dopester" of his day, Hugh Fullerton, a classic Matty, into a skeptic overnight. In the World Series of 1912, in which Fred Snodgrass authored the famous "muffed ball," Fullerton relates what happened on Tris Speaker's easy pop foul toward first a few batters later: "Anyone could have caught it. I could have jumped out of the press box and caught it behind my back—but Merkle quit. Yes, Merkle quit cold. He didn't start for the ball. He seemed to be suffering from financial paralysis. Perhaps he was calculating the difference between the winner's and loser's end."

The Rubes, whether "aw nuts" or "gee whiz," would influence the new breed of reporters like Dick Young and Jimmy Cannon, iconoclastic "new journalists" like Jimmy Breslin, and the irreverent group of writers called "chipmunks," all of whom came to prominence after World War II. In "Bring Back the Real Mets!" (1969), Leonard Shecter, one of the early chipmunk journalists (the origin of the term is unknown but it seems to have something to do with the way these writers nibbled away at the edges of a story and the quality of incessant funny animal-like chatter that went into their writing and repartee), recalls the portent-filled first game the New York Mets played in the Polo Grounds in 1962:

> Brian Sullivan of the Metropolitan Opera and the St. Camillus Band rendered "The Star-Spangled Banner," but not together. And when the lineup was announced on the P.A. it was the wrong one, and then the Mets lost the game when Jim Marshall came off first base to take a throw he just couldn't wait to reach him and Richie Ashburn and Gus Bell let a ball drop between them in the outfield. It was also discovered after the game that Casey Stengel's undershorts were still emblazoned with the emblem of the New York Yankees.

Matties and Rubes, it should be noted, are examples of writing *excellence*. Within their ranks, however, are writers who possess, as Joseph Epstein said of Theodore Dreiser, "an aluminum ear (one down from tin), an unfailing penchant for the purple, an oafish wit, and the literary tact and lightness of touch of a rhinoceros," but like Dreiser's novels, their baseball prose may "tell more in the way of elemental truth about American life and character, and tell it in a consistently persuasive and powerful manner." Writers like Bob Considine and Roscoe McGowan fit this description. Considine, writing in *Cosmopolitan* on the subject of pinch hitters, shows less concern for style than for a greater appreciation of the game: "Whatever his background, the pinch hitter is blood-brother to every other man who stepped up to the plate. For in his soul seethe the passions and torments of a full game, and he prays feverishly to spend all these accumulated emotions in his one-split second on stage." Arthur Daley won a much-resented Pulitzer Prize in 1956 for turning the Matty style into awkwardness and affability. In relating the story of the day Connie Mack traveled to Punxsutawney to sign Rube Waddell, Daley wrote: "Just before the train rumbled in a half dozen men walked briskly down the platform. 'Good gracious,' exclaimed Connie. 'What now?' They formed a semi-circle around Mack and the spokesman stepped forth. He shook Connie's hand fervently and thanked him for taking Rube out of town."

By the late forties, most notably under Stanley Woodward's tutelage at the *New York Herald Tribune*, sportswriting style had taken a turn away from opinion and essay toward greater objectivity and factual reporting, influencing Matties and Rubes alike. In the forties, both styles reached their apotheoses in the newspaper columns of Red Smith and Jimmy Cannon, while essayists like Heinz and John Lardner turned to feature writing.

Woodward himself had written the definitive news beat baseball story in 1947 when he uncovered, at no small risk to his paper's credibility, evidence that several St. Louis Cardinal players were planning to strike rather than take the field against Jackie Robinson and the Brooklyn Dodgers. Both the story and the follow-up article the next day contain elements of the familiar essays and brash editorials of Westbrook Pegler and W. O. McGeehan: "The blast of publicity which followed the *New York Herald Tribune*'s revelation . . . probably will serve to quash further strolls down Tobacco Road. In other words, it can now be honestly doubted that the boys from the Hookworm Belt will have the nerve to foist their quaint sectional folklore on the rest of the country."

Though Red Smith was Woodward's true protégé, Woodward's ideal journeyman scribe on the mound was Frank Graham, who wrote for the *New York Sun* and *New York Journal-American* and was the author of a best-selling biography of Lou Gehrig. Woodward described Graham as "a master copyist, [who] gives you scenes and conversations with the greatest faithfulness to fact. . . . He can sit on the bench for half an hour before a ball game and recreate everything that occurred. What's more he can make it interesting. Some of his best columns have been written about ordinary and unepisodic interludes. No one can bring the commonplace into focus as effectively as he."

But the most exciting voices were those that continued to draw from the older traditions even as they kept within the new parameters of the sports pages, which afforded them less latitude in style and craft than had been available to journalists like Lardner and Kieran and Pegler. Like the Rubes before him, Dick Young, the controversial and talented writer for the *New York Daily News*, sought out the unusual angle for his stories. Imitating sportswriters' occasional use of Brooklynese, for instance, Young wrote a 1954 story entirely from the point of view of a souse: "Lasht year, when the Brooks were losing game after game, Cholly Dressen told the boys to go out an' have a few drinks to loosen 'em up. So, after the way the Brooksh losht to St. Louish tonight, I figgered it wash a pretty good idea. The score was . . . jusht a minnit. Hey, wha wash the score? Oh, yeah, 6–5, an' that makes 'em six in back of the Giants, and two in backa Milwaukee." More often, though, Young went after a scoop and the clubhouse quote.

For Matties who worked consciously in the objective style, pellucid prose was not uncommon. Al Laney, who was one of Woodward's great writers and had once been amanuensis to James Joyce in Paris, never failed to capture the mood of game: "The extraordinary World Series of 1947, which has provided perhaps more thrills and more hysteria than any other, finally came down to a pleasant, sunny afternoon on which people could sit back and enjoy an ordinary ball game without having their nerves worn raw or their emotions too heavily involved. This was a straight-forward game with reason and logic in it and never once did panic sit up and make a noise."

As the baseball essay found a home in the late fifties and early sixties in mass-circulation magazines and sports journals, including the *Sporting News*, Matties and Rubes began to give their prose a more contemporary feel. Gay Talese, as he had done with boxing pieces on Joe Louis and later Floyd Patterson, worked deliberately, according to George Plimpton, at blocking "out his stories scene by scene on a large wallboard to see if he could bring out every point he wanted to make via a scene rather than historical narration." If Matties had learned something from A. J. Liebling, young Rubes borrowed from Liebling's counterpart at the *New Yorker*, James Thurber, whose brand of "emotional chaos told about calmly and quietly in retrospect" suited their methods, just as the game on the field often reflected Thurber's notion of skillful disorganization.

From the very beginning, though, baseball provided all of its writers with something indispensable: the simple notion of point of view. It has been at the heart of the great conversation and is part of the mystique of the game. "For the adventures of 'dem bums' of Brooklyn," wrote Philip Roth in "My Baseball Years" (1973), ". . . to be narrated from Red Barber's highly alien but loving perspective constituted a genuine triumph of what my English professors would later teach me to call 'point of view.'"

Over time writers began to explore the idea that voice or self could also be projected by a piece of baseball writing. Whether authors were Matties or Rubes, old-fashioned newspapermen, letter writers, or scholars, once point of view found its way into their prose, baseball writing began to shift from its own dead-ball era to a livelier one.

CHAPTER 3

The National Myth

Several myths or themes appear repeatedly in baseball prose. By myths I mean those core beliefs and values (widely held to be true) that help shape our cultural goals and ideals. Myths are derived from real events in baseball, and writers freely draw upon the imaginative, symbolic, allegorical, or metaphorical functions they assume. Similarly, some anecdotes serve as stories or myth-narratives that express bedrock convictions. Thus, Jackie Robinson can represent not only common heroic aspects (the individual who overcomes difficulties and prevails) but also the idea that baseball is democratic, that even in the face of racism, race-consciousness, or racial pride it is essentially a color-blind game. That these myths are long-standing and steadfast explains Stephen Jay Gould's complaint regarding "The Creation Myths of Cooperstown." Baseball, he writes, "has no true Cooperstown and no Doubleday. Yet we seem to prefer the alternative mode of origin by a moment of creation—for then we can have heroes and sacred places." Wilfred Sheed thinks little of myths, but he celebrates the fans who "want to be where the myths are."

I explain in this book how various themes, which I have classified as myths, appear in influential and important works of baseball nonfiction. Although the myths can lend themselves to bathos, metaphor-mongering, and demythologizing, they are neither outright falsehoods nor always clichés.

The Myth of America

"Whoever wants to know the heart and mind of America," Jacques Barzun said famously, "had better learn baseball." Barzun has lately grown disenchanted with the game as it has begun to mirror the excesses and failures of fin de siècle American society in general. The wealth and avarice that corrupted baseball owners in their "robber baron" phase can be viewed as having finally spoiled players in their "age of greed" phase. George Will has noted, "Between the foul lines the national pastime is emblematic of the nation in many nice ways. But off the field it mirrors many of the causes of our current discontents—angry factions loudly invoking the language of 'rights,' and not even one small voice articulating the community's collective and long-term interests." Yet others see baseball as being as resilient as the nation it represents.

Baseball embodies conventional notions of the United States—for example, as a moral exemplar, a nation of destiny and prominence. It was not just in a tongue-in-cheek spirit that Roger Kahn subtitled his book *The Era, 1947–1957: When the Yankees, the Giants, and the Dodgers Ruled the World* (1993). Another American ideal is that of Yankee ingenuity: games can be won through thoughtful planning, skill, and know-how (perhaps even with the aid of modern technology), but in the popular imagination games are won in the American grain—by playing your heart out and doing your best. We admire figures who demonstrate hard work, common sense, and self-reliance. Whatever the damage done to the game by the 1994–95 baseball strike (fan resentment and lack of interest have never been more widespread), the Baltimore Orioles' Cal Ripken's new consecutive-game streak set in September 1995 became occasion for many writers to extol the oldest American virtues. Wrote Jeffrey Hart, "Amid the devastation, Cal Ripken reminds us that there was something marvelous about baseball, and maybe there will be once again." Added Cal Thomas, Ripken is "a walking definition of 'family values' and a true role model." In addition, baseball is an equalizer (both teams start out on somewhat even terms with nine players and nine innings), and a degree of failure (not hitting the ball seven times out of ten or losing 40 percent of your games) is also a measure of success.

Baseball prefers the common man to the intellectual (or the celebrity). The manager Charlie Dressen once remarked that he had never read a book in his life and he wasn't planning to start reading one anytime soon. The myth of America helps make baseball's rules palatable and explains why so often they are meant to be broken. As A. Bartlett Giamatti put it, baseball "fits America . . . so well because it embodies the interplay of individual and group that we so love, and because it conserves our longing for the rule of law while licensing our resentment of lawgivers."

In other respects, baseball can be seen as having grown with the nation; baseball, the saying goes, is America. Lesley Hazelton, an immigrant, observed, upon attending "Catfish Hunter Day" at Yankee Stadium in 1986, tangible proof that she had arrived in America: when Hunter closed his speech by saying, "Thank you, God, for giving me the strength, and making me a ballplayer," Hazelton recognized "the perfect American day, the perfect American place, the perfect American sentence." The mythic world of baseball was her first encounter with "a mythical place called America."

The myth of America also incorporates the idea of the American odyssey ("going home"). William Zinsser chose the Pittsburgh Pirates as his subject for spring training because he "wanted a team from the heartland—one that had long been a fixture of its city and its region." The journalist David Lamb in *Stolen Season* (1991) was content to stay in minor league towns, where he found ballparks scattered everywhere throughout an America united by baseball; Lamb becomes an American explorer, a stargazer, discovering "a glow of lights . . . softly through the June darkness, from somewhere behind a grove of elms and past a village green . . . [in] a little Tennessee town whose name escapes me now." The true map of baseball could be any page of a Rand-McNally atlas of America used as a dartboard.

Yet what makes the myth so provocative is largely the American emphasis on democratic action: the "radical vision of American exceptionalism, of America as an idea," as John O'Sullivan put it; the American culture's sense of orderliness; its passionate fueling of individual effort and effective teamwork; its spirit of fun and pursuit of happiness; its pride of ownership and personal achievement; its opportunity for individuals to possess a moment in the sun (or 15 minutes of fame). "Baseball," wrote the historian Francis Trevelyan Miller in his introduction to Connie Mack's *My 66 Years in the Big Leagues* (1950), "is democracy in action; in it all men are 'free and equal,' regardless of race, nationality, or creed. Every man is given the rightful opportunity to rise to the top on his own merits. . . . It is the fullest expression of freedom of speech, freedom of the press, and freedom of assembly in our national life." Or as Mark Harris put it more personally in "The Bonding" (1993): "One of the things that made me a baseball fan is its democracy. Lines of snobbish distinction go down."

It is also true that writers, before the seventies at least, rarely wrote about baseball's unsavory side—the owners' contempt for their players, the sycophancy of sportswriters, the nasty racism, the quackery of team physicians and trainers, the sleazy politicking for franchises. But even in criticizing the game for its past "clunky paeans" and present follies, Robert Lipsyte insists that the game is worth preserving: "Of all our major sports, only baseball has the capacity to explore the American ideals of individualism within a group, democracy with a goal, and good work rewarded."

The Myth of Memory

Baseball essays contribute to the vast literature of reminiscence. "Memory," writes Zinsser, "was the glue that held baseball together as the continuing American epic." Put another way by James T. Farrell, "Baseball and its memories are part of the river of our national life which flows on and on."

There are several ways to look at the myth of memory. "Those were the days for the baseball fan!" John Kieran wrote in "Baseball Memories" (1927), remembering "when no umpire would come within a stone's throw of" John McGraw "except under injunction." Giamatti saw baseball as a means of reconnecting us with memories of our fondest childhood dreams and wishes. Baseball can also be seen as a fountain of *future recollection*, as Vladimir Nabokov describes the term in *Speak, Memory* (1966). According to his biographer Brian Boyd, Nabokov (who preferred tennis and soccer) "always considered that to recognize future recollection at the moment it happened, to know with certainty that *this* particular moment would later be recalled, was somehow to cheat the tyranny of time." Thus, certain plays and games remain etched in our minds, in much the same way Jimmy Foxx wanted to get a good grip on the bat, as if he could leave his fingerprints on the wood.

Baseball calls forth *shared memory* of an important event that large numbers of people remember, even as it swells the crowd that actually witnessed the event, and *borrowed memory*, the baseball on loan to us from history and lore. "In baseball history," writes Donald Hall, "writers find connections with the past that most Americans, most of the time, ignore."

The myth of memory occurs in all forms. The ancient Hall of Famer Edd Roush, a resident of Bradenton, Florida, goes to some games and, "staring fiercely into the past," tells William Zinsser about spring training in his day, when "ballparks were little better than cow fields, full of holes." Richard Hugo's "The Anxious Fields of Play" from his autobiography *The Real West Marginal Way* (1986) is rooted in childhood memories, evoking another sentiment—that baseball can be played almost anywhere, in ballparks rough-hewn from landscapes, or from the chaotic depths, of one's mind. Hugo plays in the fields while a war rages in Europe, where housing will be wiped out, creating what might well become new playing fields (as indeed happened in Japan after the bombings of Hiroshima and Nagasaki). When he began to play for organized teams, he often "luxuriated in the memory of the game just completed" and even "visited ballfields in the fall and winter and sat alone in the car remembering some game I'd played there."

The age-old desire of every American boy to grow up to play major league baseball resides in the myth of America (the American dream), but the pleasure of playing baseball, especially for the first time (the myth of Elysian Fields), belongs to youth and future recollection.

The Myth of Timelessness

Although the end of the season or of a career or of an inning brings finality, baseball lives on robustly and fervently when it is being played in the head. "Every day was the same day," Daniel Okrent recalls, summoning the cycle of baseball seasons and other images associated with his earliest baseball experiences:

> We were American boys in the 1950s, and we played baseball. In springtime we played it in city streets as soon as the soot-gray hardpack of snow melted away. In fall, when darkness fell early, we played it against front stoops, the light from the porch illuminating the ball as it zipped off the steps. In the winter we played it with dice and playing cards and dime-store games that came with a spinner and little markers and a cardboard replica of a diamond. But in summer, when each day rolled smoothly into the next and the sun accommodated game upon game upon game—in summer we played baseball, and we did nothing else.

Just as baseball has no clock, it knows no season, no time. The myth of timelessness indulges imagination: Nolan Ryan pitches to Ty Cobb; Christy Mathewson pitches to Ted Williams; Williams plays those five seasons he lost to the war. We close our eyes and see Ben Paschal starting as a designated hitter on the already devastating 1927 Yankee team, or we unimagine that egregious rule altogether. For the briefest of moments, we see the ball not going through Bill Buckner's legs.

Baseball's myth of timelessness is its way of holding on to history and tradition, which other sports have, of course, but which are not facets of their games. That we devise "all-time great" teams from generation to generation (with but a few revisions) speaks to the fact that baseball today would not be entirely alien to the players of the dead-ball or postwar eras, though certain changes would mystify them; by contrast, basketball players of only 30 years ago would find today's NBA a very different league from the one in their day. Despite changes in baseball, the myth of timelessness holds firm, and writers try to understand it in many subtle and symbolic ways.

Consider the ball. In the old days, new balls were used infrequently, perhaps a half-dozen or so per game. Pitchers almost immediately dirtied and scuffed any new ball that came into a game to their advantage, but whether one ball or a hundred are used, the nature of the game remains inviolate. Roger Angell couches the myth of timelessness in the idea of the ball itself: "The ball is released again and again—pitched and caught, struck along the ground or sent high in the air—but almost always, almost instantly, it is recaptured and returned to control and safety and harmlessness." The myth, then, accounts for baseball's ability to resurrect itself in successive generations and helps baseball withstand its own continuing assaults on its traditions.

Though baseball is urban in origin and character, the myth of timelessness has fashioned an accompanying *pastoral* myth that draws us back to the game's earliest discernible beginnings at Hoboken's Elysian Fields, which one turn-of-the-century author, William A. Shepard, described as "a perfect greensward [where] Nature must have foreseen the needs of baseball and designed the place especially for that purpose." Calvin Griffith, the owner of the Washington Senators, believed nothing would come of night baseball; the game, he said, was meant to be played in the Lord's sunshine. Thinking of parks as green cathedrals, batters hitting the ball "a country mile," and baseball's annual "rite of spring" advance the myth of an idyllic pastime. Observes Ted Solotaroff, "The primary tradition of baseball is pastoral—not just the sunshine, swept dirt and green grass but the spacious space and slow time of the game." As life became more hectic after World War II, the pastoral myth grew more appealing.

Even in the absence of history or literature, baseball would continue to be passed down through the generations in an ersatz oral tradition and through the ritual of going to ball games. The tradition of *fathers and sons* (or any variation thereof, including coaches and players) is still the way many young people learn the game and its lore. Zinsser saw the myth in the concept of spring training ("Baseball's Annual Season of Renewal"): "I liked the fact that spring training was a time of teaching and learning. That was a process that interested me; I was a teacher myself." And through the element of statistics and a massive record book, the pursuit of the past stays charged and alive.

The Myth of the Best Game

Baseball stays timeless mainly because those who follow it, some religiously, see it as simply the best game. This myth accounts for fan books and satisfying straightforward game accounts in the absence of any sort of mythifying or abstract ruminating whatsoever. The superlative also attends another myth, that of "greatest games," which in turn become part of the great conversation.

But the myth also speaks to baseball's reconditeness and aesthetic qualities. "I don't claim to know what lights the sparks," wrote Art Hill in his fan diary, *I Don't Care If I Never Come Back* (1980). "I know only that every winter when baseball is dormant, I feel as if it's gone forever. And every spring, the first time I see a shortstop charge a slow bounding ball, short-hop it on the edge of the grass and in the same motion throw to first, beating the runner by a half-step, I rediscover its magical beauty and I marvel at my good fortune."

The myth of the best game can be witnessed in what Sheed calls "the diamond chain," which links the big leagues and minor leagues and little leagues and colleges and neighborhood pickup games. "The biggies will always be loved and returned to for their icy perfection. But for everyday comfort and satisfaction, there's a lot to be said for the game next door."

Baseball as palliative is another theme that frequently accompanies the myth of the best game. Sheed's lengthy, solipsistic memoir *My Life as a Fan* (1993) was composed during a period of what he calls "suspended convalescence" in which he began "looking forward to each game like a convict on visitor's day." The poet Floyd Skloot, in the moving essay "Trivia Tea: Baseball as Balm" (1992), details how his lifelong passion for baseball helped him adapt to the debilitating effects of chronic fatigue syndrome. The disability altered his memory; it "had grown so totally unreliable that I could neither place a close boyhood friend who had sent me a letter of good wishes nor remember my date of birth." Baseball alone allowed him to locate specific items in his memory, from a trivia question he believed that he had thought up himself (and then discovered in a book, with an incomplete answer) about Andy Pafko's falling into the stands to catch a Gene Woodling drive in 1952. In the myth, baseball becomes "a form of alternative medicine: its history and statistics are taken in like herbal remedies, its lore meditated on as a form of relaxation therapy, its long televised games approached as part of a natural healing process."

The myth of the best game holds that if baseball is only a game, at least it is better than the others.

The Myth of Heroes

The myth of heroes is baseball's most prevalent myth, yet it has largely been the creation of baseball writers themselves. As a result, in addition to frequent panegyrics, certain dubious stories arise concerning ballplayers. Nicholas Dawidoff notes in his biography of the catcher Moe Berg that John Kieran helped create the legend that "Professor Moe Berg" could speak a dozen languages (but could not hit in any of them), had a plethora of university degrees and a photographic memory, and was an expert in just about any arcane subject. Berg certainly approached doing many of those things, but his extraordinary abilities came mostly from the pen of Kieran and other sportswriters.

Early writers drew upon classical and folk models to mold baseball heroes. Writers like Giamatti saw the game as a Homeric odyssey, while "sportswriters," as Tristram Coffin noted, "have consistently turned to Yankee and tall-tale stereotypes in chronicling baseball: the sage merchant, the clever clown, the frontier braggart, the country promoter, the 'Marster and John' Negro." Coffin also observed the use of prowess heroes (Babe Ruth), trickster (rogue) heroes (Ty Cobb), and ethical heroes (Judge Kenesaw Mountain Landis).

In the current era of "fatheads who spend their first paychecks on sports cars that run on airplane fuel," to quote Leigh Montville, and "substance abusers and late-night carousers and uncoachable prima donnas," the writing has become more objective but no less mythic in scope, as in Montville's description of 44-year-old Nolan Ryan as the classic citizen-hero: "In the tie-a-yellow-ribbon Americanism of the '90s, Nolan somehow has become the perfect oak tree. The fact that he still can compete with the young and wild-eyed millionaires of his game and still can make them look silly is only the beginning. He is Citizen Ryan, a total package. . . . Here is a family man. Here is a businessman. Here is a cowboy. Here is Nolan Ryan, cut from a good bolt of denim cloth and served with a glass of milk and no apologies."

Other writers seek variations on the theme of heroes. As Jonathan Yardley observes in an essay on Christy Mathewson, "In our national mythology he occupies a place alongside Frank Merriwell and Dink Stover: a flawless hero, a paradigm. That in point of fact he was not, that there was at least a narrow gap between myth and reality, only makes him more appealing: a true hero is rarely a saint." Sheed shapes baseball heroes with a personal point of view that renders them wholly new again. Shoeless Joe Jackson, for instance, seems at once lifted from the history books and turned into a hero for our time. His banishment from the Hall of Fame "is a bit like omitting the *Tyrannosaurus rex* from the Museum of Natural History—it hurts us more than it hurts him by now, and it leaves an awful hole in the historical record."

Michael Seidel in *Streak: Joe DiMaggio and the Summer of '41* (1988) contrasts the rise of an American ethnic hero (DiMaggio) with the fall of a Waspish one (Charles Lindbergh), while Lou Gehrig's (then) consecutive-game record seems very much in mind as Gehrig lingers heroically near death in the early days of DiMaggio's historic 56-game hitting streak. Furthermore, Seidel sees the streak as a "heroic, factual focus for a land whose imagination seemed primed for increments of power" as it readied itself for war. The streak, in fact, can be viewed as a microcosm of the game, which exhibits *"aristeia*, whereby great energies are gathered for a day, and then regenerated for yet another day in an epic wonder of consistency."

The myth of heroes allows us to appreciate on-the-field accomplishments as separate from off-the-field antics, although some writers may doubt the status of baseball heroes without necessarily questioning their ball-field bravura. Florence King, whose "fond look at misanthropy" hoped to "win one for the Sonofabitch," considered Ty Cobb one misanthrope she didn't like: "I know this man. I saw him many times during my roadhouse-crawling days in Mississippi and North Carolina, and he always looked the same: a round-faced, pink-cheeked gnome of a man, a mean good ole boy biding his time until somebody had the misfortune to make eye contact with him. That's *all* it takes." Nonetheless, as Stephen Jay Gould wrote of Cobb recently, "[We] might say of him, 'This was a ballplayer!' Such a judgment should be enough to give life value. Render to Ty Cobb what he couldn't give to others. His viciousness cannot injure anyone any more; the excellence of his play endures."

Any close study of statistics reveals just how exceptional and rare baseball heroes are. Of course, heroes cut across the spectrum, appear in brief bursts, and emerge at unexpected moments, off the field as well as on, to inspire and uplift the rest of us. Hugo recalled from his semipro league experiences players who shared the same characteristics as heroes from major league baseball lore. Tied as they are to the other myths, baseball heroes are memorable and their stories constitute a true miscellany of Americana.

Baseball as Literature

A final theme that baseball writers sometimes stress is baseball's literariness. As with most sports, baseball contains allegorical and metaphorical possibilities. Moreover, sport is an important form of human activity; for some people baseball is a part of daily life for more than one-half of the year.

The theme can get rather silly at times. Some writers have thought of baseball as epic poetry, or of the ball as the "narrator" of the game, or, in Donald Barthelme's view, of baseball as art, sparked by "passion, without which neither art nor baseball would signify at all." Philip Roth's half-joking retort to the question of why he chose baseball as the subject of *The Great American Novel* (1973)—"Because whaling was already taken"—demonstrates just how far-fetched the theme can become. After all, *Moby-Dick*'s seas and distances might signify baseball's pastoral myth; the vernacular of the *Pequod*, the vernacular of the dugout; and its cetology, baseball's statistics. Players like Ted Williams are cut from the same cloth as Ishmael, an outcast who will "quietly take to the ship," just as baseball is "best suited to accommodate, and be ornamented by, a loner" (like Williams), as John Updike noted.

Nonetheless, some baseball events do border on literature. Of the Pete Rose–Bart Giamatti affair in 1990, which saw Rose's lifetime suspension from baseball for gambling followed by Giamatti's death of a heart attack shortly thereafter, Mark Harris wrote: "For me, happy playgoer, catharsis achieved, pity and terror satisfied, Rose brought down, Giamatti brought down, gods of power and fortune reduced to equality with me, no experience of theater could have rewarded me with greater pleasure. This is the pleasure tragedy brings us."

Given a subject brimming with history and drama, is it any wonder that even bad baseball prose always leaves us with something—a magnificent anecdote, an idea of the game, a miniature portrait, a quotable quote, an instant replay made of words?

CHAPTER 4

Early Innings

For the sake of argument, let's call 1858 the beginning of baseball literary history. The date falls almost exactly between baseball's ur-game between Alexander Cartwright's New York Knickerbockers and the New York Club on 19 June 1846 at Elysian Fields—"an appropriate spot," wrote Tristram Coffin, "in the inappropriate town of Hoboken, New Jersey"—and the birth of professional baseball with Harry Wright's Cincinnati Red Stockings in 1869.

The date is close to the Civil War; we know for a fact that soldiers on both sides played baseball in army and prisoner-of-war camps. "They might have nothing better for a ball than a walnut wrapped with yarn," wrote Harold Seymour. "But still their enthusiasm made up for everything." On 20 July 1858, the precursor of the latter-day Brooklyn Dodgers–New York Giants rivalry took place at the Fashion Race Course in Long Island. It was the first series people actually paid money to see, so the year marks the beginning of baseball as business, at least in the popular mind-set.

Americans were experiencing the signs of a new "epidemic" called "baseball fever," marking the year as the beginning of baseball cliché, too. A reporter covering the game between well-regarded players from Brooklyn and New York remarked that "a galaxy of youth and beauty in female form who, smiling on the scene, nerved the players to their task, and urged them, like true knights of old, to do their devoirs before their 'ladyes fair.'"

That reporter would be neither the first nor the last to use the myth of heroes to describe the game. Roy Hobbs in Bernard Malamud's *The Natural* (1952) plays for a team called the Knights. He is a man who "coulda been a king." In baseball, Malamud noted, "you have a confrontation between two forces, the batter, who's a hero, and the pitcher, who's an eternal adversary. It's much like the confrontation between two knights in a tournament, where it can end with a single blow, like the knight cutting off the head or the ballplayer hitting one into the stands or striking out."

In addition, 1858 marks the era of Henry Chadwick (1824–1908), who earned the appellation "Father of the Game." The English-born Chadwick, a reporter for the *New York Clipper*, was not just the first notable baseball scribe, he was also its chief critic and guardian during some of the early crises and revolts. He would write and edit the first baseball guide, the first weekly, and the first hardbound book, in addition to numerous manuals and pamphlets on the game. "In the mid-1850s," notes Jack Lang, "William Trotter Porter gave a decided lift to the game with extensive coverage in his publication *Spirit of the Times*. Until Porter's reports began appearing regularly, baseball in America was ignored in most publications."

Baseball literature had also begun to appear in popular song, church sermons, pulp novels, and letters to the editor. When A. G. Spalding sold the great Chicagoan Mike "King" Kelly to Boston in 1887, Clarence Darrow and Eugene Field were among those writing letters of protest. By the time sports pages began to stand out with original drawings, box scores (invented by Chadwick as a "system of short-hand reporting for movements made"), and first-rate writing, sportswriting had been established, as the historian Charles Alexander concluded, "as a distinct form of journalism."

Roughly a month before the Fashion Race Course series, the poet Walt Whitman was also watching a game, this one between the Putnams and the superior Atlantics team. He wrote about it the next day, with his characteristic equipoise, for the *Brooklyn Eagle*. The losing club, he said, played "carefully and well, as the score will show," and he doubted "if any other club can show a better one in a contest with such opponents." Baseball, Whitman intimated, could be about losing as well as about winning, a theme to which later writers would regularly turn.

Whitman had come to love the game primarily for its health and recreational benefits, a notion that helped spread baseball's pastoral myth. His vision looked beyond the pastoral, however, as he witnessed baseball's remarkable growth. He said memorably, "I see great things in baseball. It's our game—the American game. It will take our people out-of-doors, fill them with oxygen, give them a larger physical stoicism. Tend to relieve us from being a nervous, dyspeptic set. Repair these losses, and be a blessing to us."

Though the *New York Times* had editorialized in 1881 that "there is really reason to believe that baseball is gradually dying out" and that it was "a sport unworthy of men and . . . in its fully developed state, unworthy of gentlemen," baseball was by that time firmly established as the national game, almost in the way that Whitman, in *Democratic Vistas* (1871), had envisioned a national indigenous literature.

American writers soon began talking baseball. Mark Twain, who dreamed up a medieval lineup in *A Connecticut Yankee in King Arthur's Court* (1889), called baseball "the very symbol, the outward and visible expression of the drive and push and rush and struggle of the raging, tearing, booming nineteenth century." He once lost a valuable umbrella (for which he offered a sizable reward) "at the great base ball match on Tuesday [18 May 1875], while I was engaged in hurrahing."

Stephen Crane, who played shortstop and catcher on the Syracuse University varsity team, left behind a few fragments on the subject. He wrote that the baseball diamond, with its nine players capriciously dressed, "presented an appearance of Joseph in Bible Days with his coat of many colors." Of his travails at Claverack College, Crane also wrote, "But heaven was sunny blue and no rain fell on the diamond when I was playing baseball." As a player, Crane was known to be "free of speech, wantonly profane," and loved talking baseball with the professional players he came to know when he was a newsman. He might have composed a baseball story in the *New York Press* of 31 May 1894 called "Decoration Day Ball," though the Crane scholars R. W. Stallman and E. R. Hagemann believe "its authenticity is questionable."

Obviously, Crane was influential beyond his few baseball sentences. The gritty realism of his novels and short stories, his expressive use of language and dialect, and the fictive techniques he employed in his newspaper articles and sketches became a model for later journalists and authors. Although Crane covered college football games for the *New York Journal* in 1896, his short story "The Monster" (1899) provides the best example of how he might have written about baseball teams. Henry Johnson, the black groom who saves his employer's son from a deadly fire and ends up disfigured and mentally impaired, becomes a kind of "boy of summer," a hero who comes to be forgotten, even shunned, over time as he copes with life's problems away from baseball. The talk in Reifsnyder's barbershop closely resembles the chatter of the hot-stove league. Local boys extol the exploits of their neighborhood fire teams, watching "their heroes perform all manner of prodigies." Crane also voices the parochial loyalties and rivalries, the way local baseball teams would become synonymous with cities: "In that part of the little city where Number Four had its home it would be most daring for a boy to contend the superiority of any other company. Like-wise, in another quarter, when a strange boy was asked which fire company was the best in Whilomville, he was expected to answer 'Number One.' Feuds, which the boys forgot and remembered according to chance or the importance of some recent event, existed all through the town." Early in the twentieth century, Henry Adams would recall boys playing "a rudimentary game of baseball" in 1850s Boston, a far cry from the vision of W. E. B. Du Bois's *The Crisis* (1911) of "future 'Rube Fosters . . . romping over corner lots, batting, pitching, and learning to play the game."

But the English expatriate Chadwick remained the dominant influence in what was becoming "the literature of base ball." He would support a rule change (such as abolishing the bound catch from fair balls) in one newspaper and oppose it in another, for only when he got the debate going in public could he try to promote the rule change. Whatever the limits of his own wooden style, Chadwick helped get the great conversation going. His reportage sometimes opened with a bit of poesy— "Everything was lovely and the game was on the fly"—and sometimes it conveyed a more serious concern, such as sportsmanship or protocol: "Mr. Ferguson had been agreed upon as umpire before the game, and no more impartial man could have been chosen for the position."

His style was nonconfrontational, the same attitude he brought to the game. Nonetheless, he still took part in baseball's first great hot-stove league controversy—whether baseball was or was not American in origin, an issue that hardly mattered to Chadwick, who knew that "from this little English acorn of Rounders has the giant American oak of Base Ball grown." (He was, according to legend, covering a cricket tournament when he spotted a baseball game taking place on the fringes of Elysian Fields.) Baseball, after all, had become American in spirit and design, and Chadwick promulgated that theory as much as anyone else. His opponents, however, led by Albert G. Spalding, an early player, administrator, and founder of the sporting goods company that bears his name, wanted no English traces in baseball any more than they believed Darwin's contention that primates are modified descendants of a single progenitor. Spalding insisted that "it would be . . . impossible for a Briton, who had not breathed the air of this free land as a naturalized American citizen . . . to play Base Ball."

Chadwick was the game's first contemporary writer as well as its first social historian. Though his prose is punctuated with his Victorian moral biases, he could write affectionately about having seen the first curveball, or invoke his own reminiscences of having played the game, in a way that first called up the myth of memory: "About twenty odd years ago I used to frequently visit Hoboken with base ball parties, and, on these occasions, formed one of the contesting sides; and I remember getting some hard hits in the ribs, occasionally, from an accurately thrown ball. Some years afterwards the rule of throwing the ball at the player was superseded by that requiring it to be thrown to the base player, and this was the first step towards our now National game."

Chadwick established the place of the writer in baseball lore. He could find encouragement in Whitman's simple reference to "A good game of base-ball" in *Leaves of Grass* (1855–92), but he would eventually have to make way for the racy vernacular of the very players he disdained, the ones, wrote a Cincinnati newspaper, who "uttered oaths and curses until a number of ladies left the stand." Chadwick continued to write baseball until his death from pneumonia (supposedly after a rainy ball game) in 1908. His more prominent contemporaries and heirs included Jacob Morse, a Boston newspaperman who founded the long-running *Baseball* magazine, and Francis Richter, a baseball visionary, born 30 years after Chadwick, who hoped to revamp the minor league system and liberalize the majors. He started up *Sporting Life* in 1883, the precursor of the *Sporting News*, which was founded in St. Louis by the Spink brothers in 1886.

It was the entrepreneurial Spalding, however, who, though much flattered by writers, would publish one of the game's most important books in 1911. *America's National Game* is a truly remarkable work, not simply because it solidified the Doubleday creation myth, but because it clutched at metaphors ("Base Ball is War!") that equated baseball with other American myths and values. It comprises chapters on the history, origins, techniques, and the business operations of the game, in addition to chapters on the poetry of baseball, and baseball in Japan and other countries. Furthermore, there are, as the sub-subtitle suggests, "personal reminiscences of [baseball's] vicissitudes, its victories and its votaries." Though Chadwick and Spalding's secretary, William D. Page, are believed to have had a hand in writing this massive work, baseball historian Benjamin G. Rader notes in his introduction to a new edition of the book that "nearly every page of the final edition bears the unmistakable imprint of Spalding."

Spalding felt no imperative to argue that baseball was America's national game, for it was already "like a solemn declaration that two plus two equals four." He extolled the democratizing features of the game: "The son of the President of the United States would as soon play ball with Patsy Flannigan as with Lawrence Lionel Livingstone. . . . Whether Patsy's dad was a banker or boiler-maker would never enter the mind of the White House lad." And baseball seemed right for the age of imperialism: "It has followed the flag to Alaska, where, under the midnight sun, it is played on Arctic ice."

At times Spalding could strive for poetic heights: "I claim that Base Ball owes its prestige as our National Game to the fact that as no other form of sport it is the exponent of American Courage, Confidence, Combativeness; American Dash, Discipline, Determination; American Energy, Eagerness, Enthusiasm; American Pluck, Persistency, Performance; American Spirit, Sagacity, Success; American Vim, Vigor, Virility."

Spalding's prose seems at times sprung from Whitman. If there was an alternative voice to Spalding's, it belonged to O. P. Caylor of the *New York Herald* and *Harper's*, whose vituperative wit and sarcasm earned him the nickname "Cucumber Head." Though essentially a conservative like his friend Chadwick, Caylor often described games in Rube-like fashion: the Giants without Amos Rusdie, he once said, would be like *Hamlet* without the melancholy Dane. By the time of Caylor's death in 1897, what was happening in the newspapers was a different story entirely.

The Bugs

After 25 years, baseball prose, particularly in the newspapers, needed an antidote to Chadwick's antediluvian style. There were other problems as well. Unlike Chadwick, some early journalists knew even less about the game than the typical fan. Second, the teams had begun paying the way of the sportswriters and expected (and often got) favorable press. The quid pro quo, which lasted well into the next few generations of baseball writers, eventually became part of game's early lore. John Wheeler would recall how "[Ring] Lardner and Hugh Fullerton seemed as much a part of the old Cubs as Frank Chance himself." Writers traveled with the players almost on a daily basis and soon became part of the game— several of them served as official scorekeepers. Furthermore, baseball and American journalism were in a period of transition as the new century approached. New technologies were changing the newspaper industry. Joseph Pulitzer's *New York World* in 1883 and, 12 years later, William Randolph Hearst's *New York Journal* had established separate sports sections and made other innovations that set the standards for newspaper journalism as we know it today.

The "organized" game was only in its second generation, and it awaited those writers who, unlike Chadwick, had grown up with the game. They were the "bugs," the ones who had played the game from earliest youth and knew the rules. The bug, wrote Spalding, was "a ver-

itable encyclopedia of information on the origin, evolution and history of
the game. He can tell you when the Knickerbockers were organized, and
knows who led the batting list in every team of the National and
American Leagues last year. He never misses a game."

These younger writers would be able to separate fact from legend,
though the use of legend (and anecdote) would provide them with the
extra literary dimension they needed to breathe new life into baseball
prose. "Legend," wrote Coffin, "is the only form of folklore in the her-
itage of ball players. However, there will be a wealth of minor, folk-liter-
ary forms: a lot of jokes; many superstitions and beliefs; a host of
customs; a few proverbs, proverbial sayings, and truisms; and a cant—
all working to maintain the homogeneity and ideals of a life separated
'by the foul lines' from the main culture."

The "foul lines" would prove an appropriate enough pun, for more
than anything else the younger writers were attuned to baseball jargon.
By the late 1880s, that is, by the time the roots of both the National and
American Leagues had been planted, writers were using dialect in baseball writing. By 1899 even the courts agreed that "swearing was so
much a part of ball playing that a club was unjustified in suspending a
player for using opprobrious language, because he was entitled to summon up stronger words than ordinarily used by the average citizen."

There was also a conscious effort on the part of some newspapers,
mostly in Chicago, to make baseball and other news more appealing.
Often a reporter's "bug" knowledge was not even necessary if he had a
keen sense of what might make an interesting story about a particular
game or player. The newspapers would now be "written largely in the
language that the wild growing young city understood," wrote
Fullerton. "They were boisterous, at times rough; they lacked dignity,
perhaps, but they were readable, entertaining and amusing." The new
language of baseball went well beyond the quaint lists of baseball terms
Chadwick had often composed.

"Cap" Anson's White Stockings, then a National League club and,
according to Warren Brown, the "forerunners of the Cubs," were rife
with material for a such a new style of writing. Wrote Brown, "If A. G.
Spalding succeeded in getting National League baseball started in
Chicago in the grand manner, it was Adrian C. Anson, his protégé, who
kept it going on the field with a bang."

By 1887 Finley Peter Dunne, the American Irish-dialect humorist,
and Leonard Dana Washburn were covering Anson's club for Chicago
papers. Washburn is usually given credit (by Fullerton and others) for
changing the rhythms and texture of baseball prose, primarily because

he wrote baseball (without a byline) longer than Dunne; the humorist lasted only one year before moving on to politics, but in all likelihood he approached the new style slightly ahead of Washburn. Where Dunne tended to be digressive, Washburn stuck to baseball. Washburn wrote for the *Chicago Inter-Ocean*, starting about 1887 until his accidental death in 1891. The writers who came after him, including Ring Lardner, surely absorbed his voice. Washburn opened up the possibilities of the comic simile. When he covered games on "the big diamond of pompadour grass," the cumulative effect of his metaphorical expressions could be riveting: "He hit the ball a lick that brought tears to its eyes"; "[Hutchinson] slammed balls down the path that looked like the biscuits of a bride"; "a dull, stifled squash like a portly gentleman sitting down on a ripe tomato"; "Mr. Fields lacerated the ethereal microbes three times out of four to get solid with the ball"; "Mr. Staley . . . did not have speed enough to pass a streetcar going in the opposite direction"; "His balls wandered down toward the plate like a boy on his way to school"; "Kitteredge . . . got a strong reverse English on the leather and started an artesian well in faraway left."

In time the Washburn style became widely imitated and, eventually, hackneyed. The papers looked to local men with writing talent and a technical knowledge of the game. Among the better "partisan" writers of the time cited by Fullerton was Boston's Tim Murnane, a former player who "established a school of experts—men who knew the game perhaps better than the scribes of other cities."

About 1911 John Wheeler of the *New York Herald* began collaborating with the New York Giants pitcher Christy Mathewson on several pieces about "inside baseball" for the McClure syndicate. The articles were published a year later as *Pitching in a Pinch*, with Mathewson on the title page as the author and with a foreword by Wheeler. The book would become a classic, baseball's first legitimate "as told to," primarily because, as Red Smith noted, "Wheeler was conscientious enough to consult Matty before putting the pitcher's comments on paper." Long before the invention of the tape recorder, ghostwriters either wrote the player's words entirely themselves or (to paraphrase the novelist Mark Harris) promised to restrain certain of their enthusiasms. In describing the famous championship playoff game forced by the Merkle boner, Mathewson/Wheeler put their respective talents together. One can hear the voice of the scribe at his best, providing a classic newspaper-type lead, his prose enhanced by parallelism and by Chicago-style, if restrained, humor:

The New York Giants and the Chicago Cubs played a game at the
Polo Grounds on October 8, 1908, which decided the championship
of the National League in one afternoon, which was responsible for the
deaths of two spectators, who fell from the elevated rail-road structure
overlooking the grounds, which made Fred Merkle famous for not
touching second, which caused lifelong friends to become bitter enemies, and which, altogether, was the most dramatic and important
contest in the history of baseball. It stands out from everyday events
like the battle of Waterloo and the assassination of President Lincoln.
It was a baseball tragedy from a New York point of view. The Cubs
won by the score of 4 to 2.

The player's voice is also detectable, in a style no less dramatic or
amusing or articulate. The Bucknell University–educated Mathewson
turns the player into a poet-philosopher: "Did you ever stand out in the
field at a ball park with thirty thousand crazy, shouting fans looking at
you and watch a ball climb and climb into the air and have to make up
your mind exactly where it is going to land and then have to be there,
when it arrived, to greet it, realizing all the time that if you are not there
you are going to be everlastingly roasted?" *Pitching in a Pinch* was a popular and influential book with writers for years to come. "*Pitching in a
Pinch* became my constant companion," Roger Kahn recalled. "No one
has ever read a baseball book harder. . . . I read nothing else, no Dickens,
no Twain, no Swift. Mathewson (with help) created a baseball world that
added humor to the earnest and heavy baseball cosmos of my fantasy."
In *The Southpaw* (1953), Mark Harris gets inside the head of his narrator-
pitcher Henry Wiggin in Mathewson-like fashion: "Did you ever look
down at yourself, and you was all brown wherever your skin was out in
the sun, and you was all loose in every bone and every joint of your body,
and there was not a muscle that ached, and you felt like if there was a
mountain that needed moving you'd up and move it. And your hands!
They fairly itched to hold a baseball, and there was not a thing you
could do once you had that ball."

Matties like Murnane and Wheeler followed the Rubes of the
Chicago school on the baseball beat. They picked up some of their
humor and figurative expressions but kept mostly to clear, concise
English sentences. Murnane, in his account of the final game of the 1912
World Series, wrote: "Mathewson, the baseball genius, was heartbroken
and tears rolled downed his sun-burned cheeks as he was consoled by his
fellow players." With a style of writing already becoming trite, the
Rubes, on the other hand, clearly needed a new pitch.

The Mark Twain of Baseball

Charles Dryden (1860–1931) was the preeminent Rube throughout the early and mid-1900s; in an otherwise peripatetic career, he wrote for both the *Philadelphia North American* and the *Chicago Tribune* during that time. His writing nonetheless defied classification and delivered consistently witty and innovative baseball prose in which point of view, almost always ironical, really began to appear.

Dryden would describe "a corking good game" in a way that seemed fresh at every turn: "So far as genteel deportment goes, a ping pong game in a deaf and dumb asylum would be a fierce and boisterous proposition. The Giants did nothing but chew their cuds and play ball, and they did both well, much too well for our bald athletes." The casual tone, the air of self-confidence, the compactness of the sentences, and their classical rhythms are all hallmarks of the light essayist, but Dryden rounds out his lead further with a novelist's eye for detail and color:

> It was a hot and spicy show from start to finish, a deadly struggle without words, and Mr. Mathewson won it himself with a belated swat through the pent-up infield in the ninth.
>
> That was keeping the populace guessing some. The big crowds had hopes of the Phillies up to the last sad moment. Mr. Duggleby and his faithful fried elbow were doing noble stunts for the cause, and had the Giants panned until the closing scene. Then the weak sisters broke out in a hitting spasm and Matty, after making two navy yard home runs [foul balls], touched off a single that tallied two runs and won the game.

Called the Mark Twain of baseball, Dryden introduced a highly original style of writing. His literary credentials were impeccable: he was the author of epic verse (*Swanson, Able Seaman* [1901]), an autobiography (*On and Off the Bread Wagon* [1905]), humorous tales ("Percy the Trained Flying Fish" [date unknown, but probably 1919]), and a profile of Robert Louis Stevenson in his Samoan island bungalow. His one baseball book was *The Champion Athletics*, written in 1905. He could distill the events on the field, "making ball players," as Fullerton said, "famous or ridiculous by a single yarn," such as the day Irving "Young Cy" Young, "built like the gentleman who tosses cannon balls at the circus," made his debut against the Phillies: "The game was swift and tabascoish; but the locals couldn't hit the new-moon delivery of Young Cy. It was deceptive and likewise provoking. But four men reached first in nine rounds and they have a somewhat hazy notion of how it happened."

He was fond of coining names (Charles Comiskey was "The Old Roman," and Frank Chance was "Peerless Leader") and inventing phrases: "Washington—first in war, first in peace and last in the American League." Readers did not know when to take him seriously or not. He once claimed that the term "southpaw" was derived from a left-hander who hailed from Southpaw, Illinois—but no such place could be found in the state.

Dryden relied little on dialogue and quote. His humor was droll and conventional but strikingly new to baseball. His pieces sprang from the contiguous events of the game or any extracurricular goings-on. He wrote what he termed "rainy day" pieces and bogus interviews in which he cast his subjects in his own light and voice. Thus, Connie Mack is seen "seated in his cozy apartment reading collect telegrams from minor league phenoms and waiting for the clouds to roll by."

Dryden's attitude was always clear from the outset and defined his material. In covering the 1906 intercity World Series, or "civil war," between the Cubs (Spuds) and the White Sox, Dryden demonstrated his insouciance toward postseason games, which he considered "monkeying with the national pastime" and "a battle for the world's horse blankets" (a reference to "the handpainted blankets with which boss athletes drape skinny black horses while touring the provinces"). His account of the 1908 Merkle boner is almost a study in the minutiae of mob hysteria, "the facts in the case gleaned from active participants and survivors" and "the spectators who had swarmed upon the diamond like an army of starving potato bugs."

Dryden always chose his words to suit the occasion—for example, when the other team "backed into victory": "Mr. Mack's tired toilers lost today, 10 to 4, but they can do the shouting, since St. Louis cleaned up Chicago. The double-header here tomorrow carries no terrors. If necessary, we can drop both games while the White Sox pound away at the Browns until they are blue in the face. Nothing more doing until the post-mortem series to decide which is the dead one—Giants or Athletics. Let us all emit three cheers, anyhow, for luck."

He became famous for his use of slang, which he saw as a way of getting more quickly to a point. He coined some, but not most, of the words he was credited with coining, but he helped popularize their usage. He consistently wrote lines that were pungently funny (more reminiscent of Ambrose Bierce than Twain), especially in his leads: "What a shame those Phillies are not in the show business," he began a page 1 story, "for they play the kind of ball that turns people away." The routine events of a game did not interest Dryden; sometimes he wrote about a game from some eccentric perspective—the Chicago stockyards or the battle of San Juan Hill. He tightly wound the thread of any joke or image from one moment to the next: when the "bugs" surrounded a player, another player, "an expert on bacteria . . . rushed in to help"; New York was "burning red fire" the night the Giants won the series in 1905 because Christy Mathewson, who pitched his third shutout, "had his stick of solder and the hot iron in his repertoire today." Dryden's comic similes and metaphors, though less frequent than Washburn's, were every bit their equal: "Like the lunch hour in a local chop house, the action was fast and effective but not as clean as it might have been. . . ." "Over in the stockyards district, where gentle deeds and smells are rare, the Cubs dragged the Sox around their own killing beds and slaughtered them to a finish."

Dryden had lived life and been to sea; he was no budding youth when, at the suggestion of Finley Peter Dunne, he first came to write baseball. He had read books and brought his knowledge with him to the "diamond stage," as he called it. He had known other men in other walks of life, and his canvas was broad and his perspective wide because of the man he was. On numerous occasions he was kicked out of club-houses and forced to cover games from park benches (where fellow writers fed him material) or up on Coogan's Bluff overlooking the Polo Grounds.

After retiring from the *Tribune* in 1915, he wrote for the Chicago *Herald* and *Herald and Examiner* until 1921, when he suffered a debilitating stroke. Dryden died in relative obscurity in 1931. "The name of Charles Dryden rings no bells," wrote Stanley Frank in 1944. "But to old subscribers and sport historians, Dryden strikes a clamorous gong awakening remembrance of baseball's first humorist and perhaps the greatest."

If you want to read someone funny, Ring Lardner said, read Dryden. Ironically, it was Dryden who paved the way to prominence for Lardner, who, noted Donald Elder, "literally sat at his feet," Cubs players calling him " 'Charlie's Hat' because he went everywhere with Dryden." What Dryden suffered in the way of anonymity, Lardner would make up for in a popularity no baseball writer has experienced before or since.

CHAPTER 5

Ring Lardner's Diamond

The year 1913 signaled the change in American journalism brought on by a large influx of gifted writers (many of whom later branched out into other areas of literature), primarily in Chicago. Literature was happening in America—in Chicago, and in the newspapers. Wrote Frederick Lewis Allen, still the best and most reliable historian of that period: "Gradually military affairs and foreign affairs and politics began to yield first place in newspaper coverage to scandals, crimes, disasters, human dramas, and sports. . . . Something like a World-Series-week spirit—a contagion of delighted concern over things that were exciting but didn't matter profoundly—was dominant."

If we define modernism, as Julian Symons does in his excellent study *Makers of the New* (1987), as the attempt of artists "consciously to change the form, language, or subject matter of literature, sometimes all three," then something of a modernist spirit was penetrating the newspapers, where "a number of energetic literary journalists were ready to give the new American writing columns of praise in the *Chicago Tribune* and elsewhere."

In New York, Don Marquis, who had worked alongside the young Grantland Rice on the *Atlanta Journal* and later wrote some classic pieces on golf, was very much aware of the new literary movements in Chicago and elsewhere. Writing for the *New York Sun* and later the *Tribune*, he punched out (in lowercase letters) his popular *archy and mehitabel* columns. Burton Rascoe, an admirer of Ring Lardner's, became literary editor of the *Tribune* and was said to champion the American and European modernists. Harriet Monroe was also writing an art column for the newspaper. The American language, particularly its vernacular (its "slanguage") appealed to the young writers.

As Symons notes, the new writing in America exhibited "a national quality" and rejected "European models as irrelevant to American life and landscape." Hart Crane's bridge might have easily been the Polo Grounds, Ebbets Field, or some other urban ballpark. Literary modernists did rail against certain elements of small-town American life, but they were not willing to abandon baseball. Alfred Kreymborg, the poet and playwright, recounted in his memoir *Troubadour* (1925) one of baseball's earliest literary anecdotes, foreshadowing a later literary baseball outing between George Plimpton and a much older Marianne Moore. Kreymborg accompanied a youthful Moore to the Polo Grounds "for one of [those] ancient frays" between the Giants and the Cubs. He was hoping he could finally stump the perspicacious and articulate poet. During their "descent into the world of the lowbrow," Moore talked to Kreymborg about Ezra Pound and Richard Aldington "without so much as a glance toward the players at practice grabbing grounders and chasing fungos." Kreymborg was sure she would not be able to identify the Giants' pitcher that afternoon. Moore had never seen the pitcher before, she said, but suspected "it must be Mr. Mathewson." She had read *Pitching in a Pinch*, she revealed, and noted with pleasure "how unerringly his execution supports his theories." Kreymborg, Moore's "victim," ends the anecdote in the accents of a Matty humbled to a Rube: "'Strike three, batter's out!' concluded the umpire and, as Shorty Slagle slunk away, glared toward the Chicago bench for the next victim."

Journalists could now speak comfortably about a baseball past. Their own experiences had been formed by the earliest incarnations of sandlot ball, barnstorming teams, and the semipro leagues of rural America. Lardner would write of having seen a much-touted "Cy Young" pitching for the Cleveland Spiders during a tour in Ohio. When he began covering the major leagues years later, he happened to see that same "Cy Young," who "had changed his name to Bobby Wallace, his position to shortstop, and his summer home to St. Louis."

"Newspaper writers," Jimmy Breslin points out, "particularly the good sportswriters, concentrated on getting anecdotes into their stories, for they formed the word of mouth in the neighborhoods, on the stoops and bar stools, especially the bar stools, of the city. It was this need to talk, to hear stories, much more than the need to drink, that filled the speakeasies and saloons."

Though most of the new talent was concentrated in only a few writers—the majority of whom, observes David Quentin Voigt, "could easily be written off as a baroque continuation of the styles of" Henry Chadwick and John Montgomery Ward—many other writers developed a wider latitude of narrative modes. They could praise the manager John McGraw's "inside game" or knock it; they could write from the perspective of the fans or re-create the game through individual heroics. They could be argumentative and critical or cynical and wistful: "Write in the pages of World Series baseball history the name of Snodgrass. Write it large and black. Not as a hero; truly not. Put him rather with Merkle, who was in such a hurry that he gave away a National League championship. Snodgrass was in such a hurry that he gave away a world championship." Though by and large their notion of what "off the record" meant was very different from the modern definition, the early literary stylists were helping to define the national image of baseball in the early innings of its prose.

"I Am Still a Baseball Writer and Always Will Be"

As with Western philosophy to Plato, much if not all of baseball writing consists of a series of footnotes to Ring Lardner (1885–1933). Noted Lee Allen, "Almost every anecdote about the illiteracy of players dates back to the period before WWI when Lardner was using his genius to describe the genus." Lardner's impact on American literature is without question. "Ernest Hemingway denied that Lardner had influenced him," writes Matthew J. Bruccoli in his introduction to *Ring Around the Bases* (1992), "which is proof of the influence." That influence surely did not begin only when Lardner started writing fiction.

Lardner was not formally a part of the Chicago-Midwest literary movement, and he was not especially influenced by it. The writers who moved to Chicago to become part of the literary renaissance there had come from all over the Midwest; Lardner came from Niles, Michigan. There was no conscious attempt on anyone's part to form a "movement," although a literary circle did develop around Harriet Monroe and *Poetry* magazine. Writers worked and matured independently. "If in the end he became a greater iconoclast than any of the self-conscious rebels of his generation," writes Donald Elder, "it was not the images of Niles, home, family, or childhood that he shattered. He remained faithful all his life to the values of his early environment; it was the world he found outside it that was to repel him. He was seeking self-expression or personal freedom through writing. It was a professional matter with him."

Growing up in the waning years of the nineteenth century, Lardner lived a life of literature, music, baseball, and, ultimately, drink. He could gleefully write the lyric "Gee, It's a Wonderful Game" in 1909 and ten years later, inebriated in a Kentucky roadhouse on the night of the second straight White Sox loss in the 1919 World Series, sing his parody "I'm Forever Blowing Ball Games" ("I'm forever blowing ball games, pretty ball games in the air"). He fell into newspaper writing after flunking out of engineering school and plying some blue-collar trades. After he finally landed a job on the *Chicago Tribune*, following stints on other Chicago papers, including the *Inter-Ocean*, he would cover both Chicago teams at one time or another until the end of World War I. He took over the late Hugh E. Keough's column, "In the Wake of the News," which made him famous overnight.

Lardner, by all accounts a dedicated journalist, took the genre of baseball writing in a whole new direction in his articles and columns. He relied on conventional stereotypes but introduced the vernacular in a way that made it sound indigenous to baseball—written, said Tristram Coffin, with "the cold perspective, all the scornful wit, of a seventeenth century courtier." He practically reinvented the anecdote at a time when the anecdote was just coming into use on the sports page.

He could meld vernacular and anecdote and lend a quality of legend to his stories about baseball men, even though he was "absolutely positive that the players are just common human beings and that some of them are really no better than ourselves." At the top of the order were the likes of Mathewson or "Tyrus [Cobb], the Greatest of 'em All" (1915); on the bench were the bushers and nickel-nursers. In his piece on Cobb ("Sit down here, kid, and I'll give you the dope on this guy"), published in *American* magazine and built solely upon anecdotes, vernacular, and the conceit of baseball talk, he kept the hero in perspective: "If you'd ever saw him play as much baseball as I have, you wouldn't be claimin' he was overrated. I ain't goin to come right out and say he's the best ever, because they was some old timers I never seen. (Comiskey, though, who saw 'em all, slips it to him.) I just want to tell you some of things he's did, and if you can show me his equal, lead me to him and I'll take off my hat."

During his sportswriting days between 1905 and the early 1920s, Lardner began publishing his fictional epistolary series, which later came to be known as *You Know Me Al*, beginning with "A Busher's Letters Home" in the *Saturday Evening Post* in 1914. He had begun experimenting in vernacular when he was writing his "Pullman Pastimes" in 1910–11 and editing (rather unhappily) the *Sporting News*. He continued with the style through his *Chicago Tribune* columns, such as in this opening-day piece in 1914: "I wisht I had time and I would go a round and see these here federal league men and warn them they should not ought to make no rash challinge to the white sox to play them for $25000 because Comiskey is pretty sure to except because he is out after the money and of coarse they would not charge no addmission to get in to the games and if the white sox won the serious the federals would be up against it."

Baseball's low comedy belonged to the bush leaguer. Crude, crass, ignorant, mean, yet not entirely unlikable, the busher was a man held down not so much by lack of talent (he did possess more than a modicum) but by an exaggerated sense of his own self-worth. Other writers might have patronized such characters, but Lardner fleshed them out, introducing a new persona to the sports page. He observed in ballplayers what Edgar Lee Masters saw in the small-town inhabitants he wrote about in his popular *Spoon River Anthology* (1915). The con men and bank presidents who appear in *Spoon River* become the gamblers and club owners in Lardner's world. Just as Masters dwells on the idiosyncrasies of Midwest natives (such as the condemned man who memorizes the encyclopedia), Lardner focuses on the dime-tippers and alibi artists. Masters might have written an epitaph for Jack Keefe.

No one had yet synthesized the new methods into a literature of the game. Like his "In the Wake of the News" predecessor, H. E. Keough, Lardner could describe a rainout in a casual tone and language suited to the occasion: "No game, for some reason or another. It was wet grounds, or rain, or something just as effective, and it certainly made a hit in this Cub camp. Nobody is going to protest when he is deprived of an hour's ride over to Washington Park, on Long Island, two hours or more of baseball, and another hour's ride back to this same metropolis of these here United States."

The rest of the short piece is loose and disjointed. Lardner provides the requisite five *W*s of journalism; they are not the cornerstones of the piece but a function of it. The players are scattered, some of them heading "over to the racetrack to do some donating." But the focus of the piece is a hot-stove dialogue between two ballplayers trading inflated anecdotes that puncture the myth of memory.

A few years later, writing for the *Chicago Examiner*, Lardner described another rain delay, this time in paragraphed verse. He often used doggerel ("Ed Walsh, he stopped in Meridian to see his two kids once again"), but sometimes (as Yardley observed) rose well above the occasion:

It didn't rain so awful hard, it didn't rain so much; there wasn't any blizzard that could really be called such; we asked most everybody

that we met upon the street and couldn't find a single soul who'd
swear that there was sleet; we asked some information from the man
who gathers mail, and he said that nowhere on his route had he
encountered hail; we ran across a pioneer who'd lived here since a boy,
and he vowed he'd seen a stronger wind sometimes in Illinois; but the
awful combination of the wind and rain and all, it rendered quite
impossible the scheduled game of ball.

In yet another piece, Lardner lampooned his own vernacular style by
describing a conversation between a Frenchman and a "Wake" correspondent:

> "I have always been derange to see Les Cincinnati Rouges jouer a
> la balle."
> "Cincinnati is your favorite neuf?"
> "Certainement," said M. Joffre. "But I like the Petits l'Ours also.
> That must have been une grand jeu journee. It was tough luck for
> Jacques Vaughn, though."
> "What happened?" inquired the correspondent.
> "Why M. Vaughn et M. Toney each pitched une non frapper jeu
> for neuf innings. Then les Rouges got two hits in le dixieme and
> copped. Are the Petits l'Ours a bon team?"
> "Bien," replied the correspondent. "But they have too many
> artists who frapper gaucher."

Lardner, as usual, delivers the pertinent information about the game,
rather crucial in this case since both pitchers threw no-hitters for nine
innings ("une non frapper jeu"). Aside from the linguist play (the "Petit
l'Ours" for the hometown Cubs, "le premier basehomme" for first baseman), the essential facts are always in place—just rarely at the top of the
journalistic pyramid. Rather than aggrandize the extraordinary game,
Lardner's hybrid French gives it a Rube-like quality of burlesque.

Lardner could turn his attention to a balloon flight or a sunset when
a game failed to hold his interest. He opted for the offbeat metaphor and
never attempted to match the frenetic pace of Washburn's similes. He
used slang when it suited his prose, as in the phrases "Cobb's wallop,"
"Purtell poled," and "Payne pegged." Even his passives seemed purpose-
ful: "For a brief moment it was hoped that Dougherty would catch the
ball." Sentences like "Red Kelly was cracked in the trunk by a pitched
ball," mixed with active sentences like "Freddy Payne struck thrice in
vain," caught the ebb and flow of the game. Like Dryden, Lardner

"seemed to cover a game from all over the ball park—from the press box, from the stands, the bench, the plate, the pitcher's box, the umpire's position, the infield and the outfield." During the off-season, he reported from taverns, hotel rooms, barbershops, and street corners.

Though his modernist impulses were unmistakable, he was also rooted in tradition. The creative spellings, always operative, such as "skedolled" (scheduled) or "differents" (difference) were prime examples of written American slang and dialect humor. He had read and admired the works of George Ade, whose characters, unlike Twain's, resembled the midwestern people Lardner had known and grown up with, and Charles E. Van Loan, whose short stories in the *Saturday Evening Post* were to Lardner a prose model. He learned from Dryden, but they were born a quarter-century apart and had different ideas about humor. Lardner's vernacular depended upon diverse points of view, whether coming from "a athlete" or "from the bugs in the bleachers." His seamless, punctuation-free stories in newspaper columns and magazine stories predated similar efforts by a variety of twentieth-century modernist and postmodernist authors. He mingled fictional characters with historical ones: Jack Keefe lives and breathes with the real Walter Johnson.

We can take with a grain of salt F. Scott Fitzgerald's assessment that, "however deeply Ring might cut into it, his cake had the diameter of Frank Chance's diamond." Frank Chance's diamond could cut a nice-sized slice of America. Wrote Eliot Asinof, "Lardner gave baseball class, just by being part of its world."

The "Wake" columns contained a number of new departures: a baseball novelette, Miss Lonelyhearts letters, news about the wife and family. Lardner introduced yet another type to baseball lore—the person next to us in the stands, with a loud mouth and an opinion on everything.

Though he often said that there was nothing on earth more depressing than an old baseball writer, he once reminded a gathering of the Baseball Writers Association of America, whose annual meeting he crashed years after he quit reporting, that he was "still a baseball writer and always will be."

Nine Men Out

By the time of the 1919 World Series between Chicago and (what Bugs Baer called) "Cincinnutty," Lardner was writing the "Weekly Letter" for Jack Wheeler's Bell syndicate. Initially optimistic, his columns revealed a gradual, deepening suspicion. Nonetheless, Lardner continued to supply readers with his usual irony and humor, employing puns, malapropisms, and misspellings throughout intentionally ungrammatical stories about the travails of "agonized baseball" and the "world serious" in particular. The wordplay takes on greater significance here, for Americans took their World Series very seriously.

When he cites (Adolfo) Luque as the only name pitcher on the Cincinnati team, he must suppose the others to be Matthew, Mark, and John. (In the myth of heroes, baseball stars were at least apostles, if not gods.) Occasionally a pun is close to being literal. During a heavy downpour, he notes that he "was wading along Clark st." for someone. At other times, he relies on apothegms or dry wit to render an evaluation: "Dick Kerr throws left handed and hits the same way, while Grover Lowdermilk throws right handed and hits seldom."

He gives just the amount of exposition he feels to be necessary and turns instead to running themes such as gambling (which proliferated in baseball circles, especially at World Series time, and was a part of the game's urban reality). Lardner himself bet on ball games. The "author" figures into the narrative as an "expert . . . under a heavy strain," as a presenter at a banquet at which Reds players are given Rookwood vases ("which you should ought to pronounce vases on acct. of them being $2000.00 worth of them"), and as a kind of oddsmaker: "Lardner Aids Chisox," he titled one column, because he finally bet on the Reds. Lardner talks neither up nor down to the "gents" to whom the pieces are addressed but rather poses as one of them, a regular fellow who has turned "kind of a dapple gray since the serious opened up."

Lardner describes the "holy cost" that would be game 1 of the series, which Chicago lost 9–1. As for the seemingly never-ending fourth inning, Lardner suggests that "the White Sox only chance at that point was to keep the Reds in there hitting till darkness fell and made it a illegal game." The word choice is telling. Lardner may also have been implying something in calling the White Sox's second-game loss to the Reds "the biggest scandal of a big year of baseball scandals."

When the White Sox take the third game of the series, he suspects that Chicago won probably as a result of his not betting on them; had he bet on the Reds, he imagines, the score would have been worse. His game account appears in the form of verbal gymnastics; writing again of Luque, "it Luques to me like he should of went to Fisher's relief earlier in the day." Of the inning Luque pitched, Lardner reports "in pure Cubanola: El Lieboldo whiffoed. Si senor Collins was outo . . . Bucko Weavero outo . . . No runos. No hittos, no bootos."

If humor continued to carry Lardner through the sixth game, which Chicago won, it was partly because in large measure the series should have been over by then. Lardner was so disheartened by the alleged fix, he unleashed his most obvious and biting allusions. In an earlier rainy day story, he had remarked that the railroads "had their trains all fixed to start for Cincinnati tonight," but he began this time with a lead that he knew, for a variety of reasons, he could *not* yet develop into a factual story: "This is the most scandalous and death dealing story ever wrote about a world serious ball game. They have been a whole lot of talk in this serious about one thing and another and it finely remained for me to get at the facts."

Lardner then proceeds to tell an anecdote about a Cincinnati player who had so much trouble hitting a National League baseball that he asked the umpire to let him look at one. Lardner states that he now owns that very ball, which looks "soiled on the northwest side," and he laments that "I will worry my life away wondering who put a dirty finger on that ball." By the final game, Lardner is totally disinterested in the "exhibition," noting that the family history of the dukes of Normandy makes for better newspaper reading than the account of this game; he announces that "it is probably the last world serious I will ever see."

As Jonathan Yardley notes, Lardner hinted that his interest in baseball "died a sudden death in the fall of 1919," but "to say that the scandal was not a profoundly disillusioning act is to ignore the intimate association in Ring's mind of baseball and his youth. It is also to deny that he saw baseball as a small universe with its own inviolable order, an order which would endure no matter how venal or petty some of those who lived under it."

Long after Lardner had feigned disgust with baseball, he began a column on the 1923 World Series with an allusion to 1919 ("win by the Cincinnati Reds greatly to their surprise"). The game-by-game account takes the reader on a jaunt from the Polo Grounds back to 1919 Chicago, up to Connecticut, where Lardner's wife needs a fur coat, down to Lansdowne, Pennsylvania, where the Eddie Collinses live, and back to New York, where he hopes "they boys . . . will not have no meetings in no hotel rooms between now and Wednesday" (even the double negatives eventually right themselves) so he can bet on the games with peace of mind and get his wife that fur coat she's been waiting five years for.

The fur coat becomes a running gag in subsequent columns, in which Lardner wrote very few words about the "serious" itself. During one outing, Lardner relates that the weather was so perfect that anyone would be a fool to buy a fur coat for it, and he ends with a few comments about the game itself, including one pitcher's decision to throw only slow pitches to Babe Ruth, annoying the crowd because the pitcher thus demonstrated his ability to think.

His next column again picks up the thread of the fur coat motif in something of a shaggy dog story. Having bet on the losing Yankees, he will be forced to skin his cats (which will produce, one furrier tells him, "the most satisfactory and handsome coat that money can buy"). He will do that whether the Yankees win or not. He then gives an extraordinarily brief account of the game itself; he remarks smartly that he would have discussed the game in more depth had it not been "played in such darkness that I was only able to see a few incidence." As the Yanks win the series, Lardner nonetheless calls upon readers to search their cellars for old family albums and to send him the plush from their covers: "They nothing more attractive than a black and red and tan blocked coat made out of plush albums."

One of the few straightforward baseball essays Lardner wrote was an article for *Collier's* magazine in 1912 called "The Cost of Baseball" in which he attempted to explain the business of baseball and "why a 'piker' would stand no chance in the game." Lardner found it difficult to view ballplayers as exploited and suggested that fans be "less envious of the gentleman who gets that dollar or half dollar of yours on a summer afternoon."

Lardner's attitude toward the fans was problematic. On the one hand, he thought they talked too much about things they knew nothing about. On the other, he knew that talk was the heart of the game. In one of his most poignant baseball pieces, "Oddities of Bleacher 'Bugs'" (1911), he asserts that whatever advantages come with being a reporter cannot match the thrill of "scraping up the necessary quarter, or half dollar, and knowing you are going to SEE a game, not report it." The joy of baseball lies at least partly in the myth of the best game, in the fans being happily deceived; the true bug is not your run-of-the-mill know-it-all but the blissfully ignorant fan, wrapped up in the language and images of the game. "They go out there to have a good time and they have it." No better description—or tribute, whether or not Lardner is being facetious—of the true fan exists:

> The real article is the man who knows most of the players by sight, as they appear on the field, but wouldn't know more than one or two of them if he saw them on the street, struggles hard to keep an accurate score and makes a mistake on every other play, or doesn't attempt to score at all, disputes every statement made by his neighbors in the

bleachers whether he knows anything about said statement or not, heaps imprecations on the umpire and the manager, thinks something is a bonehead play when it is really good, clever baseball, talks fluently about Mathewson's "inshoot," believes that Hank O'Day has it in for the home team and is purposely making bad decisions, and says, "Bransfield is going to bat for Moore" when Walsh is sent in to hit for Chalmers.

Lardner's style contrasts directly with that of some writers—especially ghostwriters—who would clean up a player's voice. Ford Frick could get Ruth to sound Dickensian in describing his earliest days in old Baltimore: "Crowded streets they were too, noisy with the roar of heavy trucks whose drivers cursed and swore and aimed blows with their driving whips, at the legs of kids who made the streets their playground. And the youngsters, running wild, struck back and echoed the curses. Truck-drivers were our enemies: so were the coppers patrolling their beats, and so too were the shopkeepers who took bruising payment from our skins for the apples and fruit we 'snitched' from their stands and counters."

Many of Lardner's later essays were autobiographical and rich in anecdote, such as the one about the pitcher who suggested to another pitcher that if Mordecai Brown could pitch so well without a forefinger, the other pitcher could do twice as well if he cut off his whole hand. Baseball looms in these essays as both background and center. In them, Lardner discovered the myth of memory, which helped keep his love of baseball alive. In "Meet Mr. Howley" (1931), we are privy to the hot-stoving of old-time players (including Honus Wagner) discussing how they might have hit in the era of the lively ball. Lardner writes affectionately of a time "before the era of deuces and treys wild, the lively ball, and mellow, twenty-hour old Bourbon, distilled and aged in the Blue Grass of Little Sicily."

Arguably the most famous is Lardner's *New Yorker* piece of 1930 called "Br'er Rabbit Ball," in which he admits his reluctance to attend ball games except "for the alleged necessity of getting my innumerable grandchildren out in the fresh air once in awhile." Other than covering World Series games, for which he was richly paid, Lardner spent afternoons at the park reading "a handy pocket edition of one of Edgar Wallace's sex stories because the events of the field make me yearn for a bottle of Mothersill's Remedy." To see this piece as a bitter indictment is to read it too literally. In the era now of Ruth and Gehrig, Lardner laments that the games have become too high-scoring and fast-paced for his taste. He prefers the dead-ball game, before the introduction of the "crazy ball" or "TNT ball" or "Br'er Rabbit Ball," as he calls the lively ball on different occasions; in a dead-ball game, one could see "efficiency rewarded." Breaking a couple of fingers is merely "a superficial injury for an infielder of the present," and the modern hitter, "with the old ball, would have been considered too feeble to hit fungoes on one of these here miniature golf courses." Even the long-ball hitters are overpaid stars only "because of the lofty heights to which they can hoist a leather-covered sphere stuffed with dynamite." A vicious low-line-drive hitter of old like Nap Lajoie would be so dangerous to the modern game that there would be "a general walkout if that big French gunman were allowed in the park again, even with a toothpick in his hand."

The essay works the hot-stove-league theme with references to Frank Schulte, who "would just about treble" the number of home runs hit by Babe Ruth. Lardner's argument lies in the metaphor of the lively ball itself. The essay ends with a reference to Ruth, who asserts that "there are at least fifteen outfielders now playing regular positions in his own league who would not have been allowed bench room the year he broke in." And so the great conversation and the myth of timelessness carry into the next generation, as they will in the next generation and the one after that.

Lardner's Willie Clough columns for the Bell Syndicate in 1931 and his Danny Warner stories of 1932 (featuring Casey Stengel) collected in *Lose With a Smile* (1933) are of passing interest but are mostly pale imitations of *You Know Me Al*. Virginia Woolf recognized in Lardner's writing "the quickest strokes, the surest touch, the sharpest insight." Lardner's uniquely American voice was the point at which all the great baseball themes met; indeed, it was where many of them began. Baseball (or "games," in Woolf's terms) gave Lardner "a clue, a center, a meeting place for the diverse activities of people whom a vast continent isolates, whom no tradition controls." That sentiment was just beginning to emerge and be recognized by the new breed of American authors for whom baseball represented a vast array of myths about culture and language. It was material out of which good, if not great, literature could grow. The writer, too, could see himself as a ballplayer whose "only real happiness," Lardner often said, "is when he is playing a ball game and accomplishes something he didn't think he could do."

CHAPTER 6

Ink by the Barrel

The years 1920–46 will be remembered as a period when sportswriters worked on train platforms, set up typewriters on baggage trucks in Pullman cars, and used suitcases as makeshift desks. Baseball writing was arguably the dominant prose in the dominant medium of that era. In fact, wrote Jimmy Breslin, "Everybody was sure that if something ever happened to baseball, the newspapers would collapse."

Robert W. Creamer recalls that newspapers became the lifeblood of the sports fan: "The sports columnist wrote every day, or at least six days a week, and you looked forward to reading them each day the way you looked forward to seeing your friends in school or around the neighborhood." Even as radio became the foremost medium—and that was not until the 1940s—the typical fan still got baseball news from reading the newspapers. In 1908, during the World Series at the Polo Grounds, Hugh Fullerton had helped to found the Baseball Writers Association of America, partly for logistical reasons: as John Lardner retold the story, "Fullerton . . . found the press-box pews covered with cured ham, that is to say, with visiting thespians."

The 1920 Black Sox scandal, Lardner also wrote in an article for the *Saturday Evening Post*, had nearly "wreck[ed] baseball for all eternity." Fullerton, who virtually broke the story later that year, believed that the final game of 1919 would be "the last game that will be played in any World Series."

But several things saved baseball, leading to the phenomenal postwar boom in its popularity. There were the full revelation of the scandal and its resolution in 1920; the beginning of Judge Kenesaw Mountain Landis's 25-year reign as baseball commissioner; the death of a player, Ray Chapman of the Indians, when he was hit by a grungy, discolored ball thrown by the Yankees' Carl Mays; a great American League pennant race between the Indians, the White Sox, and the Yankees; and most important, the trade of Babe Ruth to the Yankees, the great left-handed Red Sox pitcher who now, wrote W. O. McGeehan, "with his bat pounded baseball back into popularity."

As a result, baseball's literary scene shifted abruptly from Chicago to New York. As Marshall Smelser pointed out, "The baseball writers of New York represented more than a half dozen dailies, plus wire services and feature syndicates. Ball players had a better chance to get publicity in New York. What happened in baseball happened more loudly in New York." Writers spoke of Ruth with reverence. By 1928, Hugh Fullerton reckoned "that 1,420,000,000 words have been written about Babe Ruth and his exploits." The "gee whiz" tradition of journalism, led by such figures as Grantland Rice and Paul Gallico, underwent something of a renaissance.

The Matties tended to be romantic or realistic or often a combination. The Rubes continued to be ironic or satirical. They neither deified players nor denied them their due. They saw themselves as baseball writers, not as house organs for the ball clubs, even though some were often in the club owners' debt. (Fullerton dedicated one of his books to Charles Comiskey, "The man to whom, more than all others, the honesty and high standard of professional baseball is due.") The gee whiz tradition lasted into the forties, when, as Roger Kahn points out, the "three New York ballclubs underwrote New York baseball journalism . . . and promotional copy . . . was the return."

The Era of Wonderful Nonsense

Three men, none of them exclusively baseball writers, began developing their talents as light essayists in the sports pages during the era of Babe Ruth. In 1924, W. O. (William O'Connell) McGeehan (1879–1933) left the San Francisco Hearst papers to become the sports editor of the *New York Herald Tribune*; there he would bring American sports journalism into the professional age. His writing was crisp and direct, and he refused to talk down to his readers. McGeehan set new standards. His assumption was that the writer should have insight, authority, and every bit as much knowledge about the subject of baseball as the players and coaches had. He moved the Rubes in a new direction—away from linguistic play and toward a more concentrated kind of baseball talk filled with strong opinions and ideas. Where Dryden's narratives were humorously digressive, McGeehan's stayed on the field: "After mature deliberation I have come to the conclusion that only those who know little or nothing about the national pastime really enjoy a World Series. The experts are interested only in the games that put non-experts into a state of somnolence, while they suffer great mental anguish at the games that produce thrills for those who know little or nothing about the intricacies of inside baseball."

McGeehan did not for a minute care (hence, the "aw nuts" label) about "the intricacies of inside baseball," such as a manager's moving the infield in. He also uses the first person more categorically, as when he refers to "the flippancy of your correspondent" who tells his interrogator that moving the infield to wherever it was did not matter since "'nobody hit where the infield wasn't.'" The voice is clearly that of a knowledge-able reporter who also happens to honor the myth of memory (hence a later reference to Connie Mack's Athletics, who "won ball games with such monotonous regularity that the customers became so wearied of seeing them win baseball games that they did not come to the ball park"). The fans—or customers, as McGeehan always referred to them—"never get a thrill out of inside baseball, and . . . the perfect game, if it could be ballyhooed in advance, would not draw a corporal's guard."

Stanley Woodward would later damn McGeehan with faint praise, questioning his more than occasional lack of objectivity in reporting sports events. Nonetheless, McGeehan, a man who, according to Grantland Rice, was never easily impressed, became a voice of modera-tion, a combination Matty and Rube, in an era when most baseball prose was vastly overwritten.

McGeehan certainly influenced, among other writers, Westbrook Pegler (1894–1969), the biting, irreverent Pulitzer Prize–winning polit-ical journalist who began his career on the sports pages of the *Chicago Tribune*, for which he wrote a syndicated column called "Speaking Out on Sports." He saved his devastating wit for other sports and sports fig-ures—Knute Rockne, among them—for what defined baseball for Pegler was its romanticism, a quality he disdained in other sports. He was lackadaisical with his facts and more devoted to craft.

In 1932 he covered the Chicago–New York World Series in which Ruth, then 36 and "as an outfielder . . . pretty close to his past tense," hit his famous called-shot home run. For Pegler, the homer was the high-light of a Ruthian day that became a "spiritual memento of the most gorgeous display of humor, athletic art and championship class any per-former in any of the games has ever presented." It is fitting that Pegler cites humor first. Even Dempsey, he says, could never "make them laugh as he stepped back from some inert hunk with a lacerated face heaving laboriously on the floor." When Pegler describes the home run, he builds upon moments of interior monologue that he has been developing throughout the story:

> Bush pushed back his big ears, funneled his hands to his mouth and yelled raspingly at the great man to upset him. The Babe laughed derisively and gestured at him, "Wait, mugg, I'm going to hit one out of the yard." Root threw a strike past him and he held up a finger to Bush whose ears flapped excitedly as he renewed his insults. Another strike passed him and Bush crawled almost out of the hole to extend his remarks. The Babe held up two fingers this time. Root wasted two balls and Babe put up two fingers on his other hand. Then with a warning gesture of his hand to Bush he sent the signal for the customers to see. Now, it said, this is the one, look. And that one went riding on the longest home run ever hit in the park. . . . He licked the Chicago ball club, but he left the people laughing when he said goodbye. . . . Many a hitter may make two home runs, possibly three, in World Series play in years to come, but not the way Ruth made these two. Nor will you ever see an artist call his shot before hitting one of the longest drives ever made on the grounds in a World Series game, laughing and mocking the enemy, with two strikes gone.

Pegler's elaborate periodic sentences are well suited to the excitement of such occasions. When Babe Ruth hit three home runs for the second time in a World Series game, Pegler wrote: "Three times he laid his crutch in the way and knocked the baseball out of the St. Louis ball park and finally, in the last half of the ninth inning, shook his groaning chassis into a wild, loose-legged run to the rail of the temporary seats in the left field, where he leaned over and plucked a foul ball out from the feathers of a lady customer's millinery for the final put-out of the World Series of 1928."

Pegler punctured the egos of baseball heroes without deflating them. Ruth was that "pale and trembling invalid." Grover Cleveland Alexander was "Old Aleck," "loose-jointed, careless, incorrigible Aleck," "the ball player who won't behave because he doesn't have to." Before his celebrated relief appearance against Tony Lazzeri in 1926, Aleck had already pitched a complete game the previous day and had "enjoyed a fairly sizeable evening, too."

On occasion Pegler could go the way of a total Rube, as he did when he covered a 1931 game from the point of view of one "Medium-Sized Girl Reporter per Westbrook Pegler." Though the piece is sexist by today's dubious standards, Pegler twisted the baseball vernacular to make a point that can be seen as parodying the notion that "baseball has always been regarded as a man's game": "I found myself pounding my escort on the arm with my tiny fist in my excitement in the fourth inning when that poor man fell down running to his goal. My escort had to smile because he said the man fell down purposely trying to slide to his goal, and, of course, I blushed my confusion because it all looked so accidental and I suppose the maternal in me cried out for the poor boy when he went down so hard." The "era of wonderful nonsense"—Pegler's term for the twenties and thirties—could stand for the myth of the best game as well as for how Pegler came to write about baseball.

John Kieran (1892–1981), who began his career in 1916 and was the first writer to receive a byline under "Sports of the Times" for the *New York Times*, was another Matty who helped baseball writing evolve into an authentic and distinct literature. A brainy and gifted writer—John Lardner blamed him "for the rash of knowledge which is sweeping the country and endangering the basic principles for which our fathers fought"—Kieran, who faintly resembled William Faulkner, was also a regular panelist on the radio program "Information Please" (the brainchild of Roger Kahn's father Gordon). In addition to clever verses and concise profiles, he wrote some of the most intelligent baseball columns of the thirties, a time when workhorse sportswriters like John Drebinger and James P. Dawson covered the play-by-play baseball action for the *Times*. Kieran graced his sentences with quick successions of adjectival bullets: "Who could suspect the slim, gentlemanly [Herb] Pennock out there with his graceful, almost languid motion?" or, "The fiery, peppery, trim McGraw of other days had changed to the portly genius of the high chair on the left end of the Giant bench."

Kieran described baseball men the way some writers write about other writers. Pennock was "always a delight to the eye, every move a picture." When Ruth hit his sixtieth home run in 1927, Kieran reprinted a familiar "versified query" that asked, "Was there ever a guy like Ruth?" Kieran saw Ruth as Achilles. Long counted out, Ruth returned to battle the ignominy of advancing age: "Supposedly 'over the hill,' slipping down the steps of Time, stumbling toward the discard, six years past his peak, Babe Ruth stepped out and hung up a new home run record at which all the sport world may stand and wonder. What Dempsey couldn't do with his fists, Ruth has done with his bat." Rather than quote a player, Kieran entered his head: narrator and player share a moment together in the great conversation, such as John McGraw's thoughts on how "the lively ball came in and any hillbilly, hay shaker or plow jockey might walk up there with a blundering bludgeon to ruin a whole afternoon of fine strategy by slapping the jack-rabbit ball over a distant fence."

Few of his contemporaries could summarize an entire era with Kieran's panache and refined humor or better shape a sports column into a light essay. A "tour of inspection" of Yankee Stadium–in-progress in 1922 turns into an object lesson on architecture, construction work, Yankee management, and baseball: to deal with the cavernous center-field, "it is suggested that Yankee outfielders be equipped with bicycles for chasing fly balls that go over their heads."

Kieran cared little for the technical side of baseball; he preferred to hear about such details in the player's own words. He said, "The most stupid ballplayer knows more, really, about the game than any baseball writer I ever knew." He thought that *Baseball: The Fan's Game* (1933) by the Hall of Fame catcher Mickey Cochrane was the best baseball book he had ever read. Though no romantic like Pegler, Kieran believed in the myth of the best game, played shortstop well himself, and, mandarin that he was, saw in baseball the possibilities of a wonderful education.

Baseball in the Roaring Twenties

The man who brought John Kieran to the *New York American* for a brief stint in the early twenties was its famous sports columnist Damon Runyon (1884–1946). Runyon, along with Grantland Rice, Heywood Broun, and Paul Gallico, dominated the gee whiz school of sportswriting during the "Age of Ballyhoo" (one of the many synonyms for the Roaring Twenties). Runyon was the only Rube among them.

Born in Kansas, Runyon seemed a more likely heir apparent to the American West of Bret Harte than to the Broadway and Roaring Twenties he later came to popularize. A roving reporter at heart, he was something of a realist, writing about the people and daily life of New York City. If his subjects were familiar, it was because Runyon had met many of them personally in the dugouts, just as he had come to know real-life petty mobsters, small-time bookmakers, and gamblers, horse-players, hoodlums, and molls from covering the sensational murder trials of his day.

On a portable Royal typewriter, Runyon banged away at copy for the *American* from 1914 to 1928. Though he often wrote under the assumption that he was simply and legitimately publicizing the home-town team and players, his prose was pungent and strong. "Runyon could do things with the alphabet," wrote Red Smith, "that made a fellow want to throw his typewriter away and go dig coal for a living. . . .

He created a new language and enough characters to people a fair-size town." He wrote about individuals as diverse as Christy Mathewson, Bugs Raymond, and John McGraw. Through baseball Runyon learned the art of character development and dialogue; he knew that the quote, at its best, could be a miniature essay. Lines like "Pitchers sometimes let their wits go wool gathering" would become in the mouth of the fictional Harry the Horse, "A guy must pay his bookmaker, no matter what."

Not surprisingly perhaps, Runyon wrote only one baseball short story. The brief description of Haystack Duggeler in "Baseball Hattie" (1936)—"no smarter jobbie ever breathes than Haystack when he is out there pitching. He has so much speed that he just naturally throws the ball past a batter before he can get the old musket off his shoulder, and along with his hard one, Haystack has a curve ball like the letter Q. With two ounces of brains, Haystack Duggeler will be the greatest pitcher that ever lives"—had been realized years earlier when he was depicting players like the White Sox pitcher Dickie Kerr: "Take Dickie Kerr, now, a wee hop o' my thumb. Not much taller than a walking stick . . . the tiniest of the baseball brood. Won't weigh 90lbs soaking wet, an astute scout once reported after a look at Kerr. Too small for a pitcher. Too small for too much of anything, except, perhaps, a watch charm."

Runyon had a sound reason for treating his subjects like fictional figures. As he wrote in "Postscript on Sports Writing": "To be a great sports writer a man must hold himself pretty much aloof from the characters of the games with which he deals before his sympathy for them commences to distort his own viewpoint. There is nothing more engaging than an engaging rogue and there are many engaging rogues in organized sports. I fear I knew most of them, and that is not good for a sports writer."

On opening day of the 1919 World Series, he caught a small piece of the myth of America:

> The crowds coagulate at hotel entrances. Soft hats predominate. It's a mid-Western, semi-Southern town. Hard-boiled derbys mark the Easterners. The streets of old Cincy have been packed for hours. People get up before breakfast in these parts. The thoroughfares leading to Redland Field have been echoing to the tramp of feet, the honk of auto horns since daylight. It is said that some people kept watch and ward at the ballpark all night long. Might as well stay there as any place in this town. They would have had the same amount of excitement. Flocks of jitneys go squeaking through the streets. This is

the heart of the jitney belt. A jitney is the easiest thing obtainable in Cincy. . . . A drink is next. . . . Cincy is a dry town—as dry as the Atlantic Ocean.

Runyon discounts the undercurrent of excitement in the city, presenting instead a sense of quietude. The noises are muted, the crowds move in slow motion. The words "soft hats," "echoing," and "watch and ward" create a different picture. Runyon, who liked to get to the ballpark before his writer pals, begins his piece in the hours before the game. He knows that games start elsewhere in time: at breakfast tables, in subway cars or jitneys, in saloons. He lets the prose, and whatever tension that might result from the anticipation of the series, build naturally. Like other Rubes, he made his observations from many angles; when he found the one he was looking for, he followed it. In some ways he helped introduce human interest stories to the sports pages. People might come and go from different places on the map, Runyon seemed to be saying, but baseball is a town everywhere. When it was time to reassess the Black Sox story years later, he wrote with deep sympathy about "the guilty ball players [who] were given the hoovu-groovus from baseball for the rest of their lives," and about Joe Jackson in particular.

His most famous baseball piece, written for the *American*, covers the opening game of the 1923 World Series; its first paragraphs of sustained parallelism are celebrated: "This is the way old Casey Stengel ran yesterday afternoon/This is the way old Casey Stengel ran running his home run" is a refrain we hear four more times in the piece. The writing continues to greater effect with more vivid description: "His mouth wide open. . . . His warped old legs bending. . . . His arms flying back. . . . His flanks heaving, his breath whistling, his head far back." For nearly 12 paragraphs, Runyon literally wears out Stengel on his way to singlehandedly leading the Giants to victory over the Yankees with an agonizing inside-the-yard home run. Focusing on Stengel's rickety legs ("twisted and bent by many a year of baseball campaigning"), Runyon has "them" crossing home plate. "Then they collapsed."

At this point the elevated narrative collapses as well, and Runyon's story turns to fierce, direct reportage.

Runyon composed the piece inning by inning, as though he were broadcasting the game. The account was supposed to begin chronologically, with "four solemn-looking gentlemen in dark, funeral blue uniforms with little blue caps [holding] a meeting at home plate just before game time." When Casey's "ball sailed out over left field, moving high, moving far," Runyon decided to invert the structure of the piece, filling in bits of hot-stove exposition ("If you are curious to know the origin of the nickname 'Casey,' it might be explained that Stengel's hometown is Kansas City") and the pertinent facts. The box scores, as he often said, tell the rest of the story. As Breslin notes, Runyon's piece "lasted by word of mouth as long as if it had been issued on a bronze plaque." Robert Creamer was surely thinking of the Runyon piece when he began his 1984 biography of Stengel with the great opening sentence, "Casey Stengel naked was a sight to remember."

Character would be at the heart of Runyon's best pieces, including the one he wrote about a drunken Grover Cleveland Alexander's striking out Tony Lazzeri in the seventh inning of the 1926 World Series. Beginning with a faint reminder of the Stengel piece, Runyon writes, "Old Grover Cleveland Alexander, with his cap perched high above his ear, shambled in out of a fog into the seventh game of the World Series of 1926." He alludes to Alexander's conspicuous absence earlier in the game ("Some say Grover had been heating himself up under the bleachers"), follows Alexander to his favorite haunts, gets him drunker than he probably really was, and sobers him up when, after the strikeout, "everybody got right up and yelled for the Grover."

Covering the first game of the 1928 World Series between the Yankees and the Cardinals, Runyon returned to the "rhythmic song" quality of prose he had been so successful with in the Casey Stengel piece. In this case his subject was Yankee pitcher Waite Hoyt: no longer the fabled 'Brooklyn schoolboy,' he was "up around 30 years now, and has been moseying around the big league since John J. McGraw signed him up for the Giants when he was about sweet 16." Again, inverting the structure, Runyon describes Hoyt's "greased old pump handle, the right arm . . ." as it "rose and fell before the amazed eyes of the St. Louis Cardinals up at the Yankee Stadium . . ." "Up! Down!" Runyon repeats ten times in describing the "irksome . . . sheer iteration" as "the funnel of [Hoyt's] fist poured speed, and yet more speed to the befuddlement of the batsmen. . . ."

Runyon clearly saw similarities between sport and the other real-life material upon which he drew. He preferred prizefighting to baseball or any other sport but always found his analogies in baseball. He likened sport to a murder trial, saying, "I find the same popular interest in a murder trial that I find in any city on the eve of a big . . . baseball series. There is the same conversational speculation on the probable result, only more of it." The "slight curiosity" that makes him want to see a murderer also makes him "eager to see . . . a great baseball player." In a way, "human life is at stake." The murder trial has an "inside game" of its own, "with something new popping up at every turn, something in the form of what you might call a new play by the State or the defense. Often it starts off as involved as a hidden-ball maneuver and it takes you a little time to figure it out before the play gets in the clear." Like any baseball team, a murder trial has its "high-priced players." Afterwards the "players," so antagonistic in court, "hobnob all friendly together, like Brown's cows, as baseball players fraternize after a game in which they have attempted to spike each other."

When Runyon finally turned to fiction—though he always remained a working newspaperman—baseball became the nut he cracked open to find a world inside.

The Book of Ruth

Heywood Broun (1888–1939) began writing in 1912, covering John McGraw's New York Giants and cheering for them, to Runyon's dismay, from the press box. His son Heywood Hale Broun once confessed that his father's "largest contribution to American culture might turn out to be his persuasion of . . . McGraw not to turn the young Christy Mathewson into a first baseman."

In addition to writing baseball for the old *New York Morning Telegraph* and later the *Tribune*, Broun wrote novels and short stories (*The Sun Field* [1923] and "The Last Signal" [1936] contain baseball themes) and familiar essays. Broun did not dwell for long in the sports pages, though he was popular and influential. He was an authentic "gee whiz" writer, but also an exemplary Matty. His careful insights and light touch won him many readers.

Yet as he moved from drama critic to political columnist, he never seemed to forget his roots. Whereas Lardner began writing purely autobiographical baseball essays, Broun viewed baseball as a serious theme for a wide variety of subjects, as a catalog of metaphors and allusions, and as an important subject in itself. On one occasion he speculated on the injustice of Babe Ruth's omission from the 1925 *Who's Who in America*. The "nearest name" was a forestry professor named Roth. "If the professor chances to be wrong, even if he is wrong three times," Broun muses, "nobody in the classroom is likely to poke a sudden finger high in the air and shout, 'You're out!'" Broun's politics stopped inside the clubhouse; the defender of Sacco and Vanzetti wrote nothing about the plight of exploited ballplayers. He left the sports beat to write his "It Seems to Me" column but almost regularly covered the World Series.

Broun was among the first newspaper writers for whom baseball had mythopoeic dimensions. In a piece on southpaws, for instance, he quotes from the third chapter of the Book of Judges. The essay is ostensibly about the oddities of left-handedness, the observation being that people "who reversed the traditional use of hands were regarded as queer folk or even a little worse than that." Yet Broun titles the piece with a baseball term and cites Babe Ruth along with Charlie Chaplin, "both of whom are completely and fervently left-handed." Broun plays on the common prejudices and symbols of left-handedness, from political radicalism to baseball's almost endemic hatred of portsiders. Nonetheless, writes Broun, a lefty himself, "the complete triumph of the left-hander comes in baseball." He returns to scripture: "Like the Roman emperor before whom Paul appeared . . . he is almost persuaded" by Ty Cobb, since Cobb bats left but, alas, throws right.

In his famous account of the second game of the 1923 World Series (beginning "The Ruth is mighty and shall prevail"), Broun consistently develops Ruth's godlike image, his "full brilliance." Managers sometimes pitched around great hitters, but the Giants' McGraw chose to pitch to Ruth "eyes front and his thumb on his nose." McGraw believed that Ruth was no better than other hitters his pitchers had faced in the National League; "ere the sun had set on McGraw's rash and presumptuous words," however, "the Babe had flashed across the sky fiery portents which should have been sufficient to strike terror and conviction into the hearts of all infidels." Nonetheless, McGraw clung "to his heresy" and refused "to kneel before Ruth," who had hit one home run, almost hit another, and walked twice. When Ruth came to bat again, he hit his second home run of the day in what would be one of his greatest World Series. For those who would count Ruth out, Broun reminds us, "Ruth crushed to earth shall rise again."

Broun loved baseball and continued to write about it until his death in 1939. Spring always heralded baseball's pastoral myth, and an April 1936 piece for the *World-Telegram* found him rooting for Casey Stengel's Brooklyn Dodgers. The Dodgers appealed to him because they were a team made up of "striplings" and "shopworn" players; they remind him of the old New York Highlanders in their salad days and of their old ballpark, both of which "serve so poignantly to remind a man of his lost youth."

The Highlanders, he recalled, once were sent a couple of aged players from the established clubs so that the team "boasted the finest collection of grandfather clucks ever seen on any diamond." Among them was the "mashie-minded" Popup John, who couldn't hit the chip shot out of the tiny park but instead would "take a full swing at a fast one and meet the ball in such a way as to drive it straight into the air." Anecdote, metaphor, and vernacular come together as he calls up one of his own lines about the Highlanders from his reporting days: "Jack Kleinow goes down to first as if he were pulling Big Bill Taft in a ricksha." The anecdote serves to justify his faith in the Brooklyn club, and he eagerly awaits the chance "to see baseball again and in the company of men of my own age."

Shortly before his death he wrote what was to be his last baseball piece for his homespun newspaper *Broun's Nutmeg*. "The Happy Days of Baseball" (1939) recounts a hot-stove "dialogue in free association" he had with a man sitting next to him on a train. They talked baseball with great ease, asking each other questions and swapping names. Their conversation turned to "tolerance," which "has done much to impair baseball as a spectacle." In the old days, "there was none of that nonsense about applauding a good play by either side." Brooklyn fans react quite differently, however. "They do not cheer even the most spectacular play by any invader and they do throw pop bottles." This aspect of Dodger baseball helped draw crowds in spite of poor standings. Most of the league had been like Brooklyn once. Perhaps only Washington mirrored Brooklyn in partisanship, but only because the transient population of the city was "disenfranchised" and required "some emotional release."

"Baseball fervor" for Broun stemmed from the myth of timelessness. The automobile had become baseball's third strike against tradition. In modern times "[e]ven the rookie . . . buys himself a car and he uses it going to and from the park in his home city." In the old days players traveled on team buses and were paraded "through the main street like circus elephants on exhibition." If the players happened to be bums, they were subject to epithets and leers, "eggs and tomatoes." Fans now shouted verbal missiles instead of throwing them. The "happy days of baseball"—"when it was frequently necessary to call out the reserves in order to limit the number of killed and injured"—had vanished.

The year 1939 and the onset of war marked the end of a baseball era. Broun's Elysian Fields were overrun with ghosts and scattered with broken bottles and rotten fruit, but underneath the debris, the field was green with the myth of memory. Just as the dead-ball era ended with Ring Lardner, the era of Babe Ruth ended with Paul Gallico and Heywood Broun.

That Veteran Sportswriter

Paul Gallico (1897–1976) wrote sports for the *New York Daily News* from 1923 to 1936, long before he became a popular novelist and short-story writer. He wrote, among numerous titles, *The Snow Goose* (1941), a book whose craftsmanship Hemingway envied; *The Pride of the Yankees* (1942); and "Saint Bambino" (1948)—his attempt, he wrote in an introduction to the story, "to bring the late Babe Ruth back from wherever he had gone, Heaven, Hell, Purgatory, or Limbo," and to canonize him as "the patron saint of baseball."

"I belonged to the gee-whiz group of sportswriters," he told Jerome Holtzman. "I was impressed by athletes, by what I was seeing and also what I was trying to do. I thought I ought to impress my public, impress the people who were reading, because if I didn't make a game that I saw, and which excited me, if I didn't make that exciting to the reader, I was a lousy sportswriter."

In an early blueprint of participatory "new journalism," his essay "The Feel," which first appeared in *Farewell to Sport* (1938), he described his experience catching Herb Pennock's pitching (and more famously, getting into the ring with Jack Dempsey). "If I knew what playing a game felt like," he wrote, "particularly against or in the company of experts, I was better equipped to write about the playing of it and the problems of the men and women who took part in it."

Gallico's daily columns (he once said that he would settle for two good columns a week) are less important to baseball literature than his essays in *Farewell to Sport*, a sort of apologia for leaving sportswriting to write fiction and drama. Two of these essays that also first appeared in *Farewell to Sport* became staples in the baseball canon, "His Majesty the King," his profile of Babe Ruth, and "Inside the Inside," his short, didactic analysis of the game. Both essays are comprehensive enough to sum up the entire sport as Gallico understood it.

Gallico's treatment of the Babe is indicative, as Jimmy Cannon once wrote, of how the myth of Ruth "celebrates American innocence in a good lost time." Gallico captures the great player at the end of his career. Washed up, Ruth was shamefully neglected by the baseball establishment. Gallico evokes the popular image of Ruth with references to "Mr. and Mrs. Average Citizen" and overblown similes like "the crowd caught fire like a blaze running over a dry meadow." He describes how girls and boys chase after Ruth's fungo flies for "there was magic on those baseballs."

Gallico saw Ruth as a kind of pagan god. Like Enkidu of the Gilgamesh myth, "he was kneaded, rough thumbed out of earth, a golem, a figurine that might have been made by a savage." Put words into his mouth, however, and he was one of Emerson's teamsters, speaking the vernacular of the "asphalt and gutter world." Ruth the human being worked hard to pay the debt he owed to baseball and to the young fans who admired him, although he never fully abandoned his vices. If he had done so, he would not have been Ruth. He slowly came to understand what it meant to be always in the public eye and learned how to behave when the public watched, while "perform[ing] his peccadillos in strict privacy if possible."

Whether intentionally or not, Gallico perpetuates several Ruthian myths: Ruth's orphanhood, the "bellyache heard round the world," the sickbed visit to Johnny Sylvester, and so forth. When asked to visit little Johnny, Ruth did so in earnest, believing absolutely in the part he was playing and unaware even that he might be playing a part. (Years later, however, when someone reminded Ruth about the boy, he responded, "Who the hell is Johnny Sylvester?")

Gallico came to love Ruth for his essential manliness. Sports were *macho*. He remembered even the tennis great Helen Wills for her "great concentration, will-power, and stamina and powerful legs and shoulders, a cool, calm, finely chiseled Grecian beauty with the perfect profile of an Athenian statue." Ruth could never have lived up to the myth of heroes, which the writers had created, if he had not believed the treacle written about him. In spite of his flaws, he demonstrated his greatness, coming through "when there was something important at stake, when it meant the most, when the greatest number of eyes were upon him."

He earned the awe of fans not just for his home runs but also for "the energy, power, effort, and sincerity of purpose that went into" his strikeouts, which were "the absolute acme of frustration." Any action Ruth performed might bestow the gift of future recollection—"a curious double rejoicing in which the spectator celebrated not only Babe's feat and its effect upon the outcome of the game, but also his excellent luck in being present and with his own eyes beholding the great happening."

Gallico's Ruth is a "king" drawn from fiction and fable. Like Rice and others, Gallico claimed to have seen Ruth call his home run shot in the 1932 series with the Cubs, and he was convinced that Ruth knew exactly what he was doing. By 1938, when he wrote the essay, Gallico must have known that the claim had become suspect. The Ruthian myths become, appropriately, like various biblical strands: when we piece them all together, even if they are contradictory, they reveal a larger truth.

If Ruth personified the myth of heroes, there was still nothing better than "the things that take place on the field." "Inside the Inside," an early technical analysis of the game, can also be read as a poetics of baseball. Gallico believed that knowing inside baseball spelled the difference between fascination and boredom. Baseball is every kind of theater, with "cause and effect, crime and punishment, motive and result, so cleanly defined." It is Greek theater as staged at the Festival Dionysus—a spectacle highly original and given to certain rituals and practices. "It is endlessly intriguing, and when the human element is added to the weird mechanics of the sport, the wise, foxy veterans, the brash cocky young kids, the eccentric and screwy characters who play the game, it becomes truly a part of the national scene."

Baseball has its own *orkestra*, the diamond, which "is no diamond at all, but actually a square set up on one of its points." There is pageantry ("One team dresses in white, the other in gray") as well as choreography: "There is nothing prettier for timing and rhythm than to watch a shortstop or third baseman . . . come in fast for a slow roller, and as he is moving, swoop on the ball like a gull dropping for a fish." The frequently shifting advantages and disadvantages pitchers and batters find working for or against them lead to many reversals of fortune. Baseball's action rises and falls and includes climax and denouement: "The consequences of a single error or failure pyramid inexorably as the game goes on and finally prove to be the events that have won or lost the day."

Baseball's heroes have "moments of pure glory and unadulterated satisfaction," but they must also mollify meddling gods, as "when an obviously astigmatic umpire, with two out and none on base, calls what was obviously a third strike a fourth ball." And finally, there is the groundling, "to heckle, hoot, cheer, and advise the player to his heart's content," and the crowd, which plays "the role of Greek chorus to the actors on the field below." Catharsis may arrive at any moment: "a great roar turning into a groan that dies away to nothing—a potential home run, with too much slice on it, that just went foul. The crowd lives the actions of the players more than in any other game."

Inside baseball—"the plot behind the patterns"—creates a play-within-a-play. Onstage the catcher plays the role of interlocutor, and any game can be "as full of surprises as a mystery play." The myth of timelessness assures the spectator that, for all its tautology, the game "never seems to be twice the same."

The essay form let Gallico make a clean break from the pressure to remain fresh. "I was beginning to find I was repeating myself in my column," he said. "I was scared stiff of becoming an old sportswriter, a veteran sportswriter. I could already read and hear, 'Gallico, that veteran sportswriter.'" Runyon and Broun—and to some extent, Ring Lardner— had felt the same. Pegler moved over to politics, and even McGeehan chased other beats. Of all the major writers who covered baseball between the wars, only one, Grantland Rice, never left the sports page.

The Dean of Sportswriters

The fame of Grantland Rice (1880–1954), creator of heroes, could have matched the myth of any baseball hero. He wrote sports through five decades and died at his typewriter at the age of 74. An oft-injured athlete at Vanderbilt, he barnstormed with some semipro ball clubs before accepting a job in 1901 on the fledgling *Nashville Daily News*, where he started breaking up his columns with verse, a knack he developed by "scanning . . . Latin poets" in his student days and nurturing his own love of great poetry. In his time, notes his biographer Charles Fountain, "Rice was one of the most popular of American poets—not only one of the most widely read, but one of the most widely praised as well."

His early life is well detailed in his best-selling posthumous autobiography *The Tumult and the Shouting* (1954) and more recently in Fountain's *Sportswriter* (1993). The literary influences on Rice (as well as his prose style) are removed by time and history: they include the heroics of the Confederate general Nathan Bedford Forrest, and Latin and Greek studies. "As for English," he wrote, "I honestly can't recall having studied it."

Rice would work with Don Marquis, Joel Chandler Harris, Frank L. Stanton, and, in New York, with what must have been the literary brat pack of its day: Rube Goldberg, Franklin P. Adams, Deems Taylor, Irwin S. Cobb, Broun, Runyon, and O. O. McIntyre. At the *Atlanta Journal* in 1904, Rice covered the young Ty Cobb (who repeatedly sent Rice flattering telegrams about himself, either unsigned or falsely signed) and claimed credit for Cobb's "discovery," which became part of Rice's own legend. Rice's big break came in 1910 when he took a job with the *New York Evening Mail*, a job that would lead him to the *Tribune* a few years later and ultimately the long-running syndicated "Sportlight" column.

Rice's contribution to sportswriting was enormous. He was famous for his quotes and memorable lines (it's "not that you won or lost—but how you played the game"). To some extent he popularized the use of the historical anecdote in sportswriting in his numerous essays for *Collier's*, *Look*, and *Sport* as well as in "Sportlight." He had been around so long by then, he had many anecdotes to tell. He was one of the last of the old-style Matties, "with his enthusiasm and kind word for every event," as Stanley Frank wrote. Where Charles Alexander in his 1984 biography depicted Cobb as "sensitive, distrustful, courageous, often arrogant, and sometimes mean," Rice painted him as a model of Emersonian self-reliance, "flint hard, perhaps, but not so cold."

Often Rice got the words perfectly, as when he described Walter Johnson as a big train roaring through, Dizzy Dean as "a beggar with a bullet through his spleen," and Christy Mathewson as "the knightliest of all the game's paladins." On the death of Babe Ruth he wrote poignantly and simply, "Game called on account of darkness."

His writing can be studied in three stages of development, not counting his early verses: his reportage, his essays, and his reminiscences. The reportage was always firmly structured along classical lines. Between the exordium and peroration lay the game account. Thus, his rendering of the winning game of the 1923 World Series began: "The Yankees rode through the storm at last to reach the shining haven where the gold dust for the winter's end lies ankle-deep in the streets." The body of the story gives the facts, mounted by classical and literary allusions: in the eighth inning, "there were massed and concentrated the fall of Rome, the destruction of Carthage, the feast of Belshazzar, the rout of Cyrus, the march of Attila, the wreck of Hesperus and the Chicago fire." In the game's penultimate moment, "here was Babe Ruth at bat, with the bases filled and two runs needed to win—Ruth standing 'amid the alien corn,' as Keats once put it, yearning 'for home.'" Ruth's heartbreaking strikeout ("Oh, what a fall was that, my countrymen!") announces the concluding section of the piece, as well as the game's climax when the Yankee's Bob Meusel, "amid the reverberating clamor of the multitude, ripped a sharp bounder through the box." Rice patented a style that Stanley Walker called "magnificent and may God bless us all, pretty terrible."

His essays and profiles were more conventional in style but no less varied in tone. In his "Open Letter to Ted Williams," published in *Sport* in 1947, he could sound like Polonius to Laertes, offering sententious chunks of wisdom to the bad boy of baseball: "You have your way of life, and you have your way of baseball," "Stick to the Williams system," "The only thing that can hurt you is yourself," "They never boo a bum," and, "Baseball needs you more than you need baseball." A *Sport* profile on Bob Feller a year earlier found Rice at his most sentimental, echoing the familiar theme of fathers and sons. Speaking of Feller's father, also a subject of the piece, he began, "Every father who has ever lived has had a dream for his son." For a 1951 *Sport* essay on the Yankee dynasty he called upon his stock of anecdotes and imagery, such as the story about the turn-of-the-century player who argued a call by stepping on the umpire's toes, or his description of the diminutive Yankee manager Miller Huggins as a man on whose ill-fitting uniform "the letters that spelled out 'New York' across his chest always drooped as they did when the shirt was hung over a peg in the locker room."

In his long reminiscences, most of which he saved for chapters in his autobiography, Rice remained largely anecdotal, for he had been present himself at many significant moments in baseball history. Rice takes us back to spring training 1919. The young Ruth, then a pitcher, circled the base paths by "mincing along with short, pigeon-toed steps" like "Man O'War's gallop." Rice remembers how "that Giants series put the exclamation mark on Ruth." He retells the old myths and legends: the called-shot home run, Ruth's startling Mrs. Walter Lippman with profane language, the "Duke Ellington for Duke of Wellington" gaffe on radio. One anecdote leads to another; many sentences begin simply, "I recall. . . ." About any negative characteristics of men like Ruth, Cobb, or John McGraw (from cop punching to drunk driving), Rice is nonjudgmental. "And so it went," is his only dry comment. Rice betrays no friendships and suspects that Babe is "kicking his heels around on some king-sized cloud." Rice, always the classicist, adhered to Plutarch's approach in his life of Cimon. Though Ruth's flaws were ones of "natural effects of vice" rather than "shortcomings of some particular virtue," Rice undoubtedly believed that, "since it is hard, or indeed perhaps, impossible, to show the life of a man wholly free from blemish, in all that is excellent we must follow truth exactly and give it fully."

Rice's prose was widely copied and parodied and much maligned over time, but his style had developed from the rigors of a sound liberal education: Homer, the Bible, the Koran, Shakespeare, Keats, Shelley, Carlyle, Emerson, Kipling. James Whitcomb Riley was about as contemporary as Rice got. His imitators and detractors often lacked his depth of knowledge or sanguine point of view. "Rhythm, the main factor in both [verse and sport]," he said, "is one of the main factors of life. For without rhythm, there is a sudden snarl or tangle." What he said of Christy Mathewson was true of himself: "He handed the game a certain touch of class, an indefinable lift in culture, brains, [and] personality."

By the end of World War II, a good many new faces had already entered the ranks of baseball journalism—well beyond the borders of New York City, too. The focus of the sports beat gradually shifted away from the writer's voice and stylistic inventions toward more biting, objective, quote-filled stories with an "angle." Matties like Al

Laney and Rubes like Dick Young worked brilliantly while digging for truth and reporting the facts.

Black sportswriters, too, it must be noted, made a solid contribution to baseball literature that has been too often overlooked. Jim Reisler, in his important anthology *Black Writers/Black Baseball* (1994) describes these "talented journalists pursuing their work with professionalism and a kind of folksy humor rare on today's sports pages. Baseball was a refuge from the often blaring headlines in black newspapers of the day, which, in true tabloid fashion, seldom shied from the truly horrendous toll of misfortune generated by the concept of 'separate but equal' and other forms of racism, which the writers themselves were not spared." Even though organized black baseball, as Wendell Smith of the *Pittsburgh Courier* wrote in 1938, was "still in its infancy," many of the great baseball themes could be found in their prose, particularly the myth of heroes. Rollo Wilson, who also wrote for the *Pittsburgh Courier*, observed in a 1927 piece, "Some of these days, I'll see a greater and more versatile ballplayer than the Cuban Stars' Martin Dihigo, and when I do, I'll write, wire or phone the details to each reader of this Colyum, collect." Baseball, black or white, was still the best game, and black writers could write imaginative spot reporting with the best of them, as evidenced by this line from the 20 August 1927 story by Chester L. Washington, yet another *Pittsburgh Courier* columnist and perhaps as fine a Rube as there ever was: "Homestead Gray stock soared 'sky-high' Sunday when the Pittsburgh club, not only raided the value three points by three victories over the Lincoln Giants in Smoketown, but invaded the very meat of the 'market' itself, and incidentally the spacious abode of the Giants' Protectory Oval, and snatched an 8–6 triumph together with the heart of the fans present."

Covering almost exclusively Negro Leagues baseball, writers like Smith, Sam Lacy, Dan Burley, Joe Bostic, Wilson, Fay Young, and Washington challenged or helped reinterpret baseball's myth of America. While integration of the big leagues became the overriding question for most black sportswriters in the 1940s, men like Bostic of Harlem's *The People's Voice*, though attuned to the "idealistic and democratic point of view," reminded readers that it would also be impractical to "subject any player to the humiliation and indignities associated with the problems of eating, sleeping and traveling in a layout dominated by prejudiced-ridden southern whites." Bostic preferred that an all-black team join one of the two leagues, stressing economic factors, and even Smith, one of the pioneers of baseball integration, had chided his fellow blacks in a 1938 column: "With our noses high and our hands deep in our pockets, squeezing the same dollars that we hand out to the white players, we walk past [black] parks and go the major league games. Nuts—that's what we are. Just plain nuts!" By 1942 writers like Washington in "An Open Letter to Judge Landis" were addressing the issue openly, directly, and optimistically (as blacks were now being asked to serve their country in time of war), urging baseball "to catch the spirit of the times" and be "broad enough to realize the trend toward democracy in practice as well as in word, in all of our American institutions."

Despite the continuing focus on the serious racial issues affecting baseball prior to and immediately after Jackie Robinson, black sportswriters often demonstrated the essential colorblindness of baseball. Wrote Dan Burley of the *Amsterdam News* in 1947, "The boys who are sure to follow Robinson in the big show will have to . . . concentrate on being a great player, as is Robinson, and as are [Hank] Greenberg, the Italians, the Poles, the Irish, the Germans, the Hungarians, the Czechs, the French, the Swedes, the Bohemians and others who have made baseball a racial polyglot of personalities, religion, race and background."

The map of baseball was becoming too big to be contained within nine-inch columns. More than half a century of history and some changes in the makeup of the game (integration, for starters) had given rise to complex issues in baseball. Postwar writers also tried to put their personal stamp on baseball prose and to revitalize the genre in ways that could make it stand out from other types of sportswriting. To accomplish this, they would turn to the thematic nature of baseball prose as well as to the influences of their literary ancestors.

CHAPTER 7

The Heart of
the Order

Ernest Hemingway thought Jimmy Cannon (1910–73) was the best of
the new breed of sportswriters. Cannon paid back the compliment by
citing Hemingway as the country's greatest writer and a great sportswriter in his own right. Cannon, however, seems to have been lost on
many contemporary readers, who view him as something of a period
writer or men's writer and deem his short, clipped, colloquial style to be
as passé as Rice's.

His world, New York's Lower West Side (where he was born), is
indeed a lost world. He wrote of a man's world filled with gamblers and
drinkers. He captured their mannerisms and nuances, not just as gamblers and drinkers but as working stiffs and harried husbands who needed to get things off their chests. He learned as much from Gallico as
from Runyon. A newspaperman from the age of 16, he soon began writing for the *New York Post* and later the *Journal-American*. When he died at
the age of 63 in the winter of 1973, there were only three newspapers
left in New York City—one of them the first paper he ever worked for,
the *Daily News*—and he had published only two collections of his
columns, *Nobody Asked Me* (1951) and *Who Struck John?* (1956).

His world was also the world of talk ("Nobody asked me, but . . ."
was his famous tag line); it was talk as a kind of art form, and baseball
naturally became an important part of it. Yet he was not a typical hot-
stover. "The act of baseball is only a small piece of it," he once wrote.
"There are mornings and afternoons before games and the deep nights
after them. The ballplayer isn't created by the game and he exists
beyond the borders of its movement."

Cannon found his material in those late afternoon shadows and early
morning sun. His obituary of Connie Mack, who died in the winter of

1956 at the age of 93, begins like a prose poem to ancient history, old men, and "waltzes danced long ago": "Is a man fortunate who lives so long that the years make him a stranger in the time of his life? Aliens populate familiar streets when a man survives beyond his generation's span. The graveyards are the friendly places because the dead share the used-up seasons. The world beyond the cemeteries is noisy with youth. The tombstones become calendars for those who mysteriously dwell in the night of time." The references to "familiar streets" and "friendly places" and the terms "used-up seasons" and "noisy with youth" are as appropriate to the world of baseball and ballparks as they are to the world outside. The opening paragraph starkly parallels the final passages of the piece, in which Mack's Shibe Park is "empty a lot . . . across the barren summers" when rookies "got off trains and were played before they had checked into a hotel." Mack has died, the Athletics have been sold, "and people forgot that Eddie Collins and Eddie Plank played for them long ago." Even Babe Ruth, as a dying old man on his way to "Babe Ruth Day" at Yankee Stadium, "walked as a stranger under the stands." Modern times, Cannon believed, made the myth of timelessness less romantic.

Cannon's baseball columns often reflected the world and the people in it. *We* are the "multitude" both fascinated and alienated by "the cruelty of Cobb's style"; "we are people who pine to be what Marilyn and Joe DiMaggio are." "Jimmy Cannon found room in a sports column to do everything he wanted," wrote Wilfrid Sheed: "war, his old neighborhood, show-biz friends, all in the style of a sports column—with friction, vitality and loss all playing their licks and winding up together on the downbeat."

One 1969 essay in which Cannon attempted to define baseball became a lament for what baseball no longer was. He tried to appeal to the myth of memory and to put the game in terms that not only he could understand but anyone who knew what it was like to ride to "the end of a trolley line." Baseball was once no more complicated than "Willie Mays running with that rocking gait, his back to home plate, as he chases down a fly ball hit over his head"; but owing to "rich men whining," "a glowing screen," and "green carpet," baseball now dwells in "a time of wavering faith." It has ceased to be "a simple proposition, an heirloom of a nation." Baseball once meant "standing at a bar and talking about unimportant matters," but it has become symptomatic of what ails our nation, whose "institutions are no longer venerated because of their age." Cannon's essay defies orderliness and organization because it is about loss. Baseball is no longer a clean, well-lighted place, "a sanctuary from the ferocity of the world."

If, like Ring Lardner, Cannon grew disenchanted with the game, he also found occasional moments of redemption in the myth of heroes. Players like Roberto Clemente showed the game "in all its innocence for a little while longer. . . . Once again it becomes a ballet performed in a metropolitan meadow by thrilling men." As a sportswriter, he remained objective but refused to stay exclusively on the field. "You close the world out," he said, "and the world must be let in. The thing I try to do is get the world in over the bleacher walls."

He thought of himself first and foremost as a newspaperman. He disowned the "new journalists," who nevertheless viewed him as one of their literary fathers; he disliked their technique of massaging quotations rather than recording things as they actually happened. He was certainly a protégé of Runyon's, but he dismissed the notion that Runyon influenced his style. He admired Runyon's moxie and cleverness—for instance, Runyon's use of Paul Waner's batting stance to describe a prosecuting attorney's demonstration of how a murderer swung a sashweight to kill his victim.

He never used the "new journalistic" technique of getting into a ballplayer's mind, but he did try to get the average fan to imagine being the player: "You're Roger Maris who isn't Babe Ruth." "You're Mickey Mantle. You're a bubble-gum kid in a chew tobacco league"; "You're Willie Mays, of Fairfield, Alabama, who is part of the small talk of New York." "You're Ted Williams who never wanted partners. You're in business for yourself."

He rarely used anecdote; metaphor and analogy were more to his liking. "Baseball is music played on an adding machine," he wrote derisively in 1969. In a *Post* article on the 1955 World Series, Cannon wonders about the differences between a player of lasting greatness and a player who lasts for only a short while after he "gets hot." He draws an analogy between such a player and a poker player with a hot hand: "All guys with hot hands get the ride until the straights stop filling in the middle. The cold wind blows away the aces and deuces are in the hole. Bet the hot hand before the cold wind freezes your fingers." To read these lines today is to hear what the novelist William Kennedy described as "that jazz language that came out of a Jimmy Cannon column."

The remarkable achievements of Joe Louis and Jesse Owens and the integrated barnstorming tours in the previous decade had given a handful of writers both white (Pegler, Jimmy Powers) and black the impetus to argue, either directly or indirectly, for an end to segregated baseball. Jackie Robinson's entry into the major leagues in 1947 would force baseball writers to rethink certain views and attitudes, though dealing with the issue proved to be problematic for some of them. Almost all of the New York sportswriters, Peter Williams asserts, "set conditions for Robinson that would not have occurred to them had the player in question been white." Nonetheless, Jules Tygiel concluded, in his in-depth account of *Baseball's Great Experiment* (1983), that "overall the desegregation of baseball received highly sympathetic coverage. Even the *Sporting News*, whose editorials at best revealed a patronizing attitude toward blacks and whose illustrations could be tasteless, generally covered the integration saga with exceptional thoroughness and objectivity."

Whatever his prior views on race, Cannon would start from scratch in the years he covered Robinson and other African American players. He looked back critically on the days when "organized baseball was in another land. The frontiers were well guarded. No one could sneak in." The old Negro League was a place where curves and sinkers and sliders "had no names." These early thoughts on the Robinson saga lay those times to rest in the myth of memory.

Cannon covered Robinson's hitless regular-season debut for Brooklyn on 15 April 1947, a day when the "dignity and compassion" of the crowd mirrored Robinson's own. He did no more than interview Robinson after the game, leaving social commentary to "someone such as Norman Corwin." Later, however, Cannon would call Robinson "the loneliest man" he had ever seen during that first season. When he wrote about Robinson's induction into the Hall of Fame in 1969, Cannon cited Robinson's accomplishments on and off the field, noted his "precious gift," and admitted that "we are a better country because of it."

If a great player had limitations, Cannon said so. "Unless you lied to yourself, you had to praise Ted Williams as a hitter. That's as far as I intend to go." Describing his good friend Joe DiMaggio, on the other hand, he could sound admittedly "sentimental and foolishly romantic": "You, who pay your way into ball parks, will probably never forget him." When it came to evaluating ballplayers, he relied on observation, not statistics. "The arithmetic is meaningless."

Cannon covered other sports and other subjects, but baseball was his first love. As he expressed the myth, "It is the best of all games for me. It frequently escapes from the pattern of the sport and assumes the form of a virile ballet. It is purer than any dance because the actions of the players are not governed by the music or crowded into a formula by a director. The movement is natural and unrehearsed and controlled only by the unexpected flight of the ball."

Cannon's own voice was also natural and unrehearsed, giving his columns a tendency to unevenness. He saved his best lines and most

Rube-like cynicism for his columns of epigrams called "Nobody Asked Me, But . . ." and "Guaranteed to Happen . . ." Here he mastered the apothegm: "Maybe the Senators should try soccer next season?" or, "If baseball goes for pay television, shouldn't the viewers be given a bonus for watching a ball game between Baltimore and Kansas City?" He cared little about the "guy who had a bad year" or "endless discussions about the balk."

He was, on the one hand, a journalist concerned with "telling the truth—and writing it with vigor and clarity." On the other hand, he was a poet whose business it was, as William Congreve once said, "to paint the folly and vices of human kind."

The Closest Man Has Ever Come to Perfection

Walter W. "Red" Smith (1905–82), a Notre Dame graduate, dominated the sports pages for nearly 40 years. He began his career, after brief stints in Milwaukee and St. Louis, by covering the last-place Athletics and Phillies for the *Philadelphia Record* from 1936 to 1945, when Stanley Woodward lured him to New York and the *Herald Tribune* during the heyday of the great Yankee, Giant, and Dodger teams. He worked there until the paper's demise in 1965 and later joined the *New York Times*. His widely syndicated "Views of Sports" and later "Sports of the Times" columns were collected periodically. He rarely forgot his baseball roots. How could he, having grown up in Green Bay, Wisconsin, during the time Casey Stengel won a batting title there? "Ninety feet between home plate and first base," he was famous for saying, "may be the closest man has ever come to perfection."

Smith counted many influences, but chief among them was Joe Williams, who perfected the art of the folksy, anecdotal lead and brought to the pages of the *New York World-Telegram* a hot-stove style of writing lush with history and the myth of memory and southern charm ("Some of the boys were talking about McGraw and the old Giants," "We were sitting in a cafe drawing moist circles on the bare tabletop with the bottom of our glasses," "We sat in a crude pine-board dugout of the Boston Red Sox training camp and gnawed the gristle with James Emory Foxx of Sudlersville, Md., today").

By the time Red Smith began writing sports in 1927, he had already absorbed most of the work by those who would one day become his colleagues. He learned his moves, as he said, from Runyon, Williams, Pegler, and E. B. White, who passed on to Smith his idea of the essay: "although a relaxed form, [it] imposes its own disciplines, raises its own problems." Smith consciously imitated these writers until his style became his own. He was a writer both influenced and greatly influential. By the time of his death in 1982, he was perhaps the most widely read sports columnist in the world.

He wrote for the groundlings because he thought of himself as one of them. He wanted to be a good reporter no matter what side of the paper he worked on. "I've always had the notion," he said, "that people go to spectator sports to have fun and then they grab the paper to read about it and have fun again." He believed that the individual game was irrelevant, that "sports isn't Armageddon." He remained cognizant of "the world outside, beyond the fences, and . . . let that awareness creep into the column sometimes."

Smith's essay writing was deceptively simple and routine, but the result was never tiresome: a descriptive lead, often anecdotal; in the body, faithfully objective reporting of only the most significant events; and a memorable fallaway line or quotation for a conclusion. When, for instance, he speculated on the probable outcome of the Players Association's challenge to the reserve system in December 1975, he concluded: "It will be acted upon exactly the way similar advice has been acted upon in the past: 'These,' the owners and their lawyers will say as they have said time and again, 'are matters best left to collective bargaining.' Then they refuse to bargain. Yes, and Merry Christmas to you, too."

Smith knew that well-chosen words intensify a piece, especially words the reader is unlikely to discover elsewhere in the sports pages. The typical sports-page prose was not his style. When the Phillies beat the Dodgers to win the pennant in 1950, Smith suggested that the Phillies had "toppled headlong into the World Series." Having led the National League most of the season before going into a tailspin, the Phillies had performed "the tallest, steepest, swiftest, dizziest, daredevil, death-defying dive ever undertaken by a baseball team." He carried the metaphor, and his thesis, further by stating that by managing to win on the very last day the Phillies "had qualified handsomely for off-season employment—substituting for the diving horse in Atlantic City." Smith generally eschewed baseball argot, preferring the well-turned phrase, metaphor, or anecdote. "His memory helped make him what he was," wrote Dave Anderson. "The mere mention of a sports personality invariably stirred a story, if not two or three." Smith could make players sound eloquent even when quoting them verbatim. He framed the vernacular, when he used it, in a way that called attention to its art. For instance, he wrote about Babe Ruth's remembering "The *naughty-word* day I hit that *naughty-word* ball into that *naughty-word* street over there." Anecdote could define character as well. Concerning Babe Ruth's conflation of Duke Ellington with the Duke of Wellington, and of Elkton (Maryland) with Eton, Smith wrote, "In the uncomplicated world of George Herman Ruth, errors were part of the game."

Consider Smith's famous account of "The Miracle of Coogan's Bluff" (1951). Bobby Thomson's home run off relief pitcher Ralph Branca in 1951 was no more important than, say, Bill Mazeroski's World Series–winning homer in 1960. The real significance of Thomson's home run, however, lay in the drama of the season and the great Dodger-Giant rivalry; Smith worked the myth of the best game brilliantly. "As far as I'm concerned," wrote George Plimpton of the piece, "that can be referred to three or four times a month."

The Giants had won 37 of their last 44 games to secure a tie on the last day of the season. Brooklyn had led by 13½ games on 12 August. In a three-game playoff, the Giants won the first game, then lost 10–0 in the second game. The score of the final game at the Polo Grounds bounced back and forth between the Giants and Dodgers, 1–0, 2–1, 4–1. The Giants were down 4–2 in the bottom of the ninth when Thomson came to bat with two men on and one man out and hit his dramatic game-winning home run.

At first Smith seems at a loss as to how to relate the story. "Now it is done. Now the story ends. And there is no way to tell it. The art of fiction is dead. Reality has strangled invention. Only the utterly impossible, the inexpressibly fantastic, can ever be plausible again." (Shirley Povich, sports editor of the *Washington Post*, would draw upon Smith's lead in this story to write the much-heralded opening paragraph of his report on Don Larsen's perfect game in 1956: "The million-to-one shot came in. Hell froze over. A month of Sundays hit the calendar. Don Larsen today pitched a no-hit, no-run, no-man-reach-first game in a World Series.")

The present tense gives Smith's story its dramatic immediacy, as in his description of a drunk who thrusts and struggles and bursts and runs and twists and kicks and shakes and crashes and weaves his way past cops and ushers until, "coattails flying, he runs the bases, slides into third." The man "at heart . . . is a Giant, too. He never gave up."

With invention strangled by reality, Smith turns to understatement: "Maybe this is the way to tell it: Bobby Thomson, a young Scot from Staten Island, delivered a timely hit yesterday in the ninth inning of an enjoyable game of baseball before 34,320 witnesses in the Polo Grounds." The scheme of the narrative is, in fact, counterpoint and juxtaposition. Thomson had almost cost the Giants the game in an early inning when he foolishly ran to second base with a runner already there and was tagged out. Smith brushes aside that miscalculation with fictive dialogue: "'Fancy,' Lockman said, 'meeting you here!' 'Ooops,' Thomson said, 'Sorry.'" When the game appears out of reach, Smith summarizes the whole history of Giants hard luck in one sentence: "Poetic justice was a phrase without meaning." Furthermore, Thomson had seemed fated from the start. The Giants could neither touch Don Newcombe nor get a run for Sal Maglie, but it was Thomson (who had hit safely in 15 straight games) who tied the game with a sacrifice fly off Newcombe (who had pitched scoreless baseball in his last 21 innings). As events unfold rapidly and the Giants struggle along, Thomson is always at center stage: "Wait a moment though. Here's Pee Wee Reese hitting safely in the eighth. Here's Duke Snider singling Reese to third. Here's Maglie wild pitching a run home. Here's Andy Pafko slashing a hit through Thomson for another score. Here's Billy Cox batting still another home. Where does his hit go? Where else? Through Thomson at third."

Near the end of the game, with the Dodgers still up by two, "Who's at bat? Thomson again?" The word *again* is prophetic: Thomson had in Game 1 hit a home run off Branca, but the "corniest possible sort of Hollywood schmaltz" did not seem even remotely possible. The Dodger manager Charlie Dressen would not tempt fate by walking Thomson. The first pitch is a strike, an ill omen. On the next pitch, Thomson is heading toward first, looking to left field, and jumping in the air "again and again." The word is important, for it has been Thomson "again and again" all along. The last we see of him, he is a "Giant," strolling casually around the bases, and we are reminded of the drunk. The piece ends with Branca walking slowly toward the clubhouse. The contrast with Thomson is subtle and symbolic. The closing sentence, one of Smith's finest, simply the word "Thirteen" (the number on Branca's back), reduces all of baseball's superstition and serendipity to a single image.

"Often [Smith's] narrative art is one of omission," wrote Donald Hall. "The teller gives *just enough* of the tale, so that one word leaps forth to do the work of a hundred."

Smith could occasionally be a moralist as well as a realist. In a column blasting both the Jim Crow statutes and "the reverse application of the same abhorrent principles" that in 1954 denied whites the right to play with blacks in Birmingham, Alabama, Smith urged the Yankees not to schedule an exhibition game there; "like it or not, baseball men now must set an example in interracial relations." He wrote the column knowing full well that the Yankees would knuckle under, wanting the revenue and having but one African American player of their own (Elston Howard), whose starting status was questionable. Blacks, of course, would have paid to see other blacks play given the opportunity, for "the pigmentation of a fan's skin doesn't affect the color of his money." Still, as Smith's biographer Ira Berkow observed, "He had not been a consistent . . . crusader, and his style often emphasized the fun, or light side, of the games. He had thought that his primary job was to entertain. . . ."

Smith had his own slant on the myth of timelessness. The designated-hitter rule change, he thought, was an assault on the poetry of baseball; Ernest L. Thayer had to be "whirling in [his] grave": *"The outlook wasn't brilliant for the Mudville ten that day,"* he mused. Every bastardization robbed baseball of its poetry, its "fairness and balance." As the age of hype approached, Smith preferred "nothing planned, nothing tawdry, no pre-arranged billing to disfigure the simple reality." Smith's label for Roger Maris's pursuit of Babe Ruth's single-season home run record in 1961 was "the great ghost hunt"—the "pursuit of Babe Ruth's ghost."

Pat Jordan described Smith, not altogether kindly, as "a white-haired, pink-faced little man whose nose is always sniffing heavenward as if in search of a fresh lead or, possibly, just a carrot" and Seymour Krim in *Views of a Nearsighted Cannoneer* (1961) actually thought Smith a bit unlettered. But he consistently wrote the best leads in baseball journalism, from his earliest pieces in 1934 ("Through the murk of cigarette smoke and liniment fumes in the Cardinals' clubhouse a radio announcer babbled into a microphone") to his last pieces in the early eighties. When he could not come up with something original, he knew which quote to use, as when he heard the St. Louis pitcher Ray Sadecki say, "'This game was invented for Willie Mays a hundred years ago.'"

When the Dodger catcher Mickey Owen dropped a third strike in the 1941 World Series, Smith opened with a virtual prose poem:

> It could happen only in Brooklyn. Nowhere else in this broad, untidy universe, not in Bedlam nor in Babel nor in the remotest psychopathic ward nor the sleaziest padded cell could The Thing be.

Only in the ancestral home of the Dodgers which knew the goofy glories of Babe Herman could a man win a World Series game by striking out.

Only on the banks of the chuckling Gowanus, where the dizzydays of Uncle Wilbert Robinson still are fresh and dear in memory, could a team fling away its chance for the championship of the world by making four outs in the last inning.

When Smith described the action on the field, he could fill each sentence with concise, concrete detail: "With two out and the bases full of Phillies, Eddie Waitkus smashes a low malevolent drive toward center field. The ball is a blur passing second base, difficult to follow in the half-light, impossible to catch. Jackie Robinson catches it. He flings himself headlong at right angles to the flight of the ball, for an instant his body is suspended in midair, then somehow the outstretched glove intercepts the ball inches off the ground."

Finally, there were the metaphors. He used them sparingly and admired writers who never used them, but they were his specialty pitch. From the catalogs of them, a few will suffice: Lefty Grove was "one of the great lobby-sitters, a graven image shrouded in smoke"; "Bowie Kuhn lifts up his hand like Moses and press releases gush forth from his office as water gushed from under the rock that Moses smote"; "To say that Branch Rickey has the finest mind ever brought to the game of baseball is to damn with the faintest of praise, like describing Isaac Stern as a fiddler."

Red Smith will be remembered as the most consistently satisfying baseball writer of this century. He favored other sports but knew that he would be around ballparks more than any other place. "Today's game is always different from yesterday's game," he said. "If you have the perception and the interest to see it, and the wit to express it, your story is always different from yesterday's story. I thoroughly enjoyed covering baseball daily."

Another One of Those Garrulous Lardners

If Red Smith and Jimmy Cannon were the best Matty and Rube writing in the newspapers, John Lardner (1912–60), an eloquent hybrid, had no peer in the slick magazines.

In addition to a now out-of-print posthumous anthology, Lardner published three collections of essays, the form he most admired: *It Beats*

Working (1947), *Strong Cigars and Lovely Women* (1951), and *White Hopes and Other Tigers* (1951). The eldest of Ring Lardner's four sons, John shared his father's gift of language and interest in sports. Not quite graduating from Harvard, he began his newspaper work at the *New York Herald Tribune* and later became a syndicated columnist and freelance writer. He wrote the "Sport Week" column for *Newsweek* from 1939 until the 1950s—when it was renamed "John Lardner's Week"—and continued freelancing for magazines like *True*, *Sport*, the *Saturday Evening Post*, and the *New Yorker*.

His modest-sounding résumé and all-too-brief life belie the major contribution Lardner made to baseball, sports literature, and literature in general. He was first and foremost a brilliant humorist and essayist and only secondarily a sportswriter. Like Smith, he was an avid reader who culled his knowledge from books and discussions as much as from keen observation and a warehouse full of anecdotes. He had a reporter's instincts and never needed or cared to hang around clubhouses. He rarely used the first person, preferring instead Woodward's "your correspondent." What he wrote about Satchel Paige was true of himself: he possessed "a dead pan, in a firm, crisp tone of voice which suggests that if you want to argue the point you will do him a favor by arguing it with someone else."

Lardner kept to the old school of Rubes, colorful but lettered. His introductions were often long and synoptic, as in his profile of "The One and Only Bobo" (1957):

> Once there was a ballplayer named Louis Norman Newsom, who called himself and everyone else Bobo. He was born in 1906, 1907, 1908, or 1909, depending on which way he told it. Early in life, he gave out the news that he was the greatest pitcher in baseball. Partly on the strength of this report—but mainly because of certain supporting evidence—he was hired 17 times by big-league ball clubs in the next 20 years. He was fired and sold just as often as he was hired, and seldom with much delay. But, in the end, no one in baseball could have said for sure that Bobo hadn't been right about himself all along.

What follows is a screaming portrait of an eccentric ballplayer—the type Lardner most admired—who greets owners with, "Bobo . . . you could surely use Bobo now." Lardner chronicles the career of a well-traveled pitcher who would win 20 games one year and then lose 20 the next, and who had an insatiable desire for the publicity that went with showing up fans or managers or even the "Goddess of Chance" who had

abused him in some way. Most astounding to Lardner was Bobo's durability—his "foolproof and painproof . . . genuine rubber arm," his knack
for winning or finishing games with a broken jaw or broken fingers and
once a broken leg—and his longevity: he won a couple of games in 1952
and 1953, when he was well into his forties. Furthermore, Newsom,
"with all his childish moods, his bombast and his pettiness . . . had an
oddly heroic quality of mind and body that led him to defy and challenge pain, and to pretend that none of the ills of heaven and earth were
a match for Newsom of South Carolina." He seemed able to back up his
boisterous and colorful boasts, winning and completing the last game he
ever pitched, his 211th major league win. In the myth of heroes,
Newsom was "a throwback," a ballplayer for whom there was never a
moment he "could not have pitched and won a ball game at the highest
baseball level."

If Newsom achieved greatness, "Babe Herman" (1952) had greatness thrust upon him. The profile of Herman is the antithesis of what
Lardner consciously set out to write about Newsom. If his baseball subject in "The One and Only Bobo" is the iconoclastic player of remarkable
durability, he is out to show the limits of the "good-hit-no-field-man" in
the Herman profile: "Floyd Caves Herman, known as Babe, did not
always catch fly balls on the top of his head, but he could do it in a
pinch." The essay is a succession of anecdotes held together entirely by an
incredulous point of view. Herman was, in hot-stove jargon, "the world's
worst outfielder, and a constant danger to his own life." Managers discarded him quickly, including one who simply fired him after "studying
his form on the bench." Not without redeeming qualities, Herman is paradigmatic of the player whom the fans "barbecued . . . one moment and
cheered . . . the next."

For Lardner, baseball was a lively art, like the cinema and theater
(about which he also wrote). He approached each subject critically and
with pregnant observation. Stanley Woodward, who had hoped to bring
Lardner back to the *Herald Tribune* to be paired with Red Smith, thought
that perhaps Lardner had "never taken sports seriously." That was not
necessarily a limitation; Woodward loved Lardner's "humor which is
based on incongruity. Whenever he writes a newspaper column he can
make you laugh." Commenting on the amount of newspaper space Ted
Williams got in Boston for every little thing he did (headlines might
read "Williams Beats out a Bunt"), Lardner noted that "there is no room
left in the papers for anything but two sticks of agate type about
Truman and housing, and one column for the last Greater Boston girl to
be murdered on a beach. As a matter of record, many Greater Boston

girls decline to be murdered at all in baseball season because of the poor press they will get while Mr. Williams, the great hitter, is swinging his bat or his epiglottis."

But one does not read John Lardner just for the lines or the laughs. Where Ring had kept company with the Chicago modernists and other authors in the Scribners canon, John found what he was looking for in the journalistic tradition of H. L. Mencken (who admired Ring) and the Lardners' family friend, the satirist Franklin P. Adams. Like George Orwell, John Lardner wrote as he pleased. People who knew him often described him as solitary—"convivial in a monosyllabic way," wrote Red Smith—and as an assiduous craftsman and perfectionist. Five drafts of one lead were discovered next to his typewriter after he died.

Few writers could use language as economically as Lardner did. Numerous books were written about wartime baseball, but Lardner could denote the era in a single, memorable clause: "Manpower was so sparse that the desperate Dodger scouts were snatching beardless short-stops from the cradle and dropping their butterfly nets over Spanish War veterans who had played the outfield alongside Willie Keeler."

Robert Frost admired Lardner's "very unusual slant on things." Roger Kahn might have been describing Frost when he spoke of Lardner's writing as "fusing sound and meaning, snatching the precision of the word with the rhythm of the phrase."

Newsom and Herman were not the only mavericks Lardner liked; he also admired Charlie Dressen, the Brooklyn manager who "passed education by, and went on using brains in its place"; Stanley "Frenchy" Bordagary, "who attempted to introduce the mustache into big-league baseball"; and Lou Mandel, the all-American rookie "who used to go around the big-league baseball training camps in Florida offering managers a chance to sign up a new Walter Johnson, i.e., himself, for any reasonable sum in five figures."

Though he relied on myths ("Up in Cooperstown, New York, where Abner Doubleday experimented with bats and balls some ninety-nine years ago"), he also enjoyed puncturing them (the Cooperstown story, he learned, was nothing but "a substitute with lacy trimmings"). He wrote a penetrating piece on the Black Sox scandal for the *Saturday Evening Post* in 1938, a splendid work of social history filled with moments of fresh, re-created spot reporting:

> Then boff! boff! boff! A run was in, and there were Reds on sec-
> ond and third. Dutch Ruether, Cincinnati pitcher, came to the plate.
> He whaled a terrific triple between Felsch and Jackson.

A few minutes later, five Red runs were in, and Cicotte was out. Kid Gleason, tough, gray little manager of the White Sox, was on the playing field, yanking his arms around, crazy with rage and grief.

The Reds won the ball game 9–1, as the Sox batsmen, each a sharpshooter, waved gently at Ruether's delivery.

Lardner uncovered the psychology and motivations of the players, who "sat talking in the hotel room with the door shut and the window open and a hot breeze and the smell of asphalt sifting in." He decried the players' irrevocable banishment from baseball as a "star-chamber affair." While the gamblers went their merry ways, the eight Black Sox skimmed "the frayed fringes of the professional game—semi-pro ball, sandlot ball, twilight-league ball," and ended up working at prosaic jobs.

The eight would never enter the Hall of Fame "until some outlaw collects enough votes to qualify him for the holy tablets." The final image is apropos, for the plaques in the Hall resemble the decalogue icon, and baseball had been defiled in the eyes of the newly created lord of baseball, "that snow-haloed, hawk-faced . . . Judge Kenesaw Mountain Landis." The whole affair was "the biggest, sloppiest, crudest fix of a sporting event that ever was known to man," and it "touched off a rash of scandal rumors that spread across the face of the game like measles." "Rash," "spread," "face," and "measles" are carefully chosen words (which abound in Lardner's prose). How serious was the scandal? Lardner believed that "the public came within a whisker's width of never seeing another box score, never heckling another umpire, never warming another hot stove."

The hot-stove league, of course, has its own beat—the after-hours bar, the hotel lobby, the club owner's little black book. There Lardner found material for his best essays. In "They Walked by Night" (1950), Lardner relates the tale of Shufflin' Phil Douglas, who was "thrown out of baseball on a quick double-play by John J. McGraw and Judge Kenesaw Mountain Landis." Douglas was provided with his "very own personal watchdog," who would report that "in the company of Shufflin' Phil there was seldom a dull moment, or a dry one."

Lardner's subject is the night walker, the player who stays up to all hours and has to be followed—"the man with a single-minded thirst and feet that pointed away from home." He records the short history of famous night walkers, who included Casey Stengel and one Charles Flint Rhem, "who reported back to his team, the St. Louis Cardinals, pale and shaken, with the story that he had been kidnapped by gangsters, locked in a hotel room, and forced to drink great quantities of liquor at the point of the gun."

Lardner, himself a heavy boozer, cherished drinking stories. The essay ends with a litany—one of the best in baseball literature—of great lines about dipsomaniacal ballplayers: the good pitcher who "'drank a great deal of stuff, so why shouldn't he have it'"; the player who "was thoughtful enough to leave a dummy in his berth for Durocher to talk to" during curfew checks; and Dizzy Dean, who somehow wound up with a black eye one night just from staying alone in his room.

"They Walked by Night" is a natural bridge to Lardner's essay on "The Baseball Playboy: Past and Present" (1958). A maxim from Shufflin' Phil introduces the piece. With the advent of major league night baseball in 1935, Lardner wonders whether baseball has become a "game for clean livers." (He could make old puns work overtime.) Then he picks up where the Shufflin' Phil essay left off, with drinking stories and tales of "hawkshaws" hired "to shadow rumpots." Lardner suggests that at the present time (the late fifties), there isn't a whole lot of sleuthing going on, except for those rare suspicious moments when "players were leaving fingerprints on martini glasses." Such a lapse, however, was "a case of atavism, or reversion to ancestral habit." For Lardner, the baseball playboy is a hard drinker, not a womanizer. His "all-time All-Star team of playboys" (like Ruth, "half man, half champagne") includes no one from the modern era, not even Don Larsen, who managed to run "his automobile up a pole, where only the shrewdest sleuth could have followed him." In an earlier era the hardest drinkers "had the good fellowship to die" before the age of 40.

The newcomers pale in comparison with the old-timers, who were drinking "the 15-cent red-eye of the [King] Kelly era, or the fresh-cooked prohibition dew on which Flint Rhem made his finest score." And since a good anecdote can be told more than once, he repeats the one about Flint Rhem and the gangsters. In Lardner's world, the main ingredient of anecdote is alcohol; without it, the "quality of imagination" would cease to exist. The hard drinkers of baseball past were true men of character, not susceptible to the modern "pressures for wholesomeness." The modern player looks shipshape for his guest appearance on "The Ed Sullivan Show"; in the myth of memory, Rabbit Maranville demonstrates his World Series slide on the vaudeville stage and breaks his leg on the orchestra drum.

Newspaper writers of the earlier era could complain that their sportswriting was not taken seriously; they felt, in Paul Gallico's words, "one grade above the office cat." Smith and Cannon cared little for each other's work. Lardner's essays were widely admired and read, but most people were hesitant to call them literature. They are, of course, and we are all the poorer that very little of Lardner's work remains in print.

CHAPTER 8

Their Baseball

Despite the presence of Cannon and Smith and several other talented veterans, newspaper writing was no longer the influential source it once had been in Ring Lardner's day by the end of the Second World War. The dead-ball era's Chicago school of writers was long gone. Stanley Woodward was fired from the *Herald Tribune* in 1949, and Grantland Rice, no longer a voice to be taken seriously, had died in 1954—the best of the new and old traditions had come to a close. The media, as the colorful ballplayer Rocky Bridges proposed, was becoming plural for mediocre.

Baseball prose had been almost the exclusive domain of the sportswriters. They had authored most of the baseball books and articles; one of them, Ford Frick, had become commissioner of baseball; and others had gone to work in the public relations offices of major league ball clubs. The Baseball Writers' Association became more powerful than it had ever been. One member's thirst for revenge kept Ted Williams from winning the Most Valuable Player award in 1947 and again in 1957, when he unquestionably deserved to win.

But a new, younger generation of writers had grown up with not only the most imaginative baseball writing but also, arguably, the best American literature. As David Halberstam observed in *Summer of '49* (1989), "In the years following World War II, professional baseball mesmerized the American people as it never had before and never would again. Baseball, more than anything else, seemed to symbolize a return to normalcy and a return to life in America as it had been before Pearl Harbor."

Consequently, Frank Chance's diamond began to cut more deeply into the imagination. Writers became more conscious of baseball as a literary enterprise. In 1946 Mark Harris, then 24 and the author of a novel about a young black army soldier married to a white girl, submitted a brief essay, "Jackie Robinson and My Sister," to a little magazine called *Flashes of Negro Life*. When Robinson had been signed to a contract with

Brooklyn's Montreal team in the International League, Harris was deter-
mined to put the issue in humanistic, if caustic, terms. When he asked
people what they thought about the prospect of a black shortstop in the
major leagues, a few "wanted to know how I would like it if my sister
married Jackie Robinson." Harris answered them curtly: Robinson was
already engaged, and out of the country, and Harris's sister, in sixth
grade, was fond of a boy named Raymie Carruci. "The whole thing," he
said, "is out of the question."

A boom occurred in the freelance market for articles in the sports,
men's, and wide-circulation magazines such as *Sport*, *Sports Illustrated*,
True (edited by Ken Purdy), *Argosy*, *Real*, *Cosmopolitan*, *Esquire*, *Look*, *Life*,
the *Saturday Evening Post*, and *Collier's*. Two major publishing houses—
A. S. Barnes and Putnam—became important players in the new
"adult" baseball market.

Now many different kinds of writers, not just sportswriters, began
tapping into baseball's myths and themes. Baseball, which had opened
up language, could be worked as a theme, a symbol, or a metaphor and
give access to the richer (or darker) complexities of American life. For
some authors, several of them established literary figures, baseball myths
became the source of narrative. For just about all of them, baseball was
something that they felt belonged to *them*.

The Neighborhoods of Baseball

Baseball had begun in the cities of America, and the writers of the fifties
would be among the first to return it to its roots. One of the publications
of the Federal Writers Project in 1939 was *Baseball in Old Chicago*. As it
turned out, two Chicago authors became among the first American novelists of note to write essays about baseball.

Nelson Algren (1909–81), the author of three gritty novels of social
protest, including *The Man With the Golden Arm* (1949), was a child
growing up in the Chicago slums in 1919, the "year . . . Shoeless Joe
Jackson was outhitting Ty Cobb." "The Silver-Colored Yesterday," published in 1951 in the *Saturday Evening Post*, and "So Long, Swede
Risberg," published posthumously in *Chicago* magazine in 1981, focus on
the theme of the 1919 Black Sox team, "as solid a group of horses asses
as were ever tricked into playing crooked in any sport on earth." The former piece is written in the hallucinatory, vernacular style that dominated
Algren's work in the fifties, with splashes of toughness characterizing
underclass life. The latter piece is more reminiscent of Jimmy Cannon;
its bulletlike sentences are weighted with gnawing cynicism.

The later story comes first chronologically, and is discussed here for the sake of comparison. Algren's neighborhood, the South Side of Chicago, is a brutal place, and his heroes are those players who resemble the neighborhood tough guys, White Sox players like Risberg and Buck Weaver, who "guarded the spiked sand around third like a territorial animal." Baseball and its myth of heroes hold the slums at bay: "Major leaguers were our gods. We weren't worshipful. We knew they were merely men like our brothers and fathers. Yet with a difference. When a father or a brother died, he left no record of himself for remembrance. But a major leaguer, even though up for only a season and most of that spent on the bench, left a batting, fielding, or pitching record for All-American time. Major leaguers possessed immortality."

The boy Algren took the nickname of "Swede" and began to walk pigeon-toed like his hero. After the disastrous World Series of 1919, when "the White Sox were still white" and in a three-way tie for first place in August 1920, Algren and a friend snuck into Comiskey Park during a game that had so many people trying to get in that "the cops were beginning to have trouble with the mob pressing the bleacher walls." It was the first game he had ever seen, and he found himself sitting on the left field grass, "almost close enough to *touch*" Shoeless Joe Jackson: "What's so important about learning to read and write after *that*?" The scandal rumors represent a loss of such innocence. "Our love of the game was not shaken by the exposure that followed. But we stopped pitching baseball cards and took to shooting dice. The men whose pictures we had cherished were no longer gods."

"The Silver-Colored Yesterday" chronicles Algren's move to Chicago's North Side (which led "directly to the alien bleachers of Wrigley Field") in the days following his adventures at Comiskey Park and just before news of the fix reached the streets. His prized possessions are an autographed bat signed by Swede Risberg and a program card from the game, but Algren's new friends want him to claim a National Leaguer as his "fayvrut" player. Algren, however, will "keep the faith in the Swede."

His reward for remaining loyal to Risberg is the "coal shed roof" of right field in sandlot games with those "worshipers of false gods." The Black Sox scandal ("my own gods proved me false") disgraces him with the gang. Though he refuses to believe that Jackson could "play bad baseball even if he were trying to," he is ashamed of Risberg, one of the unrepentant conspirators, who "bore the heaviest burden of all our dirty Southside guilt."

The boys treat Algren like another Black Sox, "stripped to the bleacher winds," and force him to choose another player. In "Hustlertown," Algren learns, "'everybody's out for The Buck . . .' Even Swede Risberg." He has "no heart left, even for right field." He will be wary of false gods from now on, but he will not pretend to stand with "every bleacher has-been, newspaper mediocrity, and pulpit inanity [who] seized the chance to regain his lost pride at the expense of seven of the finest athletes who ever hit into a double play."

According to David Sanders, James T. Farrell (1904–79), author of the Studs Lonigan trilogy and a onetime newspaper writer, was "unquestionably the most devoted baseball fan among America's significant writers." In Farrell's fiction, baseball is both nostalgia and an escape for his characters from the squalid urban environment of Chicago's South Side. In 1956 he became the first American author of note to cross genres and publish a baseball book. *My Baseball Diary* comprises essays in addition to baseball excerpts from Farrell's novels, grouped in a roughly chronological order that mimics the structure of Joyce's *Dubliners* (1914), one of Farrell's chief literary influences. These different pieces culled from both fiction and autobiography represent various stages in a baseball fan's life, from earliest childhood to adulthood and public life. Farrell recalls all of *his* baseball's imaginary boundaries: the pictures of ballplayers grownups gave Farrell, inserted in packages of Sweet Caporal cigarettes; "the grass edge of the large, rectangular skin-dirt athletic field" where he played and passionately dreamed of becoming a major league player; the 1956 Dodgers, a great team, but "the Gael who went forth to battle and who always fell." The book ends with the story of Fred Lindstrom, the only person from Farrell's old neighborhood "to rise to the rank of big league star." Lindstrom lives vividly in the memory of the splendid act of playing great ball from his earliest youth through his professional career. He is a symbol for all the boys who grew up on the South Side of Chicago who would say, ". . . there, but for the grace of superior ability went I. . . ."

My Baseball Diary is written in an unaffected, felicitous style: "We can boil all of this down to a simple sentence—we like baseball." The sentimentality of the dime novels is never repressed, though Farrell has put his "days of hero-worshipping baseball players" behind him. The player profiles—of Chicago-era stars like Ray Schalk, Eddie Collins, Red Faber, and Buck Weaver (Farrell, as it turned out, got the last interview ever with Weaver), whose sin in the Black Sox scandal was more in paying honor to a "code by which he grew up [that] cast scorn and opprobrium on a squealer"—are more mature reminiscences. When old-time players, some of whom have felt "useless, discarded, wasted, done for," pass away, it is "as though a friend were dead." Players like Collins, Farrell believes, played for *him*.

A question Farrell asks toward the end of the diary is, "Why do many of us love baseball?" Though he gets too analytical, wondering whether baseball is "fun or compulsion," he has answered the question earlier, in the familiar refrains of the myth of memory: "There are games you have seen, or plays, or innings or players which remain fixed in memory. They might remain in memory in a partly disassociated or fragmentary way. Sitting in a ball park years later, various of these memories will drift back to you. I jot some of these down at random. For this kind of remembering is one of the pleasures of baseball."

In a eulogy to Collins he writes that, as "boyhood memories crowd . . . upon [us]," we realize we are "a nation of frustrated baseball players and the literature of our childhood was of play-by-play, morning-after stories and box scores." Baseball's myth of timelessness also emerges: the Dodgers of the fifties resemble the White Sox of his youth. He feels at home in the great conversation as he thinks about "Lowdermilk . . . Alexander . . . Gehrig . . . a pitcher who couldn't get the ball over the plate, a pitcher who did nothing else but get the ball over the plate, and a sturdy block of cement at first plate [*sic*] that crumbled and withered as if by some mysterious alchemy."

His grandmother, who adored "the baseball" and "the Bostons" in particular, "even though until her dying day she didn't know what the plays meant," calls to mind the myth of America and the immigrant yearning to be part of the New World. The American myth is visible also in the "small kindnesses" one player showed him or those that "Ma" McCuddy, the tavern owner, showed to ballplayers; without such generous spirits, "the social history of baseball cannot be told or written."

Baseball begins for Farrell with conversations overheard at home and culminates with the realization that if baseball were ever to disappear, "there would be a widespread feeling that a hole had been cut in the national existence."

Somewhere in the Bleachers the Poets Are Around

In the midfifties *Sports Illustrated*, then a new Luce publication, entertained the idea of inviting celebrated American authors to write a baseball essay for some special occasion. William Saroyan's "My Baseball" was written for the 1956 World Series.

"Baseball is caring" of the most absolute kind, he begins. Regardless of what it means to the players, for whom the vicissitudes of success and failure are difficult enough, baseball humanizes the soul, whether we care for a player, a team, or the idea of the game itself.

For Saroyan, baseball "can be trusted, as great art can, and bad art can't." Its myth of timelessness has the power to resist or consume such dehumanizing forces as big business and Hollywood. The game is best experienced "on the geometric design of the fresh diamond," where we practice a secular devotion to an activity unlike anything else. That devotion lies in being part of an "anonymous crowd of the hungry and faithful, watching and waiting." Saroyan would agree with Jimmy Cannon that "baseball isn't solitude."

Some individuals could exist nowhere else *except* in the world of baseball: "I don't think you'd get Casey Stengel in any arena of human activity other than baseball, and not getting him would be a national disaster. . . . " Mythically, baseball is "the biggest and best and most decent" game ever. If the caring ceased, "for all any of us know there might soon be no nation at all." (Robert Lipsyte, nearly 40 years later, would echo this sentiment in saying, "Baseball's rhythms and values and dreams are suffocating, and when a pastime dies, what do you think happens to its nation?").

Baseball feeds all of Saroyan's well-known virtues and excesses as a rhapsodist. Like Whitman, he roots for no one team and does not care who wins. His baseball is like himself: optimistic ("there's always next year"; "something can still happen"), sentimental, impetuous, undiscriminating, impulsive, cheerfully discursive. In the myth of America, presidents may still throw out first balls, "but somewhere in the bleachers the poets are around, too."

Robert Frost covered the 1956 All-Star game for *Sports Illustrated*; in "A Perfect Day—A Day of Prowess," he addresses (as Lardner did the "gents") every "man-jack" like himself "so full of bodily memories of the experience" of having played the game. He thinks back to his own counterfeit baseball years at Breadloaf, the writers' colony, where he was the team's "relief pitcher with a softball I despise like a picture window." He recalls his baseball friends (one could throw what sounds like a slider) and his promise to write a poem for Alfred Kreymborg about Babe Ruth's 600-foot home run, which "got to going round and round the world like a satellite . . . long before any artificial moon was thought of by scientists."

The poet who wrote that home is the place where, when you go there they have to take you in, feels "never more at home in America than at a baseball game." The lore (of Walter Johnson, Gabby Street) sticks with him. Digressive at times, he still observes the game with a poet's eye for "significances"—a player's coming up to hit swinging two bats, or the fans wincing "with fellow feeling when Berra got the foul tip on the ungloved fingers of his throwing hand."

There are poetical moments of delight. The game's four home runs elicit Frostian syntax: "And they were—four of them from exactly the four they were expected from, Musial, Williams, Mays and Mantle. The crowd went wild four times." He finds symmetry in that "each team made 11 hits, two home runs, and not a single error." And he delights in occasional puns: "the ladies present . . . have many of them pitching arms and batting eyes."

As for the game in question, "it has been a day of prowess. . . ." Prowess is the ability to perform with success in games, in the arts, or in battle. The Welsh poet Edward Thomas, who came "to look on a poem as a performance one had to win," personified prowess every bit as much as Ken Boyer at third making "two impossible catches." Thus, baseball and literature meet at a point "close to the soul of culture."

Baseball in Our Town

A brief episode from Shirley Jackson's memoir *Raising Demons* (1957) illustrates the changing nature of the boy's game in the fifties. Little league, which Harold Seymour called the "quintessence of boys' base-ball," the very foundation of what he also called America's "House of Baseball" (baseball played below the professional major and minor league levels), had begun in 1939 but experienced a postwar boom. Jackson, who (long before Stephen King) usually cast occult stories in realistic settings, focused on the myth of America as it related to the bedrock values of family and community life and baseball. Her account of a Memorial Day game is a dramatization of an earlier observation by Frederick Lewis Allen:

> Baseball had long been the national game and millions of boys had learned to play it, but mostly in local sandlots, from which, if profi-cient, they might graduate to play on the town teams against a neigh-boring town. . . . Organized games which required special costumes and equipment were mostly considered affectations of the rich, and to the average small-town American any such notion as that of offering "supervised play" for boys and girls would have been quite bewilder-ing. Already this old-time tradition was breaking down. Organized games were growing rapidly.

Algren's and Farrell's sandlots have been bulldozed to make way for new ball fields, where once "kids used to start their sleds, coasting right down past third base and on into center field, where the ground flattened out and the sleds would stop." The town has built its Elysian Fields on a spot where memory has been before.

Nearly the entire town is "deeply involved in the Little League." It has fostered civic responsibility, set back the dinner hour, and further delineated family members' roles: mothers hope their sons will not be "nervous," while "there was a good deal of advice the fathers still needed to give the ballplayers." The game has the feel of a real game (the Braves are playing the Giants), from the "clean new uniforms" and the national anthem to the advertising signs in the outfield. Only the play is suspect, until "the boys began to get over their stage fright and play baseball the way they did in the vacant lots."

The crowd, as one writer would later observe about a different set of bleachers in Wrigley Field, is a "neighborhood, a bar, a depot, a beach, an office, a church, a home." The housewife vernacular, which structures most of the story, including the account of the game, seems right at home: "Marian leaned past me to tell Dot that first base was a *very* responsible position, and Dot said oh, was it? Because of course Billy just wanted to do the best he could for the team, and on the *Braves* it was the *manager* who assigned the positions." The great conversation is lively with anecdote ("the Giants took out their pitcher and put in Buddy Williams, whom Laurie once beat up on the way to school"), hot-stove jargon ("A rumor got around town that the Red Sox were the team to watch, with Butch Weaver's strong arm"), epithet ("'Put it in his ear, Laurie,' my husband was yelling . . ."), and mild reprimand ("'William,' she said imperatively, '*you catch that ball*'").

The mothers are exhausted and disheveled, mostly from trying to take moving pictures, or from having to defend their sons ("in the evilest voice I have ever heard") against hecklers, or from hoping that their children will not be humiliated ("I . . . promised myself that if Laurie struck out this next batter I would never say another word to him about the mess in his room"). The boys, for their part, are headed for more, unadorned baseball, in "a pickup game down in Murphy's lot" afterwards.

A Scholar on the Mound

Jacques Barzun's discourse on the game in *God's Country and Mine* (1954) set a new standard for scholarly baseball writing. One of America's towering intellects and—something of an anachronism today—a university wit, Barzun came to this country from France when he was 12, immersed himself in U.S. culture and values, and became a leading educator and critic of, among other things, the many bankrupt pedagogical methods he saw being used around him.

Barzun's "essay" (with its famous quote, "Whoever wants to know the heart and mind of America had better learn baseball," which Barzun became sick and tired of hearing repeated so frequently) is a pure celebration of the myth of America; in other ways it calls to mind Gallico's "Inside the Inside," which also spoke of both baseball's "purging of the passions" and its graceful choreography: "Once the crack of the bat has sent the ball skimmering toward second, between the infielder's legs, six men converge or distend their defense to keep the runner from advancing along the prescribed path."

Barzun relies on all the standard themes of baseball prose. The myth of timelessness decrees that "there is a World Series with every revolution of the earth around the sun." Writing with clarity and intelligence, Barzun sees America itself as the ideal baseball hero, expressing "the powers of the nation's mind and body": "Accuracy and speed, the practiced eye and hefty arm, the mind to take in and readjust to the unexpected, the possession of more than one talent and the willingness to work in harness without special orders—these are the American virtues that shine in baseball."

Moreover, he brings these ideas to fruition with rich verbal imagery: "The infield is like a steel net held in the hands of the catcher. He is the psychologist and historian for the staff—or else his signals will give the opposition hits. The value of his headpiece is shown by the ironmongery worn to protect it." Barzun, the foreigner, wants to experience the game the way "it is so bred into the native," to share in "our American innocence" in assuming "the world is our stage" whenever we play the World Series. That desire accounts in part for Barzun's powerful language, mastered with the help of baseball the way Conrad learned English from the sea.

No More "Boy Scout" Pieces

Born in Brooklyn in 1927, Roger Kahn began a seven-year stint on the *New York Herald Tribune* after leaving New York University in 1948. A disciple of Stanley Woodward, he covered the Dodgers in the heady years of 1952 and 1953. In 1956 he became sports editor at *Newsweek*, where he worked with John Lardner, his most rewarding relationship. (He edited a collection of Lardner's writing shortly after Lardner's death in 1960.) He wrote his first baseball book, *The Mutual Baseball Almanac*, in 1954 and continued to write profiles about sports figures and others through his years as a freelancer and a staffer at the *Saturday Evening Post* and later *Esquire*, where he could write about anything he pleased so long as he called it sports. His first serious books were not about baseball but about Jews in America (*The Passionate People* [1968] contains a fine portrait of the Cleveland great Al Rosen, who "wanted a name *more* Jewish than his own . . . to make sure that there was no mistake about what he was") and the campus uprising at Columbia in 1968.

In sterling profiles of ballplayers (and other sports figures), Kahn tries to dig below the surface of what happens on the field. He wants to know what it is, ability or character, that makes a ballplayer what he is. Though Kahn is often a sentimentalist, no one has written more passionately or understandingly about Jackie Robinson and what he meant to the nation.

Kahn is most struck by the myth of heroes, often referring to great players as Olympians and relying on anecdotes and his own experiences and encounters. In a couple of 1954 *Herald Tribune* stories, he wrote about Willie Mays as a ballplayer who more than lived up to the hyperbole used to describe him. Mays would become a lifelong friend and subject. Stan Musial's pending and premature retirement in 1960 prompted Kahn to reflect on the "disturbing paradoxes surrounding an aging ballplayer. . . . It is a melancholy thing, geriatrics for a forty year old." Kahn describes the 154th game of the Yankees' 1961 season (played in Baltimore), the one in which Roger Maris had to hit three home runs to beat Ruth's single-season record if he hoped to avoid Commissioner Ford Frick's (now-defunct) asterisk in the official record book. Maris hit his 59th and came very close to hitting another one, even though "this was the town where Babe Ruth was born, and the crowd had not come to cheer Maris." Kahn's Maris has a youthful, "combative integrity that is unusual in baseball, as it would be unusual anywhere else," unlike the "hard-looking, tough-talking" Maris often portrayed in the media.

A 1959 portrait of Babe Ruth for *Esquire* called "A Look Behind the Legend" gave shape to Kahn's theme of heroes. He became one of the first writers to reveal the person Ruth truly had been, "the huge, gross, ignorant, vulgar, insensitive, lecherous drunk that he was," as Quentin Reynolds remarked in assessing Kahn's essay. Though Kahn undoes Ruth's "image of holiness," he finds the legend even more beguiling, more sympathetic, and more human when the truth behind it is known. "Let the memory ring true, down to the last home run, down to the last bacchanal, through a small corridor of time."

In contrast a 1974 essay, "Where Have All Our Heroes Gone?," written during a period when Kahn was becoming more critical of the modern game, begins with an episode from his boyhood about the time he asked Ducky Medwick (then with the Dodgers) for an autograph: "'Get away from the car, kid, before we run ya the fuck down.' Mr. Medwick had concluded my first colloquy with a major-league ballplayer." For Kahn the event was not one of disappointment, but rather good fortune; even his father was impressed: "'Ducky Medwick?' my father said, almost shouting. 'He talked to you?'" Years later Kahn's own son cannot understand his father's "baseball reveries." Kahn puts his heroes in perpective of their day and age, which were not "any simpler or gentler than today," and players had to struggle to make a living in and out of baseball. "Baseball was quicker then, more violent, and therefore more dramatic. Drama is essential stuff for heroes." Kahn therefore understands the conflict inherent in approaching and being rejected by the ballplayer, so unlike today's player "with his warts and shaky syntax . . . overwhelmingly available . . . on too many television sets." The theme of fathers and sons connects with the myth of heroes, as Kahn remembers his own father: "We were father and son, set apart by tribal rivalries half as old as time, but at the ball park, we were held in common thrall. We both would like to have been Pistol Pete Reiser." The "new muckraking" and the booming sports industry have diffused both the games and their heroes. "There is no sport like old baseball, no single national game, no one sure seedbed for universal heroes."

With his 1960 *Sports Illustrated* essay recounting "The Day Bobby Hit the Home Run," which he had covered as a reporter in 1951, Kahn began to look at new ways of using narrative style. He took the opportunity to explore the myth of memory through an event that, with no "dramatic foreshadowing," was suddenly "thrust . . . into the private lives of millions of people, who forever after remember these events in personal terms." Kahn follows the thoughts and actions of several key players—where they were and what they were doing and thinking in the hours leading up to and shortly after the time "the ball was gone . . . into the seats in lower left." Both principals, for example, are shown saying good-bye to their mothers before leaving for the ballpark. Contrasting such quotidian scenes is an event "beyond the limits of belief." Still Kahn's re-creation of the game focuses on what the participants were thinking ("'Should have swung at that,' Thomson told himself, backing out of the box"; "'I got my strike,' thought Branca"). In the end, Thomson can utter only, "Gee whizz. . . . Gee whizz," while Branca leaves the ballpark wondering, "Why me?"

"Intellectuals and Ball Players," published in the *American Scholar* in 1957, contrasts the ways in which the "imaginative" person, or "thinking man," and the average ballplayer conceptualize each other. The intellectual, who looks upon the player as a demigod, has all the advantages. He can engage in the great conversation during what appear to be long periods of tedium and inactivity on the field. He can summon forth an anecdote or two, "only guess at the dialogue" on the mound, "come to a personal conclusion" about what the manager is thinking, and "jump . . . triumphantly to his feet" when the batter finally "hits the relief pitcher's third pitch into the left-field grandstand."

Ballplayers, who can neither distinguish one book or writer from another nor understand how major league baseball and the late Beethoven string quartets "frequently coexist in harmony," are at a disadvantage. The average ballplayer has actualized his boyhood dream of making it to the big leagues, a dream that remains for many of them "distressingly short of ideal"; "cynicism and disillusion are as common as grass." Not so the intellectual. "His dream, the one in which he strikes out Williams, Mantle, and the boss on nine pitches, is good for the rest of his life. If it dims at any time, he has only to visit a ball park for a recharge." Ballplayers, on the other hand, find themselves like characters in a "tragedy of fulfillment": once, in their high schools and towns, "when the dream was simple and vague," they had been heroes.

Until the publication of *The Boys of Summer* in 1972, Kahn, a baseball writer of great linguistic virtuosity, would make an impact mostly as an occasional essayist.

The Self-Effacing Writer

The roots of so-called new journalism are difficult to ascertain, but it goes back at least to the early fifties and the sports prose of W. C. Heinz and Arnold Hano. Bill Heinz (b. 1915) began covering sports regularly in 1945 for the *New York Sun*, where he had begun as a copy boy; he would be a staffer (and war correspondent) until the paper folded in 1949. He then went on to a successful career as a freelance writer and novelist.

Heinz's work needs to be viewed in the larger context of sports literature, where his contribution is considerable and his style better understood, especially in analyzing his stories on Rocky Graziano (and Graziano's wife) and Red Grange. Now sadly forgotten, he is sports literature's most tectonic writer, a consummate interviewer who built elegant narrative structures around moments of golden quotation. He did not just quote but actively engaged his subject in dialogue, revealing his own character in the bargain.

Heinz's "new journalism" stopped short (just barely) of the "self" but opened the doors to wider subjectivity in reporting. Heinz understood what the late Seymour Krim, the best authority on the subject of "new journalism," described as the "definite advantage to the newspaperman to use every conceivable literary avenue open to him; for his job, depending on the intensity of his sense of mission, is to penetrate ever more deeply into the truth of the story—and this can only be done if he has the instruments of language, narration, knowhow, character-development, etc., that . . . have always been associated with fiction."

In his brilliant essay "The Rocky Road of Pistol Pete," published in *True* in 1958, Heinz found Pete Reiser, perhaps the game's greatest prospect when he came up in 1941 with the Dodgers, managing in the low, low minors in Kokomo. The essay, most of which is rendered in dialogue, is structured around a thesis Heinz poses at the outset: "Maybe Pete Reiser was the purest ballplayer of all time. I don't know. There is no exact way of measuring such a thing, but when a man of incomparable skills, with full knowledge of what he is doing, destroys those skills and puts his life on the line in the pursuit of his endeavor as no other man in his game ever has, perhaps he is the truest of them all."

The narrative portion is finely proportioned exposition and character study balanced with quotations from other witnesses: newspaper reporters who covered Reiser; Leo Durocher, who managed him; and Branch Rickey, who signed him originally for St. Louis. Heinz draws a portrait of a man who played recklessly and hard (and whose style of play was costly in the 1947 Brooklyn-Yankees series), injuring himself repeatedly by crashing into walls and losing consciousness, which, along with alcoholism, washed him up before he was 30. "God gave me those legs and the speed," Reiser told Heinz, "and when they took me into the walls that's the way it had to be." Heinz recalls Reiser's every injury, every hospitalization, including the time the last rites were administered.

But Heinz reaches beyond the mere interview piece to establish scene, irony, and poignant detail. Before Reiser, who at the age of 39 walked like an old man, even reaches the waiting Heinz, the author reflects upon what is happening around him:

> I watched them take batting practice; trim, strong young kids with
> their dreams, I knew, of someday getting up there where Pete once
> was, and I listened to their kidding. I watched the groundskeeper
> open the concession booth and clean out the electric popcorn machine.

I read the signs on the outfield walls, advertising the Mid-West Towel
and Linen Service, Basil's Nite Club, The Hoosier Iron Works, UAW
Local 292 and the Around the Clock Pizza Café. I watched the
Dubuque kids climbing out of their bus, carrying their uniforms on
wire coat hangers.

Heinz was able to overcome the problem of having developed a personal relationship with his subject, a situation that, as Tom Wolfe notes,
"presents a more formidable problem than penetrating the particular
scene in the first place." When Reiser needs to see a heart specialist,
Heinz offers to drive him 300 miles to his home in St. Louis. Along the
way they talk baseball and the past. A story that begins as a reminder to
those who had forgotten Reiser ends with Heinz's coming to terms with
a friend who has known only a heroic sort of self-destruction.
    In the seventies Heinz would revisit Reiser and other sports figures
he had known, including the Yankees' Joe Page, "immaculate in those
pin-stripes, walking with that sort of slow, shuffling gait, his warm-up
jacket over his shoulder, a man on his way to work." As Charles Einstein
tells it, "Shortly before his death, Damon Runyon was asked who he
thought was the best young sports writer in New York. Runyon, unable
to use his voice, took pad and pencil and vigorously jabbed one word:
'Heinz.'"

A Day in the Bleachers

The author of numerous articles for *Sport* and sports biographies, Arnold
Hano (b. 1922) earned his reputation—though not recognition until 30
years later—with the 1955 publication of a little masterpiece called *A
Day in the Bleachers*.
    Published by Thomas Crowell, the book was favorably reviewed at
the time but sold only 3,500 copies. It was reprinted in 1982 (and
remains in print). Much has been written about the book, including an
excellent introduction to the new edition by Roger Kahn, who laments
that "almost everything the book represents has changed or vanished":
the Giants, the Polo Grounds, the bleachers themselves.
    The book's premise is simple enough: Hano went to the Polo
Grounds, sat in the bleachers, and wrote about what he saw and heard
that day, with no literary plans in mind. No other writer had written an
entire book about a single baseball game (or sporting event, for that matter), although Hano thought there was nothing remarkable about his
achievement. In the fifties, editors and publishers, if not writers, still

associated baseball books with juvenile audiences. As a result, *A Day in the Bleachers* was published by a small independent house, with much enthusiasm but not the slightest idea of how to go about marketing it. The book survived by word of mouth.

Hano had gone to what turned out to be a significant game: the first game of the 1954 World Series between the Giants and the Indians. *A Day in the Bleachers* would be what the title suggested, and those seats, "not seats at all, but long narrow wooden planks," would assume a point of view. Though the tight, six-inch spaces are further animated by the people who occupy them, they possess character of their own. The bleachers literally are "unreserved seats" designed for the common fan and purchased by waiting with thousands of people in a line that moves every couple of minutes; once inside the park the bleacher seats themselves can be "reserved by the presence of a newspaper or a hat or some small indication that the party sitting there will be right back."

From the outset Hano identifies with every other bleacherite who "felt the urge" to attend the game that day. These shared feelings and expectations are vital in shaping the "constantly shifting and exciting vista(s)" and understanding how baseball figures into the daily lives of citizens. For example, Hano demonstrates the different ways one can arrive at the Polo Grounds, as well as what Lee Allen describes in *The Hot Stove League* as "the lull in the action that permits the fan to take pause and consider what he has seen and read about." So Hano sets the stage with baseball talk about the current Giant team versus the Giants of old, and the frequently decisive nature of opening games.

Hano recalls his childhood summers in the grandstands; getting " 'shipped off' to the Polo Grounds the way other boys are sent to camp every summer," he became a "student of the game." But it was not until he bought a bleacher seat that he became a real fan and began to have fun at the games. He goes to the World Series game as that every-fan, surrounded by the myth of memory and the myth of the best game.

Hano had not gone to the game expecting to write anything about it. That spontaneity would serve him well. The long wait, the friendly banter with the fans and out-of-towners, batting practice as it gradually unfolded, all inspired Hano to take notes in the margins of his *New York Times*. It occurred to him that he might write an article for the *New Yorker* while the game was still newsworthy.

Once Hano is in the park, the bleachers immediately come to life. Long before Sal Maglie plunks the Cleveland leadoff hitter on the fourth pitch of the game, Hano offers a short contrast between fandom in other cities and the fierce loyalty and idiosyncrasies of Giants fans. Hano him-

self is one of those fans who shout wry comebacks at Giant bashers. A
Cleveland rooter seated behind him, a ubiquitous loud woman in a red
hat (who is a Dodger fan), and those who have brought their radios to
the game—all are crosses that Hano must bear; they sometimes function
like soothsayers forecasting doom, putting Hano, in his "omen-clutching
mood." But reason, mixed with a bit of hubris and the "lovely law of
averages, most divine of all ordinances!," prevail. When the woman in
the red hat yells to a Cleveland player to hit one where he lives, Hano
notes that the batter lives in Pennsylvania, foul territory from where he
sits. Hano provides no ordinary reportage but rather a saturated first-
person chronological account upon which he relates "the pattern of play
as it folds and unfolds."

Even as the game, a pitchers' duel, is being "played at a dragging
pace," the bleachers instinctively sense that what a player does on the
field might be of great importance later, as when Alvin Dark, the
Giants' third baseman, knocks down with his bare hand a hard ground
ball, "as you would a fractious animal," thus keeping the runner on second from advancing and most likely scoring on the subsequent play. "All
of this . . . ," Hano reflects, "I did not know, nor did Dark as he felt the
sting of the baseball against his flesh."

If the player feels a sting, the bleachers feel something comparable:
a mounting tension, "a ball game obeying no rules of the dramatist,
building all the time even as it fell"—which brings Hano to the moment
of Willie Mays's famous over-the-shoulder catch of Vic Wertz's drive to
the deep recesses of the Polo Grounds.

Hano crystallizes the moment by focusing on the interplay between
the imposing figure of the batter, Vic Wertz (who has had a perfect day),
and the new pitcher, Don Liddle (a victim of meaningless percentages, a
left-hander facing another left-hander), as well as on the image of the
indomitable player who will come between them, Mays himself, "not
merely *a* great player, but *the* great ballplayer of our time." We have
already seen a sample of the young Mays in batting practice and in other
games Hano can recall, making catches and throws no one else could
have made—like the famous catch in this game, which is not even the
best catch he has ever made. ("So much for Mays and the catch," Hano
will conclude.) What makes the scene more memorable is Mays's subsequent sensational throw to second base, possibly preventing a run from
scoring.

Hano follows the ball from the moment it is hit (not as hard, he
thinks, as Wertz's earlier triple) and notes that Mays runs after it harder
than usual, uncharacteristically lifting his head and nearly outrunning

the ball. The narrative, like the bleachers, embraces the action on the field and enters the minds of the base runners, who must know better than anyone else just what Mays is capable of doing. The throw holds Larry Doby at third and Al Rosen on first and sends Mays sprawling on the outfield grass. "What an astonishing throw," notes Hano, "to make all other throws ever before it . . . appear the flings of teenage girls. This was the throw of a giant, the throw of a howitzer made human."

In the crucial tenth inning we see Mays fielding another Wertz hit and throwing, always, "like some olden statue of a Greek javelin thrower" to hold Wertz to two bases. In the bottom of the inning the portents are reversed: the ominous figure of Mays is on second, as he was when the Giants last scored. This fact helps convince Hano that the game is nearly over—that and the additional fact that his "scorecard goes no further."

Dusty Rhodes's game-winning pinch home run into the wind comes like a whisper after the crash. Even the fans are not sure what has happened. Their victory roar is heard *pianissimo*, in concert with the "delicious languor" of the late afternoon hour. The great conversation will take place on subway cars, in taverns, and at dinner tables. The fans have departed, including Hano's nemeses, the Cleveland rooter and the woman in the red hat. We leave Hano alone in the bleachers to commit 29 September 1954 to future recollection. Any reader who opens the book finds himself in any bleachers, reliving again—or for the first time—"the naked, real ball field, grassy and breeze swept and still tingling warm, smelling of sweat and dry wood."

In the fifties, baseball, despite dwindling attendance, was as public a spectacle as it had ever been, and perhaps that is why writers and fans described the game in the most personal and memorable ways imaginable.

CHAPTER 9

A Few Kind Words and a Road Map

By 1958 five of the original sixteen major league teams had moved to new cities, including Los Angeles and San Francisco. The vast body of baseball literature would give the impression that only New York and Brooklyn had been abandoned, but as Boston writers Harold Kaese and R. G. Lynch wrote, "It will be long before the spirits of Maranville and Evers, Berger, Waner, and many other great National League ball players stop cavorting at Braves Field in memory of man." "What baseball needs today," wrote Tom Meany in 1953, always ahead of his time, is a "road map. The game doesn't lack for kind words." (Meany was actually quoting Bugs Baer, who was once asked by the solicitous manager of a remote southern hotel whether there was anything he needed. "Yes," answered the exhausted Bugs, "a few kind words and a road map.")

By 1961 and 1962 baseball had expanded by two teams in both leagues and raised the number of games played from 154 to 162, the first of several significant changes since the switch from a dead ball to a lively one. More and more people were watching baseball on television, and even more were watching football. Baseball could well have used a good road map to find out in which direction the game was headed. Most baseball writers clung to the old myths, but not all their words would be so kind. The new era, however, began with a tidy closure of sorts: the heroes who had defined the baseball past were going away.

The Kid and the Man

John Updike, then only 28 and the author of *The Poorhouse Fair* (1959) and the soon-to-be-published *Rabbit, Run* (1960), was more a student of Ted Williams than of baseball. He had come to Fenway Park on

Wednesday, 28 September 1960, for what was to be Williams's last game in Boston. Updike's account of that day is now considered the most famous literary piece in the canon of baseball literature; it is surely the most widely anthologized piece, though it is beginning to wear thin with the years.

Written for the *New Yorker*, "Hub Fans Bid Kid Adieu" (as it was called in Updike's essay collection *Assorted Prose* [1965]) is an apt title for a piece about a man who was "known to the headlines as TED, KID, SPLINTER, THUMPER, TW, and, most cloyingly, MISTER WONDERFUL" (though no headline copyist would have used the term "adieu"). On a purely emotional level, the essay reflects Updike's and Boston's lifelong adoration of one of baseball's greatest players, though the relationship between Boston and Williams had been less a "summer romance" than "a marriage, composed of spats, mutual disappointments, and, toward the end, a mellowing hoard of shared memories."

Updike seizes the moment: this is the last game Williams will play in his career at Fenway Park ("the last time in all eternity," as it turned out). Updike begins with a grand description of Fenway; taking up the old hot-stove topic of whether it is a good ballpark, he calls it "a compromise between Man's Euclidian determinations and Nature's beguiling irregularities." The allusions are a reference to Fenway's fences: the short left-field fence, which had come to symbolize the wall between Williams and everybody else, and the deep right-field fence that kept many of Williams's prodigious blasts from leaving the park.

Updike projects three stages to Williams's career, "Youth, Maturity, and Age," which he renders in terms of the myth of heroes through classical analogies ("Jason, Achilles, and Nestor"). Updike sees Williams as a "child who spake as a God" and who would have liked to play with no fans or detractors sitting in the stands. The Achilles phase began after Williams gave four-plus years of his prime to World War II and Korea. He is now "the hero of incomparable prowess and beauty who nevertheless was to be found sulking in his tent while the Trojans (mostly Yankees) fought through to the ships." Indeed, Williams's postseason and pennant-determining games are "the Achilles' heel of [his] record."

Metaphors surprise the reader. Williams's home run off Rip Sewall's famous blooper pitch in the 1946 All-Star game "was like hitting a balloon out of the park." Including every important anecdote, statistic, and pertinent fact about Williams's life makes the prose less belletristic at times, but at the heart of the essay is a central thesis, an idea of Williams that transcends any one feat or the present occasion. For Updike, Williams personifies the game's inherent loneliness—that is, baseball divorced from contest, standing as nothing but itself, the myth of the best game in its purest state. Each game presented an opportunity for Williams to perform to his limit, and every game mattered to him in the same way. No clutch hitter, no manager's dream player, Williams brought with each trip to the plate "that intensity of competence that crowds the throat with joy." Williams was the player whom most boys who could not make the grade wished they could be.

Williams seemed always to be returning from somewhere: from war or illness or injury. He was continually plagued by reporters, divorce, and the "Williams shift" (loading the right side of the infield), which he stubbornly hit into rather than away from. Poking singles to wide-open left field would have easily beefed up his already stellar batting average. Nonetheless, now in his Nestor phase, he is "the best *old* hitter of the century."

Statistical irony surrounds Williams as well. Williams holds no batting records yet is considered one of the greatest hitters to have ever played the game. Updike wonders what Williams would have done if he had not missed those years given to military service, if he had been healthier, if the Boston owner Tom Yawkey had moved in the right-field fence, if Williams had outsmarted his opponents instead of challenged them.

Updike sweeps the camera of his prose over the stands, batting practice, the "sentimental ceremony" honoring Williams before the game, and Williams's own opening salvo delivered to the "knights of the keyboard." Updike sees Williams in terms of classical art. Standing on third, Williams is "Donatello's David," and the bag is "Goliath's head." Williams at the plate is "like having a familiar Leonardo appear in a shuffle of *Saturday Evening Post* covers." Suffering a stiff neck, Williams swung "like a Calder mobile with one thread cut."

In what surely will be his last at-bat, Williams hits a tremendous home run. He is greeted by "pure applause": "There was not a boo in it. It seemed to renew itself out of a shifting set of memories as the Kid, the Marine, the veteran of feuds and failures and injuries, the friend of children, and the enduring old pro evolved down the bright tunnel of 22 summers toward this moment." The moment is, unlike Ruth's called-shot home run, "a perfect fusion of expectation, intention, and execution." Despite the cries of the fans "to be saved," Williams's refusal to acknowledge them becomes as mythic as the home run itself. To Williams, the homer is really no more satisfying than any of his others because this game is just like all the others. Anyway, "gods do not answer letters."

The remainder of the game, however, is anticlimactic. Fans depart, and the crowd generally makes the proper "aesthetic decision" not to watch Carrol Hardy, who has replaced Williams in left field. Updike revised the piece and added lengthy footnotes; its two endings are markedly different. In the original version, Williams is still the loner but always doing things in his own fashion. Deciding not to play the last three games of the season in New York, "he knew how to do even that, the hardest thing. Quit." The revised version takes something of the personal away from Williams and leaves him, in the final analysis, humbled: "He had met the little death that awaits all athletes. He had quit."

Updike had done a little bit of everything in his piece except provide an insider's point of view. The essay is often thought to be a supreme poetic evocation of Williams ("Updike's Great WASP God," wrote Kahn), but it is often expository and direct. It owes at least a debt of gratitude to the influence of Red Smith. The myth of memory, Updike's boyhood recollections of Williams, "radiate . . . from afar, the hard blue glow of high purpose." Updike substitutes those illuminating moments, deep and mysterious, for the postgame facts and quotes of the beat reporter. He worked with scant research materials. "Whatever residue of truth remains . . . ," he wrote, "those of us who love Williams must transmute as best we can, in our own personal crucibles."

Updike tells us that Williams gave it up after the last game, but in a 1961 *Sport* essay called "The Kid's Last Game," Ed Linn—an excellent freelance writer of the period and later the collaborating writer with Bill Veeck and Leo Durocher on their autobiographies and the author of two full-length studies of Ted Williams—reminds us that Williams had almost quit at least twice during the regular season. Whereas Williams assumes godlike qualities for Updike, for Linn it is "the gods who always set the scene most carefully for Ted Williams." Williams is no Nestor, but simply a man whose career is on the verge of collapse for no other reason than his tendency to injury even when "he is doing nothing more than jogging around the bases."

Updike reports from the stands, while Linn gives the story from the locker room. For Updike, Williams is a lonely, solitary figure; for Linn, Williams wants to be at center stage. Linn is well aware of Williams's contempt for the press and hostility toward him, so it is with a bit of fun that Linn's persona becomes "the man from *Sport*," and the old journalistic convention of "this reporter" and "our correspondent" takes the place of "I" throughout the long essay.

Linn describes Williams with an eye for detail, from his leathery face to the "soft roll of loose fat, drooping around the waist." Williams is constantly sought after by autograph seekers and photographers, all of whom he curses ("as an oath-hurler Ted never bats below .400"). In the minutes before the game, Linn recognizes the underlying truth of Williams's character: "On his last day in Fenway Park, Ted Williams seemed resolved to remain true to his own image of himself, to permit no sentimentality or hint of sentimentality to crack that mirror through which he looks at the world and allows the world to look upon him."

And so, the act of *not* tipping his cap after his last at-bat will become a conscious, symbolic gesture. Even as Williams finds himself ignored by the very photographers he has shooed away, he gradually raises his voice to call their attention back to him. At one point Linn overhears him say, "I guess I forgot to tip my cap."

As Williams prepares to accept the accolades during the pregame ceremonies, Linn flashes back to Williams's first spring training in Sarasota, a memory belonging more to the writers like "our man from *Sport*" than the fans, who could not have known why, "as if by some common impulse, all sideline activity stopped that day in 1938."

For Updike, Williams's departure was a last glimpse of a legend, but most sportswriters were glad to see him go. When Linn asks Williams if he even thought about tipping his cap to the fans, especially when his manager Mike Higgins sent him out a second time, Williams responds icily. Unlike Updike, Linn shows Williams ducking out the back entrance, chased by a handful of idolizing women who let out a scream, "as if Ted had been somebody of real worth, like Elvis or Fabian." The Kid's last game, like Williams himself, will soon become part of the great conversation. Williams leaves the game as he entered it, his epitaph fitting: "He was sometimes unbearable but he was never dull."

Three years later, in 1963, Arnold Hano was on hand in St. Louis to cover Stan Musial's last game for *Sport*, but it was W. C. Heinz in *Life* who captured perfectly the workmanlike Musial. Compared to Musial, Updike observed, Williams was "an icy star." Musial's common-man stature had always been set against his extraordinary talents. On the final day of his career, the "air was so clean and cool that it seemed it might, at any moment, shatter with a tinkling sound like thin plate glass."

Heinz contrasts the present and the past, recalling specific moments in Musial's outstanding career. When a man tells him that he hopes Musial will end his career with a home run, Musial replies that he will settle for anything that day. Heinz immediately recalls the time in 1948 when Musial got five hits in one game. As cameras greet Musial when he enters the Cardinals' clubhouse, Heinz shifts back to the first time

Musial walked into that clubhouse and met his idol, and later friend, Terry Moore. When Musial walks onto the field for practice, "the shouts and the applause rolled down to him." Heinz remembers the one and only time Musial was booed in St. Louis; "the next day ten fans bought space in the St. Louis press and apologized." Musial ends his career not with high drama and controversy but with his usual consistency and aggressiveness. He gets two hits (the last his 3,630th) and a run batted in. The crowd laments when he leaves the game in the sixth inning for a pinch runner. In the first game he ever played, as Musial himself remembers, he also got two hits, and the Cardinals also won 3–2. Heinz closes the circle on an era and a man.

If Williams ends his career by hitting a home run and then quitting, Musial ends his with a simple gesture: reaching into his locker and removing "the shirt with the number 6 and MUSIAL on the back." It is the way all careers begin and end in the big leagues, only Musial's uniform "will go to the Baseball Hall of Fame."

Hano covered the story alongside Heinz, and in fact, each man appears in the other's story, unidentified, sitting in the backseat of Musial's car. Hano's linear narrative helps demonstrate the routine with which Musial went about his business. Musial is "a creature of habit, a man made comfortable by old, worn things." The uniform, too, takes on greater significance in Hano's piece. Musial comes to the stadium early to dress but hesitates to do so, as though "you could read what you wanted to read into his reluctance to do something he would never do again."

As the heroes became human, nonfiction writers looked for other realistic ways to portray the familiar baseball myths to the more literate postwar and baby boom generation, for whom Roy Hobbs and Henry Wiggin had replaced Frank Merriwell and "Baseball Joe" in fiction— even though all of them had been cut from the same cloth.

The Professor

If Christy Mathewson's *Pitching in a Pinch* set a literary standard for the "as told to" book, Jim Brosnan, half a century later, set one for the player-diary.

It came as something as a surprise that Brosnan, a pitcher for the Cubs, Cardinals, Redlegs, and White Sox from the mid-1950s through the early 1960s, actually wrote his own material. Then again, the well-read Brosnan, called "the Professor" by fellow players, was an off-season advertising copywriter who had been keeping journals off and on prior to publishing a review of Mark Harris's *Bang the Drum Slowly* (1956) in a little magazine edited by S. I. Hayakawa called *ETC*. When Brosnan was dealt from Chicago to St. Louis in 1958, he wrote an insider's view for *Sports Illustrated* of what it was like to be traded. The magazine then published a second piece by Brosnan about his experiences with his new manager, Freddy Hutchinson.

Evan Thomas, an editor at Harper, asked Brosnan to try to maintain his insider style for a whole season; thus, the idea for *The Long Season* (1960) and later *Pennant Race* (1962) was born. Many consider the latter book better than the first, because it is better written and edited, but *The Long Season* actually is superior. Jimmy Cannon said it was the best book ever written about baseball. As Brosnan himself said, "I didn't try to record everything I saw or heard." As a result, *The Long Season* presents a freewheeling and relaxed narrative, focusing on the major league experience from the point of view of a ballplayer-writer with a big league arm but a less than willing attitude and less than total desire. The narrative moves about, from the clubhouse, the batting cage, the general manager's office, to the beach (where Brosnan and his family rent a house).

With the success of *The Long Season*, Brosnan began taking notes for the follow-up book, but the events of *Pennant Race* took Brosnan by surprise. He had had his best season ever, and his team won a championship. Consequently, his writing is more strained, more self-conscious. In *The Long Season*, Brosnan relies heavily on memory, most of his observations having been internalized only once. The extra material in *Pennant Race* dilutes what is an original and enlightening voice in *The Long Season*. Brosnan eventually wound up with more material than he could use, and he was forced by the Harper attorneys to delete much of it anyway. At best, he managed to leave in a few good quotes in *Pennant Race*. Though a good story, the book is more of a conventional sporting account. *The Long Season*, however, stands out as baseball's premier player chronicle. It is also a faithful record of baseball at the end of an era. "Who can doubt that the sixties and seventies saw a transformation of big league baseball?" Brosnan wrote in a new introduction to the book in 1983.

If there is a theme at work in Brosnan's diary, it is the theme of frustration—not frustration overcome by success or effort but through humor and a measure of casual indifference. In a controversial 1952 article for *Life* magazine, Ty Cobb had already lambasted the great modern-era players for not being as tough as the players of his era, and here was Brosnan (at best a middling talent) saying it was true. The diaries record the thoughts of an individual who, though an interested student of the game, never really put his heart or head into it. In that respect, Brosnan represents a large category of major league ballplayers who, as Kahn had described them in "Intellectuals and Ballplayers," never lived up to their promise.

Brosnan, a journeyman, reports to us from midcareer; each season may be his last. The long season begins when his contract arrives. Brosnan wrote during the period just prior to free agency, when a player could easily be "enfiladed through [his] own careless impatience." The myth of (middle-class) America abounds: the book is filled with references to family, children, and friends, both inside and outside of baseball. We see Brosnan packing to move from one place to another, visiting relatives, sharing apartments, as well as confronting current social issues. The reader gets to know the richly described characters as Brosnan projects us into their heads and hearts. He learned from Frank Graham and Arthur Daley, listening to conversations and recording things of interest. He later thought that technique might have limited him in *The Long Season*, but he was being selective without his fully realizing it. He may have missed a few good lines here and there, but his diaries have the impact of organic narration: nothing is interrupted just to tell a gratuitous story or drop a one-liner.

Two other themes are introduced at the outset of *The Long Season*: the fact that "every baseball family eagerly awaits the new season" (his own as well as the extended families of baseball), and his discovery that he will be the Cardinals' long man in the bullpen, "'the lowest form of pitcher.'" Brosnan's frustration at being long man in a long season sets the tone for the entertaining journal and creates parallels between his own struggles as a pitcher and those of any major league ballplayer.

In addition to these themes, Brosnan includes several meditations on the game. He wonders why pitchers can't hit and takes a grueling turn in the batting cage to discover the answer. He wonders about coaching signs, managerial loyalty, team physicians, the therapeutic effects of playing handball in the off-season, the plight of players at the end of their careers, and the general fretting over simply trying to make the roster. Take all the bonus babies, minor league stars and lifers, aged veterans hoping for one more year, and it "makes you shudder to think how easily you can be put in your place before you even get a chance to play in a major league park."

As a writer who happens also to be a ballplayer, Brosnan demonstrates his love for baseball language, which appeals to him almost as much as the intricacies of the game. The book opens with a self-styled "Glossary." His wife refers to him as "Meat," which he defines as "a term of indiscriminate affection." A "gopher ball" is "similar to the ordinary, legal-sized baseball but dangerous for pitchers to handle. Invariably, it can be observed sailing over an outfield fence in fair territory during a game. Should be avoided." As he attempts to improve his hitting, his coach tells him that he *lounges* at the ball. "Perhaps he meant 'lunging,' but then I might just as well have been lying on a chaise longue, criticizing Iron Mike's [the pitching machine's] control." Brosnan is a Rube with his ear to the mound. He is not a poet, but an amateur linguist who gets what the players and coaches say exactly right. "Man, if baseball has a language of its own, it has a Southern drawl," he writes.

Brosnan relies heavily on sexual euphemism, referring to "a strenuous exercise or two." Though scrupulous, Brosnan was not quite ready to test the "public figure" caveat in libel law, so nothing in his books is damaging to anyone in particular. *The Long Season* recalls a time when you could still play ball in Havana, when martinis and gin were the ultimate vice, and it was not unusual to have a wife who didn't like her husband to swear.

When he is on the mound, Brosnan takes us deep into his mind. It is not just the mechanics of pitching that he tells us about—indeed, that aspect is secondary—but the frustration of facing a tough hitter ("He took it again, eh? Lay one there, buddy boy. Make it a strike"). He sees himself as a man trying to make sense of his work and finding himself constantly baffled by it. He can perform the simplest of acts—throwing a baseball—better than most men could ever dream to, and yet that is not enough.

Brosnan sympathizes with the older players who know that admitting to a manager that they are in pain might end their careers. The words "'Skip wants to see you in his office' can unleash the torment of harassed, frustrated ambition." Brosnan underscores the importance of playing in pain.

The long season officially begins when the short season (spring training) is over; Brosnan cuts his modest clippings, those "artifacts of an expiring career. Those inches of print that measure relative success." The actual diary begins with a short meditation on opening day on 9 April 1959: "The most jaded old pro has his emotional weak spot—the first 'Star-Spangled Banner' of the season; the catcher's peg to second base that signals the end of springtime playtime and the start of business; the sudden realization that from this moment on, everything goes into the record book." Morton Grove, Illinois, where Brosnan lives, and Staunton, Virginia, where he visits his wife's family, are within driving distance of a bad injury or a high ERA.

He continues his thoughts and meditations on sundry aspects of the game: what a player eats before a game; the big league banter; the unfair advantage hitters have over pitchers; the fickleness of fans; kids whose dream is to one day "wear one of these monkey suits"; the waning days of Stan Musial's great career; the use of fines to punish players for mistakes rather than positive monetary reinforcements (these were the days before "incentive clauses"); the proper way to chew tobacco; those "miserable fans" in Philadelphia; the efficacy of the spitball; the precarious nature of ERAs; the psychological effects of "bad calls" and "Silent Screaming" (the tactful way to argue with umpires); and the existential life of bullpen pitchers, who must go there "because they weren't successful with the pitches they already were throwing." Despite the hoped-for adoration in the big leagues, it "doesn't take very long, really, to lose your confidence."

Brosnan portrays himself as an outsider, a learned man who likes the traditional American humor of Mark Twain, James Thurber, E. B. White, and Peter DeVries. The long season has long days as well, when "a wife looks good at the end of a two-week road trip." A player, "a negotiable asset rather than just a normal human-type business employee," can be uprooted at a moment's notice. He can find himself driving 90 miles from his recently mortgaged home in the town that drafted him to the ballpark where his new team plays, or he can find himself suddenly back in the low minors. Brosnan reduces the myth of the best game to pithy maxims: "When you aren't exceptionally able, you don't dare see yourself as others see you," "It's an ill wind that blows straight out from home plate," and "He who gets an umpire hot gets burned." His prose is graced with other short bursts of inspiration,

> You make your pitch, and if it's right, it works . . . most of the time. If it's the wrong pitch, you find out soon enough, and they tell you soon enough, also. If you don't believe them, they send you somewhere else so they don't have to listen to you; and so you can ponder by yourself the misfortune that has struck you.

and insight:

> But for the most part my arm worked like a well-oiled machine. The batter came to the plate. My experience classified him. My mind told my arm what to do. And it did it. It seldom happens precisely that way.

By mid-June, his season disappointing so far, Brosnan is traded to Cincinnati: "The second time you're sold, you don't feel a thing." He weighs the impact of the move on his family as well as on his career. Uprooted at a moment's notice, he is expected to get to work immediately and to show initiative—not, as his new general manager warns him, to vacillate: "Good God in the foothills! A general manager who uses the word 'vacillate.' That's enough to give anybody enthusiasm. We hustled out of town."

Brosnan brings us closer to a major league player than we have ever been before: he learns why he was traded (vague references to his unfulfilled promise) and gives the inside dope to his new teammates about his old ones. He gets to know certain players and is reacquainted with others; he develops a special relationship with a black player, Lawrence Brooks, based on their shared appreciation of jazz. He pokes fun at the major league mind-set regarding integration and admires the natural humor and cockiness of most black players. Brosnan recognizes that prejudices still exist among the players, and he punctures those as well, although he is the kind of player who is likely to "agitate" his teammates, both black and white.

Brosnan becomes reacquainted with Fred Hutchinson, the legendary manager, who "disjoints furniture instead of dismembering his failing athletes," and the "depth" of whose "frown is in direct proportion to the length of his losing streak." When Brosnan wins but pitches terribly ("Any old club in a storm, I always say," Brosnan writes), he must endure the snide remarks of the radio commentator as well as the "contemptuous snarl" of manager Hutchinson.

One could easily compile a short list of Brosnan's many puns ("I treasure novelty 'isms' like the beatniks. Now, there's a pitch. I'm susceptible. I already feel beat") and quotes: when his friend S. I. Hayakawa cannot make a game Brosnan expects to start, Hayakawa remarks, "I could come tomorrow. Could you pitch then?" Other chapters function like miniature essays, with thesis and development. In one such "essay," Brosnan considers the relationship between thinking and pitching. The majority of great baseball books have been written by or about pitchers, as it turns out, yet in a little bullpen scene Brosnan recounts the folly of thinking about how to pitch to Henry Aaron:

> "Knock him down, first pitch," said Pete.
> "Curve him away," said Willard.

"Jam him good. He'll swing at the ball a foot inside, sometimes," said Brooks.

"Change up on him once every trip," I suggested.

"Boys, I think Pena just struck him out on a spitter," said Deal.

"Good pitch," we agreed.

The Long Season closes with the metaphor of an empty locker, for every ballplayer must recognize that any game might well be his last. What makes the long season long is that, for the most part, it is uneventful. But even for the frustrated, "the last day of the season baseball is a game that professionals really do *play*; it no longer seems like work to them. It is virtually impossible for a ball-player to convince himself that he will never play the game again. On the last day of the season, baseball, truly, is in his blood."

After *Pennant Race*, Brosnan continued to write articles for *Sports Illustrated*, the *Atlantic*, *Esquire*, and *Playboy*; all his pieces were characteristically lively and farcical but dealt with credible or serious (baseball) matters. An essay entitled "Nobody Likes the Dodgers," written during the 1961 season, "purported to reflect the general opinion of millions of baseball fans and hundred of ballplayers, some of them wearing Cincinnati uniforms."

The Most Abject Kind of Humiliation

Regardless of the frustration Brosnan experienced (and notwithstanding his shutdown of the Cubs to help clinch the pennant for the Reds in 1961), he, like all major league ballplayers, was a member of an exclusive club to which only a handful of men have belonged among the millions who have yearned to secure membership.

Ostensibly a work of participatory journalism in the tradition of Paul Gallico, *Out of My League* (1960) by George Plimpton (b. 1927) was, as Ernest Hemingway said in advance praise of it, "the dark side of the moon of Walter Mitty." But the overall theme of the book is the real reluctance of professional ballplayers to accept outsiders (especially writers) into their fraternity.

Plimpton, editor-in-chief of the *Paris Review* since its inception in 1953 and the author of numerous "encounters with the professionals" of sport, tried to enter the closed society of professional baseball players to see "what it was like to be, even if briefly, a member of a team and thus privy to what ballplayers chat about in the dugout or on the team bus;

or being party to the exchange, for example, that takes place on the mound when a pitcher is lifted."

Plimpton sees himself as a sort of Spanish *espantáneo*, the man who hurls himself impulsively into the bullring to win the crowd's applause. Generally speaking, American fans, "a vociferous people, to be sure," stay in their seats, but what intrigues Plimpton is the myth of America, "those half-forgotten boyhood dreams of heroics on the major league diamonds."

He learns of a postseason exhibition all-star game in Yankee Stadium that he hopes will not be taken so seriously that, for the purpose of writing about it, he couldn't pitch an inning or so. He would be facing genuine all-stars, including Mantle and Mays. Taking his idea to *Sports Illustrated*, Plimpton recalls something James Thurber once said: "The majority of American males put themselves to sleep by striking out the batting order of the New York Yankees." The editor, prophetically as it turns out, sees the idea more as a nightmare than a dream. He worries less about arrangements, details, and technicalities, which Plimpton frets about, than about Plimpton's physical condition, which does not worry Plimpton.

With the magazine's halfhearted blessing, Plimpton gets off to a good start, getting back into the game, studying it intently by watching Early Wynn as "he performed . . . with a mean toughness, a pathological hatred of the batter." Along the way, Plimpton digs into the vault of baseball anecdote and personal experience. The contrast between his last pitching experience (a softball game in a French meadow) and Wynn's feral pitching seems to excite his desire (or his folly).

But Plimpton is no Brosnan, let alone a Wynn. He recognizes immediately what separates him from all grades of professional players: he lacks the motivation to practice. The promoter of the event worries about legal responsibility should Plimpton get hurt or kill someone. It is finally "the *paterfamilias* of sports in New York City," the restauranteur Toots Shor, who gives Plimpton the idea to have *Sports Illustrated* put up a $1,000 purse for the team that gets the most hits off Plimpton. In the end money talks, and not even the specter of Chapman-Mays will keep a player from trying to make a few extra bucks.

Plimpton must also understand that he can neither borrow equipment from ballplayers nor talk to them personally about their families or their batting slumps. When he purchases the glove he will use, he recalls a Boston pitcher who "once blamed a streak of wildness on a new glove he'd just finished breaking in; . . . he strode from the dugout shouting at the glove, 'It's your fault, *your damn* fault,'" and then proceeded to rip it apart piece by piece.

Ironically, on the day before he is scheduled to pitch, a cool day better suited to football, Plimpton and a colleague break in Plimpton's new glove, a $4.50 Gil McDougald, which quickly comes apart and winds up stolen the next day. He has done little to get himself in shape and leaves for the park with a pair of spikes and a uniform that, fittingly, has no team emblem. After a futile search, he finally finds a friend's ratty old mitt, which, his friend tells Plimpton, should "be about as useful to you up there as a dead owl."

As players begin to come into the locker room, Plimpton recalls his own autograph-seeking, a touchstone for memory as he later watches the all-stars sign boxes of baseballs. He once got Johnny Mize's autograph and noted the little circle that dotted the *i*, something he imitated "until the teachers at St. Bernard's stopped it." Most startling, though, are the wan faces of the ballplayers, "devoid of expression, as blank as eggshells, yet peaceful as if a mortician had touched them up." Plimpton himself will wear a similar countenance when he is removed from the mound later that day; in Marianne Moore's words, it was "a tincture of Charlie Chaplin's smile of agonized gratitude in acknowledgement of rebuffs."

If *The Long Season* is a story of frustration, *Out of My League* is a tale of humiliation. Plimpton quite seriously wants "to discuss signals and try to make up what pitchers call 'the book,'" but he can neither find nor recognize a catcher; he will even have trouble getting someone to warm him up. He realizes his predicament in the clubhouse: "The sense of being an imposter is strong, and you dress furtively, like a timid bather on a public beach."

The long wait allows him to survey his meager repertoire of pitches in the context of anecdotes about famous pitchers from Sal Maglie to Satchel Paige. Nothing seems to go right for Plimpton. He quips with one player way over that player's head, fumbles his cap and helmet, and finally warms up with a batboy, who is closer to the players than he can ever be. He envies "those who had a clear-cut job to do—even if it was looking after bats, or selling hot dogs, or ripping tickets in half at the gate." He has no idea what will happen to him.

Nonetheless, Plimpton assumes the persona of the complete ballplayer (what Moore labeled "verisimilitude"), from his manner of speech and gait to his use of chaw, but playing such a role inhibits his main function as a writer. His one saving moment at practice is when he surprises (and annoys) a catcher with a curveball ("Hey, kid, dammit, when y'all throw the hook, lemme know, hey?"). Plimpton is proud for having thrown something that "had been recognized for what it was supposed to be."

As Plimpton takes the mound, many of the players, including Elston Howard, who will catch Plimpton, do not have the slightest idea of what is going on. There is not even an umpire present. When the event is announced over the loudspeaker half an hour before the scheduled game, Plimpton is introduced as "George Prufrock." If this actually happened it is extraordinary, but it seems otherwise disingenuous on Plimpton's part. It makes the book's epigraph from Eliot too easy: "I do not think that they will sing to me." It is more likely that the name came out not "Prufrock," but not quite "Plimpton."

The first batter Plimpton faces is Richie Ashburn of the Phillies, whom he promptly, inadvertently, knocks down before miraculously getting him to pop out to the catcher. What is most disconcerting to Plimpton is seeing the faces under the helmets from the vantage point of the pitcher's mound, faces that appeared "jarringly familiar" and that "one had only associated previously with newsprint and the photographs of the sports section."

With the use of more anecdote, Plimpton describes the eternity between pitches on the mound, the extraordinary feeling the pitcher gets when the infield throws the ball around the horn, and the despair that accompanies the long wait as the relief pitcher trots toward the mound. When he gets Willie Mays to pop up, he savors the moment for future recollection, which he describes in one long breathless sentence that seems measured in the long seconds it takes for the pop-up to come down:

> When Mays hit that towering fly and it was evident it was going to be caught, I stood absorbing that October instant so that it would be forever available for recall—now blurred, of course, and fragmentary like the nickelodeon films of the Dempsey-Firpo fight you see in the amusement parks, but still sufficient to put one back there on the mound: seeing again, and feeling the sudden terror of Mays uncoiling his bat, but then watching in surprise the ball rise clean and harmless, Billy Martin circling under it, hooded and efficient with his sunglasses down, catching it then and removing it from his glove to peer at it as if he'd never seen a baseball before, then firing it down to Malzone, who also looked at it, across then to Vernon for his inspection, and during this you felt coming on a maniacal grin of achievement which you had to control, knowing that pitchers don't grin after getting a man out, and so you solemnly stomped around the mound, tidying it

up, watching with sidelong glances the ball whip from infielder to infielder, the great blue-shadowed humming tiers of the Stadium out of focus beyond, until finally you remember Nelson Fox, the big orange-size chaw pushing out the side of his face, trotting into the mound, looking at the ball in his hand, jiggling it, inflicting it with magic, then popping it in the air at you and saying, "Come on, kid, easy, easy, easy."

The common fan's element of fantasy becomes a disaster on the real playing fields. With no one calling balls and strikes, Ernie Banks decides, as he would in any game, to wait on a pitch. In this moment Plimpton realizes what the main difference between pitcher and batter is and just why someone like himself does not stand a chance in such a conflict. For Banks, "the pitcher's stature was that of a minor functionary whose sole duty was to serve up a fat pitch." After 23 pitches to Banks, who keeps fighting them off, Plimpton seems like some "curious modern adaptation of the myth of Sisyphus." He has nowhere to go, no teammate who will trot onto the mound to calm him down, no manager who will call to the bullpen for relief.

A man who serves as Plimpton's statistician overhears a conversation that characterizes the boredom in the stands and on the field. The scene is reminiscent of the young boy's epiphany in James Joyce's "Araby":

"Hey, who's that guy?"
   "What guy?"
   "Guy pitching."
   "Donno. Some guy called Prufrock."
   "Which?"
   "Prufrock!"
   "Who the hell's Prufrock?"
   "Beats me."

Like Brosnan, Plimpton offers a few brief dissertations on pitching, the most interesting of which deals with the phenomenon of the curve-ball. In these moments he gets into the mysteries of the baseball. He wonders also about what pitchers say to themselves on the mound (he refers to *The Long Season* at one point). But his stream of consciousness begins to sound peculiar, traitorous, defeatist, loud, and insufferable to Plimpton.

His psychological breakdown on the mound precedes his "physical disintegration," which he offsets with some comic dialogue supposedly recorded by his statistician in the stands: "You don't suppose it's Shucks Pruett out of Higginsville, Kentucky?" someone says. As exhaustion brings him to the brink of hallucination and collapse, Plimpton remembers a rookie who nervously fainted on his first chance in the field. There is an anecdote to illuminate every baseball action. When Ralph Houk finally relieves the beleaguered Plimpton, who like most pitchers "turn[s] mulish when the manager reaches the mound," Plimpton counters what's happening to him with several anecdotes of pitcher indignation. As he sits in the American League dugout, the players ride him, "their joshing friendly, but you could tell they were pleased their profession had treated me as roughly as it had."

Houk retires six batters in a row "with simple batting-practice tosses," frustrating the hitters even more. When Mickey Vernon hits a towering drive, all the players begin "yelling at it and applying tortured body-english to try to push its trajectory into fair territory." The players do the same thing on Billy Martin's fly ball (though his is caught). Plimpton records a simple action locked in baseball's myth of timelessness. Roger Angell would report a similar moment 15 years later when the Reds and the Red Sox faced each other in the sixth game of the 1975 World Series, Carlton Fisk hitting a long ball and "waving wildly, weaving and writhing and gyrating along the first-base line, as he wished the ball fair, *forced* it fair with his entire body."

Plimpton was limited in several ways, as an athlete and a journalist, in writing *Out of My League*. For one thing, the everyman who dreams of pitching against major leaguers imagines himself as a well-conditioned athlete; Plimpton was knowledgeable and studious but otherwise unprepared to face up to his task. Second, Plimpton refrained from taking notes (not always a drawback) and from engaging the players he faced in discussion; as a result, he reports neither what they said nor what they thought, aside from a few random quotations. And those few quotes resemble fictive dialogue. Plimpton takes liberties by getting into players' heads, as he does with his "long-suffering" catcher Elston Howard, who, Plimpton assumes, "counted on his fingers and realized that if we could get Lopata out . . . he'd be able to walk slowly for the shadows of the dugout, thinking of the slight electric hum of the water cooler and how that stream of cool water would feel against the roof of his mouth, and how he'd flop down on the bench and stick his legs straight out and feel the kinks fade away from them."

Yet as Plimpton heads for the locker room, "driven to the showers before the game had even started," he meditates on the myth of the best game, the way it feels "hungry when it was all over, and the sluice of shower water on your arms, and before that, on the field, the warmth of the sun and the smell of leather."

He thinks about signing one of the Spalding baseballs just to acknowledge his debut—"even if by this sad sort of *graffiti*"—but his book also will document his presence. Later he retreats to the stands, where he is evicted for not having a ticket. He notices the great distance that lay between the box railings and the playing field where he had stood moments earlier. By the end of the game, kids rush out to the field to pretend they are players, the myths renew themselves once more as the season ends, and "the Stadium guards didn't bother to throw their protective cordon around the infield."

Plimpton showed the lengths to which a writer—one who was not even close to major league caliber—had to go to get "the 'feel' of things," as Paul Gallico had suggested. "Major-league baseball," Gallico wrote, "is one of the most difficult and precise of all games, but you would never know it unless you went down on the field and got close to it and tried it yourself." By 1962, with the arrival of the expansion New York Mets in the National League, it would seem that not even a whole team of major leaguers was immune to the sort of abject humiliation that Plimpton had endured alone.

The Worst Team Ever

As Murray Kempton pointed out in his 1962 *Sport* article "Return to the Polo Grounds," the fascination with the Mets began almost immediately after they moved into their temporary home in the hallowed Polo Grounds; the team's arrival there "was like the raising of a sunken cathedral." For Jimmy Breslin (b. 1929), a freelance writer in 1962 and the author of two previous sports books, writing about the New York Mets was a labor of love. A writer in the old Rube tradition of Damon Runyon and Jimmy Cannon, Breslin had worked for several newspapers, including the *New York Journal-American*. He had been critical of modern baseball, preferring the style of play of Enos Slaughter, whose "only hero was a major league uniform." The Mets were nothing like the "ruthless, hard-bitten pros who made every step show in salary figures," but they did represent something of a baseball renaissance.

Can't Anybody Here Play This Game? (1963) takes its title from a quote by the Mets' septuagenarian manager Casey Stengel. According to Robert Creamer and others, Breslin actually got it wrong: Stengel said, "Can't anybody play this here game?" The title is fitting since wrongness was what the Mets were about, but Jimmy Cannon criticized Breslin for writing "the way he thinks it should be. He fakes it until it becomes fantasy. Then it stops being journalism." The Mets defined ineptitude, losing a record 120 games. Rather than enrage fans, the team's sloppy play endeared the Mets to nearly a million of them. In losing, the Mets became "the most delightful occurrence . . . [in] this era of the businessman in sports." The Mets "gave sports, and the people who like sports, the first team worthy of being a legend in several decades."

Breslin's short, witty, and lively narrative begins with the construction of Shea Stadium, the initial political wrangling over the stadium (and the team), the arguments about how many toilets ought to go in— all of which, it becomes clear, are happening for one reason: "They are building a brand-new stadium for Marvin Throneberry." "Marvelous Marv" would become the paradigmatic Met; he was a man whose "teammates would have given him a cake for his birthday except they were afraid he would drop it."

The older writers seemed miffed by the Mets and continued to prefer the Yankees, but younger writers like Breslin found the stuff of legend and future recollection in players like Throneberry, whose expertise at "holding down first base . . ." was "like saying Willie Sutton works at your bank." Whereas Dick Young, for instance, had very little sense of humor about the Mets in the first season, accusing them of slacking, Breslin was openly facetious: "From the start, the trouble with the Mets was the fact they were not too good at playing baseball."

Whatever the status of his facts and quotations, Breslin was effective as a reporter, listening closely and observing. Ill luck befalls the Mets from the team's inception. The expansion draft is, says the Mets' scout, the legendary Rogers Hornsby, tantamount to "'eating out of the garbage.'" Bad omens affect almost everyone, from Hornsby, who starts having bad days at the track, to the workers on the scaffolding of Shea Stadium. Even when the season ends and Throneberry wins a boat in a hitting contest, he has nowhere to sail it and discovers he owes an earnings tax on it.

It was Breslin's good fortune to have Stengel as point man in the narrative. At the time, Stengel was, as Joe Williams put it, "too old to manage but plainly not too old to think," and Breslin quotes the Mets manager profusely.

The return of National League baseball to New York means the return to old haunts as well, the old saloons like the Red Parrot and the old memories of the Polo Grounds and Ebbets Field. Breslin tells the stories of William Shea, George Weiss, and, most admiringly, Joan Payson, a baseball daughter and Giants fan who is the perfect owner of the new

Brooklyn club, a woman who knows her way around a "joint." The miserly Weiss, from whom even Yogi Berra worried about getting a telephone call, is also characterized with some affection. But the birth of the Mets—even as it resembled "robbery in the daytime," with teams unloading for exorbitant sums of money "old guys who, in a week or so, would be around with free agents' papers in hand, looking to catch on with some club in a utility role"—occurred "for a simple reason: New York City needed them."

Both Payson and Stengel, in their own ways, keep their humor about them; they are not so much counterparts as soul mates. Stengel encourages his players to play well and "get money off the [rich] owners;" Payson, the bleacher bum in a fur wrap, hopes that next year the Mets will "cut those losses down . . . at least to 119."

Despite a brief winning streak early in the season, the Mets proceed to lose 17 straight times in remarkable, often catastrophic ways. Players with some ability, like Roger Craig, begin to self-destruct, and Breslin discusses the Mets' phenomenon through the eyes of psychologists, sociologists, the firsthand testimony of witnesses (mostly bar owners and patrons), gamblers, and other Brooklyn characters, including Runyonesque celebrities from Jimmy Hoffa to Toots Shor. Breslin describes a Mets-centric New York in which people proudly announce, "I've been a Mets fan all my life."

Bad baseball is just what baseball seems to need at the moment, Breslin implies, but no team can go on losing forever. The Mets are a brief interlude in a game that has become too conservative, that fails to keep up with the times and still dwells in 1934. It is not clear what baseball must do—or at least Breslin does not suggest anything concrete—but it must somehow quicken its pace to keep in sync with the rhythm of modern leisure time. Baseball once "put continuity back into life," as the Mets seem to be doing now. The myth of memory helped one to "keep track of time." Breslin recalls Brooklyn's Gil Hodges as a rookie in 1947 and notes that the mention of Hodges's name reminds him of his first job. When Hodges joined the Mets, "all of a sudden, from nowhere, you find he is old and shot. And you wonder where it all went." Having decried the need for change earlier, Breslin now laments the passing of "a whole way of life" for people in New York. Ebbets Field has become "twenty-two stories of apartments, and all of them are the same, and all of the people in them get to be the same after awhile."

The Mets typify the real myth of America, from the rich eccentric owner, who never was a Yankee fan, and the fabled manager, who *was* the Yankees at one time, down to the common fan:

You see, the Mets are losers, just like nearly everybody else in life. This is a team for the cab driver who gets held up and the guy who loses out on a promotion because he didn't maneuver himself to lunch with the boss enough. It is the team for every guy who has to get out of bed in the morning and go to work for short money on a job he does not like. And it is the team for every woman who looks up ten years later and sees her husband eating dinner in a T-shirt and wonders how the hell she ever let this guy talk her into getting married.

The Polo Grounds were transformed into Elysian Fields in 1962, and the Mets quickly became a metaphor for baseball of a greener age. *Can't Anybody Here Play This Game?* is not just a fractured quotation; it is an imposing, rhetorical question directed at the game's feudal lords. The Mets are "the White Hope, Inc." of baseball, poised at the moment to give truth to Bill Terry's famous observation: "Baseball must be a great game to survive the fools who run it."

An Unrelenting War of Nerves

Breslin's book notwithstanding, baseball nonfiction, like baseball fiction, had gone from being largely team-centered to focusing, in Andy McCue's words, on "a greater concern with the rights of the individual than of the society as a whole."

In the newspapers, Robert Lipsyte of the *New York Times* was most representative of the Matty school; he wrote intimate profiles of individuals on the fringes of the baseball world, such as struggling minor leaguers, in his two award-winning news stories, "The Long Road to Broken Dreams" (1963) and "Where the Stars of Tomorrow Shine Tonight" (1966). Jim Murray, the *Los Angeles Times'* Pulitzer Prize–winning columnist, kept the Rube tradition going with his hit-and-run wit and buoyant profiles of modern major leaguers. "Don Drysdale, a man of probity . . . ," he once wrote, "never hits anybody with any object bigger than a baseball."

Two baseball essays from the period helped to define the new emphasis on the individual player and also served as models for a new literary journalism (which had been recovered from the sports pages in the first place). Both essays go more deeply into the point of view of their subjects than previous essays on either figure had managed to do. One of the essays captures the realities of a player in the throes of middle age and retirement; another player is profiled in the imminency of death.

A former staffer at the *Portland Oregonian* and a freelance writer, Al Stump wrote numerous Rube-style pieces for *True* in the late fifties and early sixties and assisted Ty Cobb in writing his autobiography, *My Life in Baseball*, published in 1961. (Stump recently published a full-length biography of Cobb, which became the basis of a highly acclaimed motion picture.) "Ty Cobb's Wild Ten-Month Fight to Live," published in *True* later that same year (and now the first chapter of the aforementioned new biography), was, Tom Wolfe thought, a "direct ancest[or] of the present day New Journalism." Charles Alexander, however, thought that "Stump . . . misled his readers in implying that he had been Cobb's companion nearly all the time, when in fact he had only seen him a few times during that 'wild' ten-month period." Indeed, the opening reads like a short story: "Ever since sundown the Nevada inter-mountain radio had been crackling warnings: 'Route 50 now highly dangerous. Motorists stay off. Repeat: *Avoid Route 50*.'"

From the outset, Cobb is desperately ill—diabetic, alcoholic, malignant (an unfortunate but appropriate metaphor for his character as well), existing on a variety of drugs from Digoxin to Librium, which he took indiscriminately. At 72, he drives to Reno recklessly and drunk in a major blizzard, pumping uncontrollably into his gut from morning until night "cognac and champagne or 'Cobb's Cocktails,'—Southern Comfort stirred into hot water and honey."

The ironic thesis of the piece does not concern the well-known violent and irrational behavior of a dying man who seems bent on killing himself, but his desperate efforts to stay alive a little longer the only way he knows how, and Stump's own attempt to come to terms with a man who "off the field . . . was still at war with the world." Cobb is a complex man, the drunk who shoots up neighborhoods with his loaded Luger because other drunks disturb his sleep. People who knew Cobb warn Stump to back out of the book deal; he will live to regret knowing, they tell him, this man "who played like a demon and had everybody hating him because he *was* a demon." At times Stump does fear for his life, thinking of all the "fee-simple sonsofbitches" who crossed Cobb in the past, or of the man Cobb reputedly killed in a street fight, or of the woman whose nose he battered with a baseball bat. He also "ducked a few bottles [Cobb] threw, too." Their relationship, which was meant to be professional (built around their collaboration on Cobb's biography), is based on tension and fear. Stump puts us at the center of a great baseball figure's life, lived outside the myth of heroes. Cobb was a man alternately parsimonious and charitable: he could use the stamps that fans sent him to send back autographs for his own personal mail, and he could send generous checks to indigent ex-ballplayers.

Stump becomes Cobb's nurse, drinking companion, cook, butler, and apologist, but each scene he writes demonizes Cobb further. Cobb, a remarkably intelligent, well-read individual, is seen at the craps table in Reno, losing, winning, then getting thrown out of the casino for taking a swing at the croupier. Once in a while Stump persuades Cobb to work on the book, telling "inside baseball tales never published." Cobb's vernacular, however, loses its charm, if not its originality: "To 'salivate' something meant to destroy it. Anything easy was 'soft-boiled,' to outsmart someone was to 'slip him the oskafagus,' and all doctors were 'truss-fixers.' People who displeased him—and this included almost everyone he met—were 'fee-simple sonsofbitches,' 'mugwumps' or (if female) 'lousy slits.'" Yet Cobb could be eloquent in his despair: "'Do we die a little at a time, or all at once,' he wondered aloud."

At times Cobb seems to awaken from death (he has only experienced dizzy spells and insulin shock) and to recover spontaneously, the way he once "hit a triple, double, three singles and stole two bases to beat the Yankees" the day after he had been feverish and bedridden. The anecdotes alone make for fascinating reading.

Cobb, "the greatest of all ballplayers and a multimillionaire whose monthly income from stock dividends, rents, and interest ran to $12,000," returns to his lush mansion in California to discover the electricity has been shut off for his failure to pay a $16 overcharge. Using a 200-foot cord attached to a neighbor's outlet, Stump and Cobb work by the light of "a single naked bulb hung over the chandelier" to finish their book. Later, Cobb lies in his hospital bed, whiskey in the glass in which he keeps his false teeth, venting his rage "into a microphone suspended over his bed."

As Cobb's health further deteriorates, details about his life pour out. At the family mausoleum, Cobb reveals what others already know—that his deranged mother had killed his father. He tells us that his own children "had withdrawn from him," and "in the wide world that had sung his fame, he had not one intimate friend remaining." At the same time, he rails against "his many baseball enemies," having "beat the bastards and left them in the ditch." In the days after his father's murder, the "persecution immediately heaped" upon Cobb by the other players was "the deepest desolation a young man can experience." If baseball is fathers and sons (Cobb had defied his father to play baseball), what Cobb experienced, Stump seems to be saying, was a violation of that myth and

became for Cobb for "that father's terrible fate" a matter of personal vindication and revenge that lasted his lifetime.

On one level, "Ty Cobb's Wild Ten-Month Fight to Live" seems only
remotely connected to baseball; the intimate details of Cobb's past and
present life, however, build into a psychological character study of an
emotionally scarred and disturbed type who was drawn to the world of
baseball and whose phenomenal success in that world stemmed in part
from his maladjusted nature. Stump's essay bears out Branch Rickey's
assessment that "Cobb lived off the field as though he wished to live forever. He lived on the field as though it was his last day."

The autobiography was Cobb's one saving grace, and he lived just
long enough to "complete a baseball book beating anything ever published." Though it would be far-fetched to suggest that Cobb and Stump
developed a kind of father-son relationship, Stump was the only friend
Cobb seemed to have left in the world. Awaiting death—his bag of $1
million in negotiable securities beside him, his clothes undoubtedly
tucked under his pillow (an old trick from his baseball traveling days to
ward off theft)—Cobb lies still, the light and heat still out in his home.
It is a moment of cold, despairing passivity, unknown to Cobb his entire
life. But there is one final ignominy: "From all of major league baseball,
three men and three only appeared for his funeral."

Just a Man Trying to Get Along

A sportswriter before moving cityside in the midfifties for the *New York
Times*, where he was an outstanding reporter, Gay Talese (b. 1932) would
go on to become an accomplished author after he wrote his famous piece
on Joe DiMaggio in 1966. He had covered sports in other arenas (mainly boxing) and was at Ebbets Field on 24 February 1960 when, instead
of baseball bats, "men swung sledge hammers, the dugout crumbled and
an iron ball crashed like Pete Reiser against the wall." Talese's earliest
work was patterned after the style of John Lardner. The 1958 piece "The
Grey-Flannel-Suit Men at Bat" described a "tweedy breed of sportsmen
who are polite to a fault, never chew tobacco, avoid late hours, eschew
pinball machines and poker games, obey the scout laws, condone
umpires, sing rotary, baby-sit, subscribe to the *Wall Street Journal* and
would not think of tripping their mothers, even if Mom were rounding
third on her way home with the winning run."

"The Silent Season of a Hero," published in *Esquire* in 1966, is one
of the most unusual and widely anthologized baseball essays. Talese was

conscious of two models in writing it. One was the middle-aged father in
Irwin Shaw's *Voices of a Summer Day* (1965), who remembers "the distant,
mortal innings of boyhood and youth." A passage from Shaw's novel
starts:

> He went out and looked at the ocean. The waves were ten feet high
> and there was about eight hundred yards of foam ripping between the
> tide line, marked by seaweed, and the whitecaps of the open Atlantic.
> The beach was deserted except for a tall girl in a black bathing suit,
> who was walking along the water's edge with two Siamese cats pacing
> beside her. The girl had long blond hair that hung down her back and
> blew in the wind.

Talese opens almost identically:

> It was not quite spring, the silent season before the search for salmon,
> and the old fishermen of San Francisco were either painting their boats
> or repairing their nets along the pier or sitting in the sun talking qui-
> etly among themselves, watching the tourists come and go, and smil-
> ing now, as a pretty girl paused to take their picture. She was about
> twenty-five, healthy and blue-eyed and wearing a red-turtle neck
> sweater, and she had long flowing blond hair that she brushed back a
> few times before clicking the camera.

Talese's lead refers not only to the old fishermen DiMaggio had known
from his father's occupation but also to the aging DiMaggio himself.

Wearing his old uniform for "Old-Timers' Day" at Yankee Stadium,
DiMaggio takes a few swings, but "there was none of that ferocious fol-
low-through, the blurred bat did not come whipping all the way around,
the No. 5 was not stretched full across his broad back." Nonetheless, for
his fans, "the great DiMaggio had returned, they were young again, it
was yesterday."

Talese had pursued a reluctant and difficult subject, a much-sought-
after man who guarded his privacy ("a kind of male Garbo"). Observing
how DiMaggio brusquely handles other seekers, Talese, the omniscient
narrator, fades into the background, recalling the mythic moments in
DiMaggio's life, which "had happened all so quickly": the young boy
who would help his fisherman father so he could steal away with "a broken oar" to use for "a bat on a sandlot nearby," to his playing days, to
the turbulent, tragic years after his retirement when he was briefly married to Marilyn Monroe, and reporters "perched in the trees."

People plan their days around the wharf just in the hope of asking him, "Who's gonna take it this year, Joe?" He responds earnestly, plays his role, "preserve[s] the myth," though he could do without the adulation, without people thinking of him as great.

The essay is an amalgam of portraiture, old and newly minted anecdote, and fictive description and narration. Talese shows us the private, quotidian DiMaggio, at home with his sister in the house he bought for his parents; at his restaurant on Fisherman's Wharf, where his father, Zio Pepe, worked all his life; on the links; in his business dealings; at his haunts, his after-hours excursions with his male friends ("Look at *that* tomato!"). The "silent season" stands in contrast to the clamorous seasons of DiMaggio's past when "there was a blast of cheering that grew louder and louder, echoing and reechoing within the big steel canyon."

But it is the second model that brings DiMaggio—and his legacy— to life: Hemingway's *The Old Man and the Sea* (1952), an epigram from which begins the essay: "I would like to take the great DiMaggio fishing." Noting that there are "older fishermen who have known DiMaggio all his life," Talese reveals the ballplayer's struggles and great endurance. Like Hemingway's Santiago, he must deal with the solitude imposed upon him by retirement and by choice. There are Manolins in his life, in the shape of fans, well-wishers, and his cronies, with whom he talks about earlier times and baseball. DiMaggio can remember games during his streak when he "would be hitless his first three times up, the tension would build, it would appear that the game would end without his getting another chance—but he always would hit the ball against the left-field wall, or through the pitcher's legs, or between two leaping infielders"; in similar fashion, Santiago recalls defeating El Campeon or harpooning the marlin. There are sharks circling DiMaggio as well—the press and the Hollywood crowd who, he believes, destroyed Marilyn Monroe. In the shadow of Mickey Mantle, in the twilight of his own great career, DiMaggio's past is like the skeleton of the old fisherman's marlin. The talk in the bar is like the talk of the fishermen, and like Santiago, his strength waning, DiMaggio can now sleep and dream of the feats of "a time when you couldn't get me out of there."

Essays Behind First Base

Between the publication of Updike's *New Yorker* essay and Gay Talese's piece in *Esquire*—arguably the two most dynamic contemporary baseball essays written up to that point—the baseball essays of a little-known writer-editor began appearing in the pages of the *New Yorker*. Born in

1920, Roger Angell absorbed the literature and culture of the era when journalism and literature were match for match; oddly enough, he most admired the rococo sportswriter Richards Vidmer. His mother was Katharine White, like Angell later, the fiction editor at the *New Yorker*, and his stepfather was E. B. White (whose writing he emulated). His father, with whom he lived, was a prominent lawyer with strong socialist ties and a great influence on his son, especially in relation to baseball and politics, "not the strange mix they would appear to be today, because they were both plainly where the action lay."

In much of his writing, Angell connects with the myths of memory and timelessness: his Red Sox–Mets (née Yankees-Giants) loyalties are akin to his father's memories of Napoleon Lajoie and Addie Joss from his Cleveland boyhood. Without box scores to herald the beginning of baseball and spring, it would be "like trying to think about infinity." In other ways, the pastoral myth inspires Angell "to conserve something that seems as intricate and lovely to us as any river valley," and his decade-old accounts of games evoke a Wordsworthian "spontaneous overflow of powerful feelings."

The myth of the best game, however, makes baseball alone worth chasing around the country; in his travels, Angell watches and appreciates it from a variety of perspectives in order to arrive at its constants, which remain deep and mysterious. One such constant concerns the caliber of the ballplayer and baseball's persistent testing of each individual who plays the game. Angell tries to find moments that illuminate the myth of the best game. Such a moment may be realized anytime, but often it comes at the times of fiercest competition, as in the final game of the 1968 World Series, an intense matchup between two dominating pitchers (Bob Gibson and Mickey Lolich), who had each won two games and then faced each other, with sore arms, in a seventh-game pitching duel. Though Gibson lost the game, "his stillness, his concentration, his burning will kept him out there, where he belonged, to the end."

Most of all, as Angell notes in his foreword to *The Summer Game* (1972), he simply wanted to sit in the stands, watching baseball and "concentrat[ing] not just on the events down on the field but on their reception and results . . . to pick up the feel of the game as it happened to the people around me."

Like many other writers of the sixties, Angell finds his love of baseball constrained by encroachments like Astroturf, which has turned stadia into "giant living rooms," in contrast to "the emerald grass" of the Polo Grounds and the pastoral settings of spring training; television (watched by "home freeloaders"), which disregards tradition, the fans, and "deprives [baseball] of its essential beauty, clarity, and excitement"; and avaricious baseball magnates, particularly the "Caliguan whims" of Oakland's Charles O. Finley and Houston's Roy Hofheinz, "the Kublai Khan of the Domed Stadium."

Angell's style and language, however, re-create games in a way that makes such changes seem arbitrary. Baseball's myth of timelessness—its artful balance, leisurely pace, mathematical precision, and innumerable surprises—is awakened in his prose. Only occasionally does Angell slip into what Edward Hoagland called the *New Yorker*'s "shrinking-violet writing style," which, as the magazine's fiction editor, Angell "helped to shape."

The Summer Game collects Angell's writings from 1962 to 1972. It is a short trip back to a time before fans began to feel overwhelmed by changes; at the same time the book serves as a bridge to the nuances of the modern game. Thus, Angell discovers and rediscovers the heart of the game in the gentle discourse of senior citizens who come to watch spring training, or in a young boy's paroxysms during his first World Series, or in startling epiphanies, such as when Angell sees Whitey Ford on the mound and Warren Spahn throwing in the bullpen, "Ford exactly superimposed on Spahn [like] a trick photograph, a *trompe-l'oeil*: a 158-game winner and a 309-game winner throwing baseballs in the same fragment of space." Even the lowly '62 Mets are a poultice for all this aching change. Their "'Go!' Shouters" represent "antimatter to the sounds" of Yankee followers, who demonstrate "the smugness, and the arrogance of holders of large blocks of blue-chip stocks."

The World Series is Angell's finest literary territory and brings out his most exquisite metaphors; invariably he finds the one image that not only shows what took place but sets the pace and tone of his essay. The 1963 series was barely memorable, "like trying to recall an economy display of back-yard fireworks. Four small, perfect showers of light in the sky, accompanied by faint plops, and it was over." The 1964 series, which eluded the Phillies (they "fell apart like a dropped tray of dishes"), was played in Busch Stadium, "a seamed, rusty, steep-sided box" reminiscent "of an old down-on-her-luck dowager who has been given a surprise party by the local settlement house."

Even high expectations of a great series can produce unforeseeable results. When the young Orioles handily beat the veteran champion Dodgers in four straight games, "fans and sportswriters straggling out of Baltimore's Memorial Stadium after the fourth game suggested theatergoers who had bought tickets to a famous melodrama only to find that the bill had been changed at the last minute to a one-acter by Samuel

Beckett." The 1967 series, following an intense pennant race between
Detroit and Boston, was "The Flowering and Subsequent Deflowering of
New England" (a punning allusion to the literary work by Van Wyck
Brooks), as Boston lost to the great Cardinal team composed of men like
Bob Gibson (at times "a Redstone missile") and Lou Brock ("a tiny little
time pill that kept going off at intervals").

The 1968 series took place in the so-called Year of the Pitcher but
seemed more symbolic of the baseball age in which the Cardinals and
Tigers last played each other in a World Series (1934), especially because
"the Tiger hitters had restored the life and noise that seemed to go out of
baseball this year." The "last pre-inflationary, pre-playoff Series meant
the end of something," for Angell soon begins to hear news about "the
death of baseball" when the winter sets in.

This news prods Angell to think of baseball as "The Leaping
Corpse," and toward the close of *The Summer Game* we experience
Angell's change of heart. Despite the growing popularity of football,
Angell sees baseball as beginning to redeem itself—in a new commissioner (Bowie Kuhn) who might "force the game's Cro-Magnons into
common-sense planning and a grudging contemporaneity"; in new
superstars (best typified by Reggie Jackson), who will be attracted to
baseball by the higher salaries; by the game's centennial, which will lead
to the acknowledgment that what the "traditionalists mourn will never
come again" and that the new divisional alignments will come in time to
seem "a perfect substitute for the departed smaller leagues." Most of all,
baseball will be saved by "the rewarding and frequently riveting nature
of the baseball games." Football will continue to attract because sports
fans enjoy a variety of diverse sports and because football can be appre-
ciated on television in a way that baseball cannot. The baseball doom-
sayers sound like "the next of kin outside the sickroom door, who went
through a screeching months-long family wrangle sufficient to do in a
less hardy patient," because they fail to realize that baseball is cherished
most "for its clarity, variety, slowly tightening tension, and acute pressure on the individual athlete."

Within baseball's structure lie many joys: a free-hitting game, a
pitchers' duel, a game of surprises and unexpected happenings
(whether due to luck or superstitions or aspects of the inside game), or
the "gentle comical back-country beginnings" of a game experienced in
French in Montreal. For Angell, all baseball games are played on the
fields of memory; the modern stadia disappear into them, and the
many things that occur "are parts of the feast that the old game can
still bring us."

What makes *The Summer Game* more than just a collection of winning essays are the two appreciative essays, "Box Scores" and "The Interior Stadium," that frame the more reportorial pieces. If box scores, those "favorite urban flowers" that "burgeon and flourish," represent baseball's pastoral myth ("the arrival of pitchers and catchers at spring training camps" is not unlike "the delivery of a seed catalogue"), the "interior stadium" introduces the idea of baseball's boundlessness. Angell explores just why baseball has the effect it has on memory. Unlike other sports, in the midst of whose "successive spectacles and instant replays and endless reportings and recapitulations, we seem to have forgotten what we came for," baseball, though inured to these annoyances by now, "somehow remains the same, obdurately unaltered and comparable only with itself."

The interior stadium is, in more poetic language, the great conversation. "Restored in retrospect," baseball "has no season, but . . . [is] best played in the winter, without the distraction of other baseball news." It begins with return and recollection—a particular play or player—but eventually "gives way to reconsiderations and reflections about the sport itself." The nature of the sport, its temperament, its measure, its "clean lines," make the memory one recollected in tranquillity and lend it a certain "vividness," which retains for us a "distinct inner vision." Talk feeds our memory, as it helped Angell's father recall Nap Lajoie's giving an umpire "a faceful of tobacco juice" or "picking up a grounder and wheeling and floating the ball over to [the shortstop Terry] Turner." The imaginative possibilities—"Ruth bats against Sandy Koufax . . . [Carl] Hubbell pitches to Ted Williams"—approximate infinity, just as the game would do if a team went on hitting and hitting: "the end of this game may never come."

Baseball, Angell concludes, "is intensely remembered because only baseball is so intensely watched." It is a game, not of inches but, as he quotes Rube Bressler in *The Glory of Their Times*, "hundredths of inches." The game has no set pattern, is unpredictable, and makes up in luck and occasional impossibilities what it lacks in assurances. Rarely has a player "defied baseball, and even altered it," by overcoming all of these mysteries. Baseball is a layman's science: the numbers of a box score can be transformed into memory, and the ballfield "is one of the few places" we can see "this profoundly moving aesthetic beauty of mathematics." These complexities, whether psychological or physical components of the game, come to us in a new dimension, "marked by no clock," in which "each inning of baseball's slow, searching time span, each game of its long season is essential to the disclosure of its truths."

Hometown Piece

Angell's prose style would spawn an army of epigones in the next two
decades. The Rubes, dominated by the "chipmunk" journalists, continued to have some fun with baseball, debunking myths and deflating
heroes. (The journalist Marvin Kitman wrote about his attempt to pur-
chase the contract of the major leaguer Dick Stuart on waivers for one
dollar so that Stuart might teach Kitman's little league son something
about baseball.) The Matties, on the other hand, continued to explore
baseball's literary dimensions. As the novelist Philip Roth, writing at the
dawn of a new baseball era in 1973, put it in "My Baseball Years":
"Baseball—with its lore and legends, its cultural power, its seasonal asso-
ciations, its native authenticity, its simple rules and transparent strategies, its longueurs and thrills, its spaciousness, its suspensefulness, its
heroics, its nuances, its lingo, its 'characters,' its peculiarly hypnotic tedium, its mythic transformation of the immediate—was the literature of
my youth."

Perhaps baseball's most precious literary moment occurred in 1964
when *Harper's*, a longtime publisher of baseball prose, lent space to
George Plimpton to recount his afternoon at the 1963 World Series with
the poet Marianne Moore (and Robert Lowell, who tagged along).
Plimpton wrote the account in epistolary form, almost confiscating the
vernacular of Ring Lardner and substituting the voice of a litterateur—
somewhat ironically, because, as the piece develops, we learn just how
much Moore felt at home in the great conversation.

The essay is about baseball and about the 76-year-old Moore, whose
company compensates Plimpton (who has not met her before) for his
bad seats and the Giants-less series (Moore, on the other hand, was a
Dodgers fan). This is not just the end of an era in baseball but the close
of the modernist period in American literature. That notion is impressed
upon the reader early on as Plimpton reflects that Moore's "talk [was]
almost as anarchic as that of Casey Stengel" (about whom she had hoped
to write a poem) and that her famous poem "Hometown Piece for
Messrs. Alston and Reese" was once proposed for a monument at Ebbets
Field. For that matter, "nothing of Brooklyn went out there to
California."

Moore can shift between "a short eulogy of Willie Mays" and "an
appraisal and criticism of the Beinecke Rare Book Library at Yale." The
names of ballplayers (Koufax and Vinegar Bend Mizell) intrigue her, as
though any poetry that could come out of a ballplayer "was somehow

locked up in the name itself." The language of the game enthralls her, even a simple phrase like, "He ran out of room."

The poet, of course, is of primary interest in this essay, but baseball comes through in this study of what it means to be a fan, who can be the diminutive, erudite Moore as well as the "beefy man wearing a porkpie hat" in front of her. Though Moore had read *Pitching in a Pinch* and attended a game with Alfred Kreymborg in the twenties, it was "something of that moment" when she saw Roy Campanella during a routine mound conference at Ebbets Field in 1949, "his 'zest'—as she put it . . . [that] caught her fancy, indeed made a baseball addict of her—this when she was sixty-six." The imposing idiosyncrasies of the pitcher Carl Hubbell had done almost the same for Plimpton.

In this piece we are attuned to the perspective of a rather eccentric Brooklyn fan who has named her pet alligator after Elston Howard (the Yankees catcher). As Plimpton and Moore take their seats in a corner of the outfield, Moore seems rather pleased at having "the same advantages as the left fielder." She sees this narrow perspective as an advantage also to the poet.

Watching the game through a pair of quaint opera glasses, she assumes the point of view of a poet, not "watching directly," as the others do, but (though it may simply have been her age causing her concentration to wane) "look[ing] away from the focal point and study[ing] what was peripheral": the distance between first base and home, the "cruel . . . but necessary" double play, the injustice of player trades, "the vendors go[ing] by with their trays."

The game itself becomes a way of eavesdropping on the great conversation. Watching the pigeons out of one eye, Moore notes the names on her scorecard, "often with a comment concise and accurate, as one would expect from her." One player is "a giraffe . . . with those long strides"; she gives others an intimate air of familiarity, such as the Dodgers' Junior Gilliam, who "hates to fail, and *hates* to be called Junior."

Though she does not engage in the vernacular she so admires, Moore fills the baseball air with her own rich but simple voice, referring, for instance, to a player's "simulating *sang-froid*, . . . surely the first time that phrase has been used in Yankee Stadium." On the field, she is less interested in the score than in how certain players overcome ignominy in defeat. She would say as much again, at the age of 80, in a 1968 editorial in the *New York Times*. Well aware of the extraordinary pitching of that year and of how evenly matched the Cardinals and

Tigers were, she nonetheless would cheer for the team of the city of her birth because the Cardinals had remarkable "fortitude," as demonstrated by Red Schoendienst's beating tuberculosis, and Orlando Cepeda's overcoming "a leg so crooked it had to be broken by a surgeon and reset." In the Cardinals she would see the true essence of heroes, who were "not to be acclaimed by the eminence reached but by the obstacles overcome."

Accustomed to watching baseball on television, Moore finds the game she watches alongside Plimpton something of a disappointment; she would have preferred a greater show of "dexterity, emotion, speed, a ball player's 'zest.'" The chauffeur Plimpton has hired for the day becomes enamored of the poet and offers to drive her on her next trip— to Vermont to see musk-oxen, who "have been maligned about their smell." The chauffeur, who would like to read Moore's poems, recognizes the irrelevance of Moore's puzzlement over the score. "'Why *should* she know the score? . . . It's what she *sees* that counts.'" Plimpton, too, feels the tug of "that extraordinary poetess and her vision." Baseball is poetry for the common man in the way that poetry could once be understood (as Moore knew it could) by people without a formal education. In addition, baseball is for Marianne Moore what it was for Whitman and Saroyan, "the hurrah game." It possesses "vim," as Moore expressed it (and A. G. Spalding once described it). It is a game for people like Moore in "cartwheel sized beret[s]" and for the ordinary fans in their "porkpie" and chauffeur's hats.

After their afternoon at the World Series, Plimpton believed that he "would never look at a game quite as [he] had before," and he wrote to Moore with some additional questions; she answered them in a post-script to the essay in *Harper's* the following month. Though only a few of the ten questions concern baseball, Moore reveals that certain aspects of the game appeal to her. Dexterity, ferocity, abandon, fury, speed, and accuracy fascinate her, but not as they would in football, which seems "not so conglomerate as fifty years ago." Babe Ruth's "pigeon-toed, stubbed little trot lacked beauty," while "vim marks" Willie Mays's "every action." Grace and beauty define the game for her (fielding appealed to her more than hitting), though not vulgarity (quite different from the rhythms of the vernacular she admired), petty squabbling, or commercialism. A player's injuries remind us of the fragility of our own lives; his public persona reminds us of the value of solitude. Roger Maris grows in her estimation when he admits "that the only privacy he could count on was when taking his place on the ball field."

The Phantom

Willie Morris (b. 1934), editor-in-chief of *Harper's* from 1967 to
1971, began something of a revival of baseball's cultural mosaic by
writing a memorable passage in his autobiographical narrative *North
Toward Home* (1970); the piece helped locate a small place for baseball
in the larger genre of personal memoir and became frequently anthologized.

The boys of Yazoo, Mississippi, all want to be baseball players; they
live and breathe the game. Like Philip Roth in Newark and Roger
Angell in New England, young Morris knows rosters and statistics.
Because the majors did not yet extend to the South (St. Louis was the
favorite team of Dixie), the radio broadcasts feed his imagination.
Southern boys aspire to go north to play, to reap the glories, the way
boys wanted to become riverboat men in an earlier era. As a young white
southern boy clutching "a Jackie Robinson Louisville Slugger," Morris
dreams of such a departure. The "dream . . . of glory in the mythical
cities of the North" seems to come alive as his father shags fly balls. In
those moments he would welcome even fleeting fame, if only his dreams
were not cut short by his father's fatigue.

Morris relates his memories of being a 12-year-old sports reporter
for a Yazoo newspaper and of his first visit to a game "higher than the
Jackson Senators of Class B." He meets the players—some of whom will
one day play in the big leagues—but much as he wishes to copy their
every move, he is "disillusioned" when he hears them complain about
working conditions. In Yazoo, "baseball was all meaning; it was the link
with the outside."

The narrative takes us to "The Store," a general store for the (segregated) baseball talk of the day, though the young boy can freely extol the
recently integrated Brooklyn Dodgers at the two town firehouses, where
radio broadcasts can be heard. Even the firemen get off lazily to fires
when they are tuned to a game. Listening to the game was an itinerant
affair. Morris's father "usually started with Firehouse No. 1 for the first
few innings, and then hit No. 2 before ending up at The Store for the
post-game conversations."

Morris relates a series of poignant vignettes, like brief innings, that
bring the small southern town to life, with all its oddities, including left-
handed catchers. He talks of visits to secluded ball fields "that were little more than parched red clearings, the outfield sloping out of the
woods and ending in some tortuous gully full of yellowed paper, old
socks, and vintage cow shit."

The image of radio is important in this narrative, and not just because it connects Yazoo with baseball in the rest of the country. For instance, a local radio program runs a rising-pot baseball contest that Morris seems able to win day after day. While playing ball, he can hear "the sounds of . . . two games, our own and . . . one being broadcast." He especially remembers the announcer, the "Old Scotchman," who could report games in such a way that "casual pop flies had the flow of history behind them, double plays resembled the stark clashes of old armies, and home runs deserved acknowledgement on earthen urns." Morris is infatuated with the Old Scotchman's great perorations, and the language of baseball on the radio helps introduce him to "reading literature."

As Morris discovers the Old Scotchman's gift for invention, the narrative adopts a more fictive style. Morris learns, after listening to his father's shortwave, that the broadcasts are delayed—the Old Scotchman is always a few innings behind the actual game. For one brief moment, baseball's clocklessness becomes disoriented by time. Using this knowledge, Morris becomes "the Phantom" (a mock radio character himself), able to predict to the letter what is going to happen, pitch by pitch, hit by hit, if no "static" interferes with his "extra vision." He soon becomes the town's "full-scale oracle," guiltily winning bets and simply awing his friends. Eventually he is caught, but news of the shortwave phenomenon does not bring immediate converts, who still prefer the Old Scotchman's "unmitigated eloquence."

When Morris does finally come to play American Legion junior ball, he knows more rules and rudimentary strategy than his coaches and the umpires; he knows when a double play is not a double play. Baseball's pastoral myth deceives him. In junior ball, the Yazoo players are the city slickers; in games in outlying towns, they get their first dose of real defeat by "those sons of dirt farmers" who "rubbed our noses in our own catastrophes . . . while their elders stood around [shouting] boondock venom." He actually fears for his safety when he breaks up a no-hitter with a cheap hit. He will learn what many young professionals learn in the low minors: the reality of the game, and its occasional brutality (and boredom and anxiety), can dispel the mythic charms.

In Legion ball, Morris gains a kind of religious awakening, not in the church of baseball but in the Scriptures, under the tutelage of his coach, "Gentleman Joe." Winning the "Miss'ippi championship" becomes the high-water mark of his young life, but it foreshadows his "last confrontation with baseball." He will play on a semipro team, the Yazoo Screaming Eagles, named after a new brand of tire sold at the store that sponsors the team. He plays under hazardous conditions: "Insects bigger than fifty cent pieces caromed off the bulbs . . . and the ground . . . [was] full of holes [and] ruts."

When he misses a line drive hit to him in the terrible lighting of center field, the ball smashes his kneecap. With runs scoring and the pitcher eyeing him contemptuously, Morris acknowledges, with reluctance and acceptance, "that if I ever made it to those mythical cities of the North, the ones I had dreamed about in my Brooklyn cap, it would have to be with a different set of credentials."

The myth of America in which every boy dreams of becoming a baseball player was coming to an abrupt end at the close of the 1960s, disappearing, in effect, into the myth of memory.

Don't Say Anything Bad about Baseball

It seemed only a matter of time before the theme of disenchantment would reach ballplayers as well as fans—and by extension, the game itself. *Ball Four* (1970), the collaboration of Jim Bouton, a washed-up pitcher who kept an intimate diary of his 1969 season with the expansion Seattle Pilots, and Leonard Shecter, one of the premier "chipmunk" journalists, was as much a reflection of the antiestablishment era in which it was published as it was of the state of the game. Willie Morris had punctured the myth of America without necessarily demythologizing baseball. Bouton and Shecter went after the baseball myths and after the game.

When the book came out in 1970, after being excerpted in *Look*, it was an instant best-seller. *Ball Four* was controversial: it garnered rave reviews from Rex Lardner (brother of Ring) and Roger Angell, scathing reviews from Dick Young and Bouton's fellow ballplayers, and disregard from the commissioner, Bowie Kuhn. Mickey Mantle's response when asked about Bouton's book (which had pilloried him) was, "Jim who?"

A quarter of a century later, *Ball Four* is pretty tame stuff. Much of the humor is sophomoric. (The paternity-suit gags, voyeurism, and other antics in the book some critics so admired in 1970 might be labeled sexual harassment today.) Past writers had dealt with similar material between the lines or in puns and euphemisms. In its most irreverent moments, *Ball Four* succeeds, but an understated style was too sophisticated for Bouton to sustain at any length. It was, however, precisely because baseball (and especially the Yankees) did not tolerate irreverence or nonconformity of any kind, at least in the sixties, that *Ball Four* became such a sensation.

Ball Four removed the ellipses from published player speech and talked candidly (though not critically) of ballplayers' drug abuse and sexual behavior (and even stopped short there). As Bouton himself stated in a follow-up book to *Ball Four*, "I could have quoted all the bastards who use the word 'nigger' on supposedly happily integrated teams. I could have recorded the stupid anti-Semitic remarks. I could have shown, in much more detail, the mindlessness of it all."

Bouton attempted to poke holes in the image of the buttoned-down ballplayer ("The Grey-Flannel-Suit Men of Baseball," Talese had called them) and to replace it with "an entire ball club of clean-cut American boys . . . looking up the skirt of some female . . to the tune of "The Star-Spangled Banner." As far as the game was concerned, Bouton wrote, "there is not enough in it to occupy a man's mind"; he would agree with what one player "wrote about the game in college: 'Baseball is an Ass.'"

Though Bouton had taken notes, when it came time actually to write *Ball Four*, he "talked into his tape recorder for seven months." The idea for the book came from Shecter, who had approached Bo Belinsky with the idea earlier. *Ball Four* is more or less an "as told to" book; Shecter edited Bouton's half a million words down by two-thirds.

Short of liberating the language of baseball, which Mark Harris had tried to do in the fifties (with word "blanks" like *f——ing*), the book attempted, as Roger Angell said in his *New Yorker* review, to provide "a rare view of a highly complex public profession seen from the innermost inside." Such a book had been written before, by Christy Mathewson at the turn of the century, and by Brosnan. Shecter simply let Bouton talk at length, unfettered by baseball protocol or censorship, and allowed the story to follow its own course as Bouton goes from the majors to the minors and then back to the majors. Even the act of writing the book becomes a subject, as players not only grab Bouton's notes away from him and peer over his shoulder but also remark, "Well, just keep me out of it."

Ball Four is essentially a sixties book. It rejects the apple-pie-ism traditionally represented by baseball; it is anti–Vietnam War and contemptuous of players who are not; and it supports the puerile notion that if you have not tried LSD, it is because you are "chicken." Though Bouton details the teams' free dispensation of amphetamines ("greenies"), the book's drug message is largely ambiguous and trivialized given the problems that developed in the next decades. Baseball is an "ego trip"—the sixties term that sets the tone of his book—in which "the difference between making the club and not making it might be the length of [your] hair." Baseball bores Bouton unless he is playing it; on the professional level, it is alternately a drudgery and a dream come true. It is also a game with "Neanderthal aspects" that require conformity, so Bouton resolves to deal with the "pettiness . . . meanness and stupidity" by living up to his reputation as a flake.

Though Angell praised Bouton for refraining from "the sportswriting clichés of debunking and anecdotage," *Ball Four* does its share of debunking and is largely a collection of anecdotes and one-liners. The writing is very uneven, even lame in places: "As far as he's concerned the Marquis of Queensberry is some fag hairdresser." The cute, flippant end lines of many entries (the book is written in diary form) only drag down the pace of the narrative: "If this sounds insane, maybe it is"; "You take your ego trips, I'll take mine"; "I was only lying a little."

Competitiveness is seen as undermining, and altruism and sportsmanship as barely existing. The typical ballplayer roots for his teammates when he is sitting on the bench but does not want any of them to succeed at his expense. Ballplayers, the superstars as well as the marginal ones, will intentionally mess up plays for the player who gets on them for having made a costly error.

Ball Four begins in November 1969 on the day Bouton signs his contract to pitch for the expansion Seattle club. Bouton provides more detail than Brosnan here, depicting the parsimony of general managers and showing what it was like to be a player negotiating for himself (no agents were allowed yet) in the last days of baseball feudalism. When Bouton delves into subjects rarely seen from a player's point of view— the Yankees after they stopped winning pennants, clubhouse politics, vengeful umpires, life on an expansion team—he can be engaging. Less compelling are the frank revelations that players, even famous ones, get drunk; say "shitfuck"; close car windows on kids who want their autographs; play nasty practical jokes on each other; and go to dangerous lengths to go "beaver shooting," that is, to stare in the windows of women who are undressing ("a baseball universal" that even the great Mickey Mantle participates in). Bouton is more successful when he relies on old-fashioned, Rube-like metaphors, such as when he describes one Houston pitcher as looking "like a grocer who's been eating up a good bit of his profits." Too often Bouton calls attention to himself as a baseball apostate trying to make nonbelievers of his teammates and noting that "unorthodoxy does in baseball what heresy does in the priesthood." He would like to tell people that he wins ball games because he does not believe in God.

But when Bouton is on the subject of baseball and its effects upon the individual, *Ball Four* offers a truly fresh perspective. Removed from the scandal and from the self-serving Bouton, who revels in his own reputation as a troublemaker, we have a story of a once-great fastball/curveball pitcher who has been forced by injuries to adjust to a pitch he fiddled with when he was younger but never believed he would ever have to use. Bouton explores the feelings of a ballplayer in despair over being cut or demoted. Knowing that such rejection can happen at any time in a player's career, Bouton finds himself "holding back a little, keeping people at arm's length."

Some of the critical moments in the book are indeed sharp and pointed. If "one of the nice things about baseball is that there are no rules you can't break," Bouton revels in breaking them all, though he thinks of himself as something of a slow learner in the end. He muses about his experiences with bad coaches (Sal Maglie) and good ones (Johnny Sain) and with front-office people who won't "sit around in a situation that calls for panic." We accompany Bouton on his descent into baseball purgatory (where "managers get angry at injuries") after he has had his tastes of paradise: the major leagues, the World Series, winning 18 and 21 games in a season, modest wealth, and fame. When he is sent to the minors early in the season, he acknowledges that he is one of the "battered bastards of baseball," having once been "the guy that was never a big pheenom but that came out on top unexpectedly." The act of writing, he discovers, and having to think about himself bring Bouton "so close to the situation that [he] can't make an objective judgment of whatever ability [he has] left."

In this moment we get real internal conflict, and one wishes that this had been the major thrust of the book, a truly metaphorical "ball four" in a pitcher's career. It is at this crucial moment that Bouton decides to be "a knuckleball pitcher and nothing else" (the knuckleball, like himself, is hard to handle). Such moments inspire his best epigrams as well, such as, "In baseball you're only as good and as happy as your last appearance." When, in mid-July, he is grudgingly given a start, he gets clobbered and must reflect after the All-Star break on the anxiety of life on the mound, where the stress of pitching can be relieved only by pitching some more. When his pitching continues to falter, he is left with only the beauty of baseball's pastoral myth: in Seattle, "when a home run hit off you disappears over the fence your eye catches a glimpse of the majesty of Mt. Rainier and some of that bad feeling goes away." Added to his frustrations are his desires to make things work again, to have all of his excuses entertained seriously. He is an individual struggling to hold on to his career while those around him seem oblivious to his very existence, a man whose "sore arm . . . made me what I am today, an aging knuckleballer." It is almost fitting that the events take place while Bouton is playing for an expansion team, one filled with players like himself who "have been rescued from the same junkpile." The reader learns what it feels like to be part of a baseball team in transition; players come and go for different reasons, and other players stay simply because, with so much money invested in them, it would be an embarrassment to the club to let them go. The feelings associated with transition are intensified as Bouton goes through certain changes himself, having to start over again, to prove himself once more, late in the season when he is traded to yet another ball club.

We seem to know what Bouton means when he is on the mound and "throwing good." "Throwing well" would not work here. Pitching is an emotion, a sensuous experience that commands a linking verb. Bouton can empathize with a sore-armed pitcher having a bad season, coming off a good one, because he has been there himself. For all that ails baseball, Bouton realizes that "you spend a good piece of your life gripping a baseball and in the end it turns out that it was the other way around all the time." Ironically, *Ball Four* cannot help being a pure baseball book.

At its best, *Ball Four*, as Robert Lipsyte said of the *Look* excerpts, "breathes a new life into a game choked by pontificating statisticians, image-conscious officials and scared ballplayers." In his sequel, *I'm Glad You Didn't Take It Personally* (1971), Bouton recounts his last futile attempt to stay in the major leagues. When he was sent to the minors again, he called it a career. *Ball Four* made its mark on baseball literature. It was, like its secondary subject, a knuckleball—erratic at times and, as Red Smith said, "sometimes dull, sometimes annoying, and frequently in bad taste"—but it helped liberate the game, which was going to be liberated anyway, one way or another, from its aging sackcloth.

CHAPTER 10

The Boys Who Went Away

If Bouton found baseball empty and asinine, other ex-players saw it as disillusioning. *A False Spring*, a book about baseball in the sixties that was not published until early 1975, looks at the myth of the best game from the dark side. Written by a young former ballplayer, Pat Jordan (b. 1941), *A False Spring* is the finest account ever written about the minor league experience—a minor masterpiece, as well, of the human experience. It is a remarkable book not only for its depth and honesty but also for its excellent writing. Novelistic and autobiographical, *A False Spring* is about self-awareness and coming of age; even as he discusses baseball's imperfections, Jordan places most of the blame for his failures squarely on his own shoulders.

Jordan's account of being a 1959 Milwaukee Braves bonus baby with a blazing fastball is an artful narrative filled with long, lyrical passages that absorb most of the traditional baseball thematic material. *A False Spring* is the myth of Elysian Fields gone to seed. Jordan attempts to "resee" an unrequited baseball experience, to make sense of something that "affected the design of my life to a degree nothing else ever will."

The narrative begins with "the bird dogs," the almost-scouts (in the days before the 1965 amateur player draft), talent sniffers who throw a six-figure signing bonus at prospects as though it were "a Frisbee that we could frivolously toss into the wind." The character of the scouts is revealed in how they dress and think: "Those Haggar slacks [they wore] might have been picked up . . . at J. C. Penney's in Fayetteville, North Carolina, on the muggy evening they watched that good nigra boy hit four home runs."

Jordan is signed so quickly that we never quite get to understand this 18-year-old kid who has always thrown so hard that when he was eight years old he could split the skin on his father's fingers. Jordan wonders if he ever thought about anything else besides pitching during his adolescence in Fairfield, Connecticut. He has been unable, he writes, to separate who he is from his fastball, which, ironically, will doom him. So much has pitching consumed his life (Jordan did not like anything else about baseball besides the pitching) that he can barely recall who his friends were or what books he read. His nurturing half-brother, who functions as his mentor, coach, and agent, seems also to have supplanted his father as a figure of paternal love and encouragement. Yet, as the brother attempts to get Jordan as much money up front as he can, Jordan realizes the hard, almost prophetic truth—that "in trying to create the illusion that my talent was greater than it was, it ceased to be as good as it was." Few writers have captured the personal experience of the short-lived bonus baby era with such precise detail as Jordan has, and his book remains the best quick study of the period.

Jordan's sheltered life takes on a new dimension when he suddenly finds himself on his own. *A False Spring* becomes an American coming-of-age story about growing up and learning to cope with failure in youth. The real-life Jordan is cut from the same cloth as Updike's Rabbit Angstrom (with touches of Holden Caulfield and Nick Adams). His is a story not of lost youth, but of the loss of self and then of finding oneself after that self has been smothered in the aura and promise of a game. The story thus transcends baseball, while the importance of the game is neither trivialized nor idealized.

The figures in the book speak directly and faithfully; they sound exactly like whoever they are—managers, scouts, girlfriends, gigolos, farm boys, Dominicans, Mormons. Eloquent descriptive passages make Jordan a more imposing figure than he would normally be; after all, many baseball boys have come and gone, and we will meet others like him. From the start, Jordan has a story to tell. Though he enters a world where real heroes are being bred and molded, he bears a greater resemblance to the "immigrant" in E. B. White's homage to New York City, the young small-town boy who comes to New York "with a manuscript in his suitcase and an ache in his heart."

A False Spring is a study in failure. One critic saw similarities between Jordan's book and Jack Kerouac's *Vanity of Duluoz* (1968): "Both Kerouac and Jordan were anointed by their families to take their athletic abilities into the world and return with fame and fortune. Both encountered immediate opposition for the same reason: they didn't fit in, or chose not to. Both possessed a distant, disturbing vision. Both failed their athletic potential because their vision distracted them. Both also lacked discipline." Although *A False Spring*, unlike Kerouac's novel, is not about "moral death and resurrection," it does detail a kind of spiritual awakening.

Each chapter begins with a scene that evokes mood and tone—from the attic, where Jordan writes his memoirs, to Ma Carter's house (like Ma McCuddy's tavern in Farrell's Chicago), where "there were plates of hot corn bread and sourdough biscuits and homemade white bread and even slices of store brought bread that nobody ever touched." Jordan piques the reader's interest with memorable descriptions of players and playing fields: Yankee Stadium is "a stately dowager of tattered dignity"; the Braves' County Stadium is "the fresh-faced and inviting ingenue." Warren Spahn walks "like a duck," and Lew Burdette "like a turkey fleeing an axe." Joe Torre, then a rookie like Jordan, resembles "a Mexican villain from a Grade B movie," while Henry Aaron's skin is "the flat black tone of latex paint."

Jordan seems more saddened by than envious of these major leaguers—eternally youthful in their worn-out bodies, with spirits that seem "perfectly preserved by the game in which [they] lived." As he travels to his first job in McCook, Nebraska, Jordan is immediately impressed by the land, the horizons, the never-ending fields, which strike terror in him and seem literally to be moving him further away from the hope of "new horizons" before he even arrives at his destination. Only those landmarks that dot the American roadside (A&W and Phillips 66 signs, for instance), along with the ballfields, are familiar to him. (In the revitalized minor leagues of the nineties, David Lamb, in *Stolen Season*, would rediscover "in these hamlets of the Appalachian League and in other minor league towns across the nation . . . the face of Norman Rockwell's vanishing America—a place where, for hundreds of young men, the journey to the major leagues begins, and more often than not, ends.")

Jordan, nonetheless, is jolted by alien experiences, such as playing in a mild tornado or watching as his teammates fight over a famous Brave's uniform, disregarding the "ill fit for whatever talent remained in those dark sweat stains that could never be laundered out." These same boys root for each other to fail (as Bouton said major leaguers did) so that they can avoid returning to what would have been their normal allotments in life—a job in a bakery or a hitch in the navy. Young phenoms, they play with agonizing injuries so that their dream will not suddenly end.

Players try to adapt in ways suited to their characters. Jordan will choose "distances"; another player, Ron Hunt, who will make it to the major leagues, discovers the "superficial trappings" of a false but kind intimacy. The players' lives are contained within ball games and nothing else, as though the players exist in little glass snow domes. Jordan is not sure where he fits in. He knows the dangers of familiarity but would like to get to know others. Though he has a girlfriend back home (whose existence he does not reveal until one-third of the way through the book and whom he will later marry), his reluctance to join with the mavericks, he admits, is "due more to circumstance than inclination."

Inconsistency will plague him from the start. He fails in his first outing but seems unable to learn from the experience that a pitcher can give up two or three runs a game and still be great. Jordan, who has never known failure (and once threw four consecutive no-hitters), cannot recover from the shock of it. Life in a minor league camp resembles life in a minimum security prison or "a cell [in] the Cancer Ward." At night he is roused by "the slap of alligator tails"; white, Spanish-speaking, and black players are "quartered" separately, the last "closest to the swamp."

Little attention is given to the rudimentary instruction he was promised (though Jordan is not sure he would have taken such teaching seriously); players must simply "sink to the level of their true ability." Jordan, instead, picks up devices, such as the art of throwing at a batter's head to unsettle him to the point of destroying whatever confidence and promise the batter may have had (and perhaps terminating his career). His first minor league season is, literally, a wash, neither spectacular nor terrible; the games he pitches are "small fragments, like . . . hailstones . . . [that] have melted in the warm waters of my memory."

Failure is a key theme of *A False Spring*. The management has invested a lot of money in its players, who are treated like "small firms on the stock exchange whose entire future could be read in the morning's quotation." Jordan, who is regarded suspiciously, is given the "privilege" of rooming alone the following season, "so as not to contaminate those younger players with [his] incurable failure." He will not become like those who have become so acquainted with loss that they have become indifferent to it. For them, no loss has been worse than the initial one. Jordan needs to deal with the frustration of finding out *why* he lost his control at the time when he was growing, gaining weight, getting stronger, and picking up speed and "movement" on his fastball. The moment of recognition, "when it was all slipping away," is a turning point in the book.

Jordan realizes he lacks the necessary virtues of "self-discipline, single-mindedness, perseverance, and ambition." His fate will be sealed by how others perceive him. When he cannot impress anyone with his "stuff" anymore, he angrily tries to hit his catcher, Joe Torre, in the back of the head with a ball seconds after being chided by Torre for throwing (sore-armed) lobs during batting practice. The action, of course, earns him no respect, and he is tagged a "red-ass guinea" who will not even make it to class C baseball. Like George Orwell in "Shooting an Elephant," Jordan acted only so as not to look the fool. For once, he realizes exactly who he is. His minor league experience has been his portrait of the artist as a young man, and "red-ass guinea" his epiphany. He will now attempt to develop "a sensitivity on paper [which he] lack[s] in reality."

The first half of *A False Spring* contains an impressionable Jordan's episodic accounts of the scouts, class D (very low minor-league ball), and spring training. In the second half of the book, upon his return to the minors (and in the last two years of his three-year contract), Jordan assumes the persona of "the aloof veteran," that is, "one who has played at least two years in professional baseball," and we begin to see the action from his slightly more mature point of view.

Jordan must now make some sense of his life. He discerns meaning in the forgotten ballparks left behind in the abandonment of small-town America, populated by drifters, drunks, mill workers, farmhands, and baseball players and marked by random violence and racism. The lives of the townspeople mirror the lives of the players, who have much time on their hands and wait out the day until it is time for a game. The acquaintanceships and relationships that Jordan does develop will become irrevocably lost to him. He realizes only later that people passed "unseen, through my life, only to be remembered years later with a warmth I never felt at their moment of passing."

The deeper Jordan descends into the minors, the further away from baseball he seems to get. Managers mouth clichés rather than advice and fall asleep by the seventh inning. One manager, after years of alcoholism, sees baseball as the only way of saving his own desperately hopeless life, "as if the game, like the waters of Lourdes, could cure him simply by his physical immersion in it." Jordan is left alone to struggle with his insufficiencies, to overcome, by minute analysis, his erratic "throwing arm . . . a bazooka without sight."

In what will be his final attempt to demonstrate his ability, Jordan attends the winter instructional leagues in Bradenton, Florida, where the alternately cool and warm weather pleases him. Only later will he realize that it "had been a false spring." (The title is taken from a line in Hemingway's *A Moveable Feast* [1964]: "Life had seemed so simple that morning when I had awakened and found the false spring.") In his last significant fling with organized baseball, he meets managers and coaches, most of them baseball lifers, who appear to be capable of teaching him and restoring his lost confidence.

But Jordan, at 19, cannot see what these older men can see. The false spring becomes a metaphor for his own baseball career and his life thus far. He envies these people, not their baseball success (whatever that has amounted to) but something else—a maturity built upon self-awareness. He is especially taken with his pitching coach, Whitlow Wyatt, who, like Jordan, had a frustrating career but never lost his composure; he became one of these extraordinary people who "develop a more refined sensitivity to life's lesser details and, with greater age, even lesser ones, until finally, their satisfaction comes from life itself and every detail in it is a pleasure."

Though Jordan's story could easily be one of a struggling actor or writer, it is baseball that tests his character as nothing else can. Even as he begins to throw well and tinker with his pitches, we know that it will not be for lack of talent that he will fail. He begins to throw much better mainly because he is now seeking, "not success, even—but simply the absence of failure." But he must do so by compromising and ultimately destroying "the one thing in me that was special"—his natural ability. Few clinical studies of pitching have recorded the pitcher's problematic art with such brevity, telling insight, and thoroughness as Jordan has here through personal tragedy.

Bradenton forces Jordan to rethink things. He (like Bouton) learns the art of holding back a little. The chapter ends on a note of inevitable longing. He is married by this time, and though struggling through the relationship, he declines to sleep with a woman who owes him some money, noting that he is "no longer free to act on the whims and impulses of my youth."

When he learns that he will not be starting one night for his Eau Claire, Wisconsin, team (having slid further down the minor league ladder), Jordan abandons the team and is reassigned to Palatka, Florida, "the Elephants Burial Ground." The city is emblematic of the men who are sent there. In Palatka, which emits "an overwhelming sense of decay," baseball is played amid swamps, foliage, creeping vines, snakes, low-lying mist, and oppressive, unbearable heat. Players go mad in Palatka, and even baseball becomes something of a parody of itself there. The team "served a cathartic experience" for the inhabitants of the town, where "even the blacks in the left field [segregated] stands [could laugh at] the niggers' niggers." Unable to do much besides play ball, the young men of Palatka face a life of welfare checks and perpetual unemployment, living in garage-sized rooms in some other strange little town like Palatka.

Jordan throws his final pitches "without thought or anxiety over my lost promise." In many ways, he is fortunate. At 19, when most of the other men he knows are much older, he can ask himself the question they have long avoided: "What would I be without baseball?" Its answer, whenever it comes to him, will be the first step on his road to complete self-discovery.

Jordan had originally titled his autobiography "The Days of Wine and Bonuses," though he smartly eschewed the cutesy pun for a more thoughtful title. In the four years it took him to write *A False Spring*, Jordan found his direction by writing articles for *Sports Illustrated*. He has continued to freelance over the years, focusing on controversial topics and people (not always related to sports), such as Steve and Cindy Garvey, Pete Rose's son, and Steve Carlton. In 1984 he published a baseball novel called *The Cheat*, which he describes as "Holden Caulfield without the innocence." Several of his early *Sports Illustrated* articles written between 1970 and 1972 appeared in a collection called *The Suitors of Spring* (1973). The book is mainly about pitchers, and about pitching in general, but larger themes arise from the gracefully written player profiles, whose subjects point to varying degrees of success or failure and to different ways of dealing with it. If *A False Spring* is about Jordan himself, *The Suitors of Spring* is about others who remind Jordan about himself in some way.

The title essay is essentially a first draft of chapter 2 of *A False Spring*. We can see what was edited out for the sake of continuity and narrative effect. It is a much more expository account of the early "bird dogs" who eventually signed the pitchers Jordan profiles in *The Suitors of Spring*.

An 18-year-old pitcher, Art DeFilippis, is the subject of the opening essay. Another Jordan, he has come through the new player draft, which removed from scouting the ability to learn what a boy "had inside . . . what made him tick." Each subsequent essay represents a certain aspect of the pitcher at a different phase of a professional career. The minor leaguer Stephen Louis Dalkowski is "The Living Legend," a sensational young phenom who is hounded by ill fortune precisely at the moment he is ready to make the major leagues. In the realm of baseball, he symbolizes those whose failure "was not the result of deficiency but of excess." His ability to throw a baseball so fast that not even Ted Williams can see it or wish to hit it is for Jordan one of "those isolated, pure distilled moments of private success attributable solely to talent."

As Jordan ventures to the all too familiar minor league towns of Wellsville, Leesburg, Yakima, and Stockton, he re-creates the poignant details of minor league life: the dollar-a-day hotels with knotted-rope fire escapes, the long walks in uniform through town to the ballpark, the array of injuries and scores of player vendettas. In Waterbury, Connecticut, he encounters a 12-year veteran minor league catcher for whom success means getting a job *anywhere* in baseball. For a "young hand," the pitcher Bruce Kison, it is the major leagues or nothing. He represents the new professional who can think his way to victory and who grows more confident as he makes his way up the minor league chain. The essay compares and contrasts the organizational man with the hot prospect, and Jordan shows how the two men's futures are inexorably linked—fittingly, as a pitcher and a catcher are linked.

Kison's career is developed further in a companion essay called "The End of Innocence." Kison did make it to the major leagues and was a minor hero in the 1971 World Series. When Jordan catches up with him, Kison seems "as straight and simple and obvious as the age in which he lives is circuitous and convoluted and unfathomable." But the taste of big league life sparks a loss of innocence. How deep will that cut, Jordan wonders? Kison, the brush-back pitcher who beat his own drum and spoke in an honest, forthright way, will now have to deal with the owners, for whom he makes money; the writers, who are looking for the splendid quote; and the fans, who idolize him and follow his every move. Like Jordan, who sees something of himself in all the players he profiles, Kison learns to hold back a little and not to "tell everything you know anymore." If there is a theme for Jordan on the subject of pitching, it is Christy Mathewson's bon mot that a pitcher is a man in need of sympathy.

In "A Talent for Refusing Greatness," Jordan wonders why a pitcher like the iconoclast "Sudden Sam" McDowell, possessed of an unrelenting fastball and a curve that collapses "at the plate like a mallard shot on the wing," cannot do better than a .500 winning percentage when he is perceived to have "the best stuff in baseball." Sam McDowell resembles the kind of pitcher Jordan (or Dalkowski) might have been had he made it to the major leagues. McDowell's sense of satisfaction, we learn, comes from doing those things he is *not* expected to do. He would rather possess his fastball than allow it to possess him, and because he believes that the possibility of doing something is the same as actually doing it, "his challenges, and their eventual resolution, are very private affairs independent of the approval or disapproval of anyone else." McDowell is contrasted with Tom Seaver, who seems to embody the pitcher's most eminent qualities. Jordan uses the image of seagulls, who must grunt and struggle to earn a moment of "uncommon grace," to introduce Seaver, who seems always to achieve perfection and grace. Individuals like Seaver are extraordinarily talented and reach a level of success few men ever achieve; he is a pitcher "conscious of all those aspects of his craft [that are] within his power to cultivate." Whereas McDowell is the gifted athlete, Seaver's talents, like Koufax's before him, "are rough stones that must be painstakingly recut and repolished with every use."

Bo Belinsky, "An Angel of His Time," is the depleted talent in Jordan's pictures of an exhibition. Belinsky has become something of a parody of himself, the playboy-athlete. The public has become bored with him and his "warehouse" of clever remarks, and also with his lack of respect for his own talent. For all his cynicism, however, Belinsky acts without malice; he still loves the mythic game, which "'moves slowly in time when everything around it is rushing like mad.'"

The books ends appropriately with a profile of baseball's best pitching coach of modern times, Johnny Sain, "A Jouster with Windmills," who earned the intense loyalty and devotion of the pitchers he coached, turning a simple baseball into a thing of "possibilities you never dreamed of." He is the coach Jordan needed and desired but never had.

On the surface, *The Suitors of Spring* is a simple book of pitcher profiles. But it is also a book about the art of pitching, with whole paragraphs devoted to mechanics and style. (Jordan later wrote *Sports Illustrated*'s textbook on pitching.) It is a counterpoint played out between men who have experienced failure and those who have achieved success (though Jordan shows just how close the two points sometimes are). No other book has quite captured the essence of what it means to be an athlete, especially in baseball, a sport at which a player can never be successful without "the peripheral adjuncts to sheer ability—control, discipline, expertise. . . ."

Simplify, Simplify

With baseball at a crossroads between 1969 and 1972, the great conversation grew more intense. Mark Harris, noted for his novels, had written numerous articles from a fan's perspective, for *Sports Illustrated* and other publications, beginning in the late fifties. A piece from 1959, "Love Affair in San Francisco," recounts a game-in-progress from the point of view of every representative district of San Francisco, including the masons then building Candlestick Park. In the Temple of Heaven Saloon in Chinatown, "the bartender and his patrons gossip in Chinese but talk baseball in English," while on wealthy Nob Hill "the news is received that Mr. Raymond Lee Walls, Jr., an associate of a Chicago firm, flies out to Mr. O. Manuel Cepeda, whose winter address is Puerto Rico." Baseball fans all over San Francisco are caught up in the ensuing pennant race, dispensing opinions as they listen to the game on radio or watch it at Seals Stadium. They are fannishly fickle—down on the Giants when they aren't hitting, up on the team when they win—but everyone is completely wrapped up in the fate of the ball club, causing "a good deal of agitated shuffling of souls."

For Harris, all baseball myths are real and all are surrounded by the myth of the best game. In "Ladies' Day at the Game" (1957), which is cast in the myth of memory ("It was 1939, and it was spring"), he believes that the only way to interest women in the game is to lie, to treat the game as if it were something "sociological or literary or historical or political or aesthetic" or economic or Greek. But there always comes along the woman who has "conquered [baseball] by adopting it, by sitting and watching." Once the game's inherent simplicity has been learned, all the myths and realities of baseball become "swiftly comprehensible." Men might do better to appreciate the game the way women do, letting baseball serve "our minds and our emotions and our hunger for retreat."

Originally appearing in the *New York Times* in 1969, "Maybe What Baseball Needs Is a Henry David Thoreau" is Harris's bittersweet plea for baseball to simplify, simplify. With a new commissioner about to be appointed, baseball is gearing up for more competition from football and other sports, as well as for the impact of television, which has made baseball's abundance of "dead time" all too apparent. Harris argues that such dead time is precisely what makes baseball so extraordinary, for it is in such moments that Babe Ruth "came trotting in from the outfield . . . at the change of innings [and] captured our eyes, for we *had* to see him (he *never* disappointed us) step upon second base on his way to the dugout."

Harris makes an impassioned plea for the traditional game, an appeal to the myths of memory and timelessness and baseball's pastoral myth—"each new season was revival." He argues against the coming rule changes (designated hitters, mound declines), expansionism, the demise of the minor leagues (once "crucial connections to the provincial heart"), baseball's deference to television (the game's "landscape is too big" for TV), and the eagerness to introduce more speed into the game ("Velocity passes, history remains"). No social crisis, including segregation, has ever thwarted baseball; even the reserve clause seems justified in the scheme of things ("a changeless foundation of customs so firm it appeared to be in law") and in the loyalty it imposes on the players.

In this sense, recidivism would be a good thing, and Harris recommends a Thoreau type for commissioner (Bowie Kuhn was chosen instead). "What you need may not be expansion, but contraction, not speed but the nourishment of old roots. . . ."

On Higher Ground

As Harris had noted, the baseball world in the late sixties and early seventies was one embroiled in "loftier issues" and controversies: "Only so long as we were not merely *enjoying* ourselves could we justify our attendance at those absurd spectacles." In ruling against Curt Flood's challenge to the reserve clause, Judge I. B. Cooper proclaimed that baseball "is on a higher ground; it behooves everyone to keep it there." No other book quite captured baseball's failing myth of memory better than Roger Kahn's *The Boys of Summer* (1972). Though the book was something of an interlude between the preceding ten years and the next era of change, it struck the right chord at the right moment.

The Boys of Summer is composed like a tone poem, with largos and adagios layered upon the larger theme of memory, which is symbolized, at least initially, by "the brownish bulk of Ebbets Field." The first sounds are given to autobiography, with an emphasis on childhood, family life, the patriarch Gordon Kahn and the matriarch Olga, the New York newspaper world that the young Kahn ventures into, and the Brooklyn baseball organization in its heyday. The second part comprises 13 separate songs: profiles of old Brooklyn players, the "boys of summer in their ruin" (Kahn borrowed the title from a Dylan Thomas poem). The overall theme of the Dodgers might be summed up as "losing after great striving."

The Dodgers were invariably close to or at the top in the years between 1947 and 1957. Kahn believes that they regularly lost the games they were expected to win (to the Phillies in 1950, to the Giants in 1951), and that they won only one world championship, in 1955, with more good luck than anything else (the team's talent was older and slower by then), having also lost to Yankee teams in 1952 and 1953. The Dodgers' departure to Los Angeles created a vacuum. When teams had moved from other cities, there had always been another team left in that city; Brooklyn's move west left an open wound. Relying on the myth of memory, Kahn found more than his share of material for the ideal baseball book, even though he would not consider *The Boys of Summer* strictly a baseball book.

For one thing, the book's open discussion of race relations was unprecedented in the 25 years race had been an issue in baseball. In 1947 Branch Rickey had hoped his Dodger veterans, "hungering for a pennant, would demand that Jackie [Robinson] join the team. Never was anyone more deaf to the tenor of his team." Kahn worried about "an infinitely barren ending for the Robinson experience" when he discovered that some "Dodgers called other Dodgers 'niggers.'" Kahn had tried to report incidents of racism but usually got back orders such as, "WRITE BASEBALL, NOT RACE RELATIONS. STORY KILLED." He was vindicated slightly in writing *The Boys of Summer*, in which he provides a new understanding of the myth of heroes. Pee Wee Reese, the Kentucky shortstop whose fellow southerners expected him to join their protest against Robinson, "made an abiding peace with his conscience"; the pitcher Joe Black, whose "career on the team was both so brilliant and so brief," became an executive and lectured black schoolchildren "about the responsibilities as well as the rewards of black power." Extolling the virtues of education and nonviolence, Black, who had been ridiculed in baseball for his name as well as his skin color, decided "that hate held neither profit nor the keys to any kingdom." In an age of increasing racial tension, Kahn writes, "Burn America and you burn the achievements of Jackie Robinson."

Kahn's *Herald Tribune* memories of 1952–53, when he covered the Brooklyn ball club mirror his memories of the old Dodgers. The old city room takes on the atmosphere of the locker room, with its rituals and cast of characters (Stanley Woodward, especially), its rhetorical flourishes ("The road'll make a bum of the best of 'em. . . . And, kid, you ain't the best"), and baseball talk. In retrospect (given his efforts "to move away from baseball" as a writer), Kahn realizes that his experiences "had become part of myself . . . something to be proud of." His visits to the old Dodgers ("If they were old, then I was old myself") open his eyes to clearer understanding; like the poem by Frost he quotes, Kahn's knows that "what I would not part with I have kept."

Kahn develops the narrative with examples from a baseball youth meant at once to be personal and familiar: the young Kahn's reading and rereading *Pitching in a Pinch*, which supplanted the Dickens, Twain, and Swift encouraged by his mother (who saw the game as philistine and helped create for him "a baseball world that added humor to the earnest and heavy baseball cosmos of my fantasy"); the early summers of playing catch with his father on a store roof or in the hallway; venturing to

Ebbets Field, "always within reach"; partaking in the family's
Wednesday evening literary conversations, which conflated James Joyce
with the Brooklyn manager Charlie Dressen—all of these remembrances
rush forward in the chapter "Ceremonies of Innocence." The father-son
baseball relationship between Roger and Gordon Kahn takes on a
poignant irony when later in the narrative we learn about the hardships
between Jackie Robinson and his son, Clem Labine and his, and Carl
Erskine and his son with Down syndrome.

The purely descriptive passages of old games gain new vitality the
second time around. Describing a retaliation play led by Robinson on
the Giants' notorious brush-back pitcher Sal Maglie, Kahn writes:

> The bunt carried accurately toward first baseman Whitey Lockman,
> who scooped the ball and looked to throw. That is the play. Bunt and
> make the pitcher cover first. Then run him down. But Maglie lingered
> in the safety of the mound. He would not move, and a second base-
> man named Davey Williams took his place. Lockman's throw reached
> Williams at first base. Then Robinson struck. A knee crashed into
> Williams' lower spine and Williams spun into the air, twisting
> grotesquely, and when he fell he lay in an awkward sprawl, as people
> do when they are seriously injured.

Kahn's boyhood desire to play first base for the Dodgers vanishes
when he gets the opportunity to stand in for some of Labine's pitches; he
then realizes that all the baseball he has ever "played was irrelevant to
sinkers that hissed like snakes and curves that paralyzed." We are all
boys of summer, but most of us have come to ruin sooner than our
heroes.

For Kahn, the "road with the Dodger was a lonely, thrilling chaos,
at once seductive, free and wild." His reports of the Dodgers of that era
reflect that sensibility. But the seductiveness of baseball, so awe-inspiring
from childhood to adulthood, lingers on even in the face of death. When
the author's father drops dead suddenly from an apparent heart attack,
Kahn must drive "to the mortuary with two men, physically flawed but
living, while my father, who could see perfectly and hit a baseball hard,
lay wreathed in the faint odor of embalming fluid."

This moment stays with us into the second section of the book
when, 20 years later, Kahn revisits his heroes of those glorious summers.
The idea for writing about the old Dodgers was born of a desire to see
one of them, Billy Cox, after 15 years or so. Discovering that Cox is
tending bar in an American Legion Hall, Kahn is surprised that the peo-

ple around him do not know what a good ballplayer and great gloveman he had been. His meeting with Cox stays with him. Kahn had heard stories about other Dodgers down through the years and had also remained a close friend of Jackie Robinson.

In Ebbets Field, the Dodgers were Olympians; in the myth of memory, the heroes, just as they went from being boys to "baseball-playing men," have become ordinary men toiling at various labors, some struggling, others getting by (much as John Lardner had found the old Black Sox 20 years after the scandal). Everyone is older, wiser, a little sadder, but Kahn "does not come away from visits with them, from long nights remembering the past and considering the present, full of sorrow. In the end, quite the other way, [Kahn] is renewed." Kahn meets the boys of summer wherever they happen to be, but the heart of the book remains in Brooklyn, whose presence can be felt on every page. Clem Labine, whose son Jay lost a leg in Vietnam, has become a lapsed Catholic. Kahn finds him selling sports apparel in Woonsocket, Rhode Island, but we remember when he "snapped curves at Ebbets Field [and] the city was a cleaner, lighter place."

The boys of summer now work for the post office, tend bar, own a grocery store, serve as a corporate vice president, work in construction, manage the Mets. We see individual triumphs over personal tragedies or disasters: Jackie Robinson coping with the death of his son, Carl Furillo ending his career "in anger, lawsuits, frustration." We see men humbled, like Duke Snider, "buoyant and boyish though fifty was approaching and the farm was gone," or properly contrite, like Andy Pafko, "who wrote his name on the back" of Kahn's souvenir glove because "'I don't belong with those others.'" In overcoming defeat, finding strength in the broken places, each man in later life evokes the spirit that the team captain Pee Wee Reese had demonstrated all those years ago in Brooklyn: the "drive to win, no less fierce because it was cloaked in civility."

Even familiar subjects, like Robinson and Campanella, whom Kahn had always found difficult, change with the passing years. Roy Campanella has "acquire[d] a curious gentleness" that comes sometimes after a man "has endured great pain." Kahn describes him as "mobile in the wheelchair, beating the dead arms, twisting his trunk, growling, smiling, shrugging as he tells a story." Jackie Robinson, "The Lion at Dusk," has become a "bent, gray man" who can no longer walk briskly. Kahn wonders "who will remember the brave, fatherless boyhood, the fight for an inch of Army justice, the courage in baseball, the leadership and the triumph, of a free man who walked with swift and certain strides." All the old Dodgers stand in stark contrast to Walter O'Malley, the team owner, who "considers people, whom he manipulates, and money, which he appears to coin in incalculable quantities, while saying from time to time, 'I'm just a fan.'"

The Boys of Summer is baseball's great ode to memory, written because Kahn was afraid that people would not bother to remember "the place where Ebbets Field once stood" and "the decent team" that once played there. The book would have its imitators and detractors. Bouton criticized the sentimentalizing of heroes: "You can miss baseball all right, but you can't miss it that much. You can't, you *don't* believe your life ends when you stop playing a game." But *The Boys of Summer* remains a classic, a book not so much about baseball as about endurance in life and the gratitude we owe, to quote the famous Housman line, to those whose "name[s] died before the man."

CHAPTER 11

The Year of the Plague

In 1973, Jackie Robinson died, Roberto Clemente was killed in a plane crash, Henry Aaron came within two home runs of Babe Ruth's cherished record, attendance reached an all-time high, and salary arbitration went into effect; moreover, wrote Daniel Okrent, "it was the year of the plague: the introduction into the game's rules of the designated hitter."

The year 1973 marked a turning point in American letters as well. Postmodern and metafictional writing (Thomas Pynchon's *Gravity's Rainbow* was published that year), the nonfiction novel, experimental and other nonrepresentational and nonrealistic works, as well as polemical prose, magical realism, and the writing of marginalized groups in America, proliferated. Robert Coover had published a few years earlier what many critics think is the best baseball novel ever, *The Universal Baseball Association, Inc., J. Henry Waugh, Prop.* (1968), a serio-comic work of fabulation. Contemporary baseball writers, ironically, returned to the conventional themes and myths even as they abandoned the old modernist, formalist, and realistic styles of writing.

Richard Grossinger, who edited a special baseball issue of the counterculture journal *IO* (which marked the first appearance in print of Stephen King, then a student at the University of Maine) and later several similar anthologies, wanted to move in the opposite, more eclectic direction of Charles Einstein's traditional *Fireside Book*(s) *of Baseball* (1956, 1958, 1968). Grossinger sought "a more radical mythologization of baseball into art form and metaphor." His anthologies (which have gone the way of the counterculture) are outpourings of contemporary poetry and fiction, though for the most part the nonfiction belonged to familiar names: Angell, Jordan, Roth, Updike, Giamatti, Hall, Kahn. Grossinger wanted to bring baseball up to date and explore its cultural ramifications by accessing the large network of published and unpublished writers interested in such areas as archetypes, myths, mathematics, multiculturalism, abstractions, Zen, visions, and voodoo.

A more or less "typical" counterculture baseball piece was "Qabilistic Sex * Magick for Shortstops and Second Basemen" by Robert Brezsny, who proposed: "Just as you are about to snare the ball in the web of your glove . . . imagine ramming your erect phallus into the upturned vulva of the Second Baseman, a red-haired woman crouching on all fours." Other new-age writers attempted to modify the traditional forms of baseball prose writing in less disruptive ways. The Boston pitcher Bill Lee (known as "Spaceman" owing to his interest in Eastern thought and leftist politics) seemed a long way from the pitcher-philosophers Mathewson and Brosnan (not to mention Bouton) when he wrote in the mid-1980s, "Every pitcher has to be a little bit in love with death. There's a subconscious fatalism there. All baseball players attempt to suspend time, and the bitch of it is we're only partially successful."

Marvin Cohen's *Baseball the Beautiful* examined ways of looking at baseball from a variety of metaphysical perspectives ("The Poetic Wellspring at Its Purest on the Youthful Field," "Baseball as Scale and Structured Language to Articulate Everything by Its Coded System, Enhancing the Significance of All That Falls Within It") but arrived at a familiar conclusion: baseball is a form of art, open-ended and diverse yet contained within an orderly universe. At the center of its world are ordinary individuals whose accomplishments, always within human dimensions, require a certain grandeur. What happens in baseball is, undeniably, fact upon which we impose our myths, our ways of discovering beauty amid the chaos. Why baseball, above anything else? "Fashions come and go," writes Cohen, "and wars, and social problems, economic crises, political climates. Baseball outlives them all . . . permanent, beautiful, ever itself: insular, yet mildly reflecting, in a peaceful way, in its own terms, the changes going on outside."

Like Cohen, the majority of baseball writers who came out of the sixties generation still found it difficult to part with the prevailing myths of the national game. Perhaps they would continue to question the myths while being reassured by the mainstays of ball games and fandom. Of *Confessions from Left Field* (1983) by Raymond Mungo, a writer connected with such counterculture movements as Total Loss Farm and the Liberation News Service, Jerry Klinkowitz, wrote, "even the most devoted fan in the stands . . . knows that the hallowed rituals embraced by 'take me out to the ball game' can be turned inside out."

Grossinger, for that matter, is now an enterprising publisher, whose California house released one of the more entertaining contemporary "as-told-to" books about old-time baseball, *Rowdy Richard* (1987), subtitled "A Firsthand Account of the National League Baseball Wars of the 1930s and the Men Who Fought Them," by Dick Bartell with Norman L. Macht. As counterculture baseball prose is of little interest today, the real legacy of the sixties generation has been the pervasive deconstruction and politicization of most literature. Bibliophile Paul Bauer recalled attending an academic symposium on baseball in which a professor of sociology attacked Sharon Hargrove's *Safe at Home* (1989) as "not accurately reflecting the reality of baseball wives" since Hargrove emphasized her long and happy marriage to a Red Sox player. "Apparently, when it comes to the academic brand of feminism, only victims need apply."

Jim Brosnan, the old Rube, expressed the idea of change and modernity best. On finding so many hair driers in the locker room, he wrote in an article for *Playboy*, "Ty Cobb would have cursed. Rogers Hornsby would have raged. Christy Mathewson would have let his hair grow long. (Pitchers have always been a progressive breed.)"

Where Have All the Heroes Gone?

Baseball's pursuit of the truth forced writers to confront some realities about heroes. Robert Creamer, a writer in the old Matty tradition, cut through the numerous hagiographies of Babe Ruth to write the first serious full-length biography. The book disqualified several Ruthian myths while squarely demonstrating Ruth's impact on the game and on American cultural life.

In the index under Ruth are listed such items as "cruel streak," "fights with . . . ," "gluttony of," and "sexual exploits of." But Creamer is dispassionate in his condemnation and his praise of a man whose "occasional evidences of bigotry," for example, "were for the most part casual and unthinking reflections of his age." In the matter of home runs, Ruth "made the breakthrough and kept going, leading the way. . . . When he retired with 714, he had twice as many as the second man on the list. The home run was his."

George Plimpton's *One for the Record* (1974) examines what led up to Henry Aaron's record-breaking home run, particularly given its foregone conclusion. *One for the Record* is one of the best long essays of what might be called total reportage: completely immersed in a game or an event, and writing in a tone set against the prevailing media hype, the writer reflects on the event's origins and aftermath and renders it through a multiplicity of points of view. Thus, the perspectives of the two key participants, "The Observer" (Plimpton) and "The Hitter" (Aaron), alternate with those of "The Pitcher," "The Ball," and "The Retriever" (of the ball), and several others.

Each instance or point of view reveals a critical antecedent usually rendered by an anecdote: the man who throws the home run pitch to Aaron leads back in memory to Ralph Branca and all of baseball's "major sinners," whose "reputations were stamped irrevocably with their misfortune—as if a debt to society had been incurred which could never, under any circumstances, be absolved"; the men who caught Maris's 61st and Babe Ruth's last home run presuppose the young bullpen pitcher who catches the Aaron homer.

The portrait of Aaron builds steadily, formed by what the author hears about him, reads about him, or learns from him. Plimpton discovers that Aaron's 1957 pennant-winning homer was far more important to him than number 715, about which "he remembered only his relief that it was over with, and the vague happiness, that a weight 'like a stove' had been lifted from his back, and that his legs seemed rubbery as he took the tour of the bases." The event (a "road show" really) may have meaning beyond baseball—perhaps as a vindication of the humiliation of segregation that Aaron has suffered. The home run is one for the record, but the other record—each voice, each nuance of the event articulated in the most concrete way possible—must be preserved for the purpose of shared or borrowed memory. Aaron is less of a central figure than those individuals touched by the event: the Cincinnati pitchers, set to pitch against the Braves, who are "involved in a sort of cosmic game of Russian roulette"; the man broadcasting the game; Aaron's father; a neighborhood fan who will erect a statue of Aaron in his backyard. The home run itself is anticlimactic: people waiting in food lines miss the moment entirely, while the pitcher and hitter see the event as simply being over. As Lonnie Wheeler wrote of Aaron's "brand of excellence" in *I Had a Hammer* (1991), it "was not expelled in blinding bursts of energy but rather played out patiently and inexorably, over a whole generation."

The death of Jackie Robinson prompted some writers to move away from the myth of heroes to sometimes tendentious thoughts about politics. For Mark Harris, Robinson did more than just break the color barrier in major league baseball: he helped define the spirit that brought "unprecedented rights through union organization and other forms of professional representation." Even Roger Kahn, who had written the most passionate pieces about Robinson and "loved Jackie Robinson well enough not to have to deify him," chides Robinson for his staunch Republicanism, for once "attacking Paul Robeson for HUAC in 1949," and for his failure to know who Alan Paton was. Kahn is regretful that Robinson died before he could "rethink . . . his approach to politics, to life."

Familiar Voices

Though his style was becoming at times predictable, Roger Angell remained the genre's foremost Matty. His most memorable account from the seventies, collected in *Five Seasons* (1977), was of game 6 of the 1975 World Series between the Red Sox and the Reds, an electrifying series in which the winning team came from behind in six of the seven games. In five games, there was a one-run margin and the lead changed 13 times.

Game 6 was "Agincourt" for Red Sox fans, and Angell's essay is one of the reasons many people consider it the best World Series game ever played. The runs dispersed like "a well-packed but dangerously over-loaded canoe." With the score 6–3 in favor of the Reds in the eighth inning, Angell envisions an all-too-familiar sight: disenchanted Red Sox fans "sitting silently at home and slowly shaking their heads as winter began to fall on them out of their [TV] sets."

But the water imagery returns: game 6 had been rained out for three days, and even now "the outfield grass was a lush Amazon green." Bernie Carbo's game-tying home run in the bottom of the eighth would make the bleachers seem "like the dark surface of a lake lashed with a sudden night squall." When the Red Sox finally win in extra innings, the fans, "even in some boats here and there," celebrate in triumph. Ken Griffey's catch in the tenth inning recalls Mays's as the game (the over-loaded canoe) rocks back and forth. Ironically, it is television, which Angell dislikes, that captures the triumph of the moment when Carlton Fisk hits his game-winning home run. The same despondent Sox fans of several innings earlier have now all come alive in joy and celebration, which Angell plays to the music of the "Hallelujah Chorus," heard over the Fenway Park loudspeaker "*fortissimo.*" Despite the renewed dejection of Red Sox fans the following night when the Reds win the series, game 6 represents for Angell what baseball, which others find "foolish and childish," is still all about.

Angell concludes with a nod toward William Saroyan: game 6 explains why the commercial exploitation of baseball fans cannot rob them of "the business of caring—caring deeply and passionately—really *caring*, which is a capacity or emotion that has almost gone out of our lives." Such a feeling of caring might be worth preserving whatever it is we ultimately care about; the fact that it is so often "the haphazardous flight of a distant ball" explains why baseball's appeal endures for us.

He expressed the same sentiment differently in a 1981 essay called "In the Country" (published along with other *New Yorker* essays from the early eighties in *Late Innings* [1982]), which on the surface is about life in the semipro leagues. It is also a story about relationships; about getting older; about having to leave the game and then seeking to return to it; about Angell's affections for a young couple he came to befriend (after having received a letter from a woman named Linda Kittell), whom he calls "friends of baseball": people who had "an involvement in the game—a connection that was simply part of life itself." The Hemingway story of a similar title is not far removed from Angell's thoughts. "In the Country," like Hemingway's "In Another Country" (1927), is a story about courage in the face of loss. Just as the Major tells Nick Adams to "find things he cannot lose," Angell and his subjects find them in baseball and in each other.

The myth of the best game returns in "The Web of the Game" (1981), which concerns a Yale University versus St. Johns University baseball game that Angell attended with the nonagenarian Smokey Joe Wood, the Red Sox pitching legend of 1912 and an ex-Yale coach. The afternoon drifts past "in a distraction of baseball and memory," and we are in the early part of the century as much as we are "almost in the country." The opposing pitchers are two future major leaguers (Ron Darling of Yale and Frank Viola of St. Johns), who are locked in a pitching duel; Darling throws "eleven scoreless no-hit innings" and then loses the game on a fluke play in the top of the twelfth. Wood has already talked about a similar matchup between him and Walter Johnson. In 1981, the year of the player strike (the "sudden silence"), the "heartbreaking 1–0 loss in May 1981 and Walter Johnson's 1–0 loss at Fenway Park in September 1912 . . . woven together into the fabric of baseball," may well be the most memorable games of the year.

Angell's metaphors and similes continued to capture the spirit of baseball's high journalism. Thus, a batter never knows "which particular lepidopteran path [a knuckleball] will follow on its way past the batter's infuriated swipe"; a catcher's paraphernalia "suggests a neighborhood grocer rolling up the steel storefront shutters and then setting out the merchandise to start the day"; and "the split-finger fastball is baseball's Rubik's Cube of the eighties."

The Angell of the sixties felt that his writing about baseball had "not yet come close to its heart." By the eighties he'd tell an interviewer, "I've written about what we've lost and what we're losing, but I don't think about baseball with a catch in my throat. I don't have sentimental thoughts about the grand old game. I resent some of the changes, I am wary of others that I think are going to come, but so far the game is played just about the way it always has been." Still, Angell has always managed to find something (the color of the ball, the size of home plate, a retired Bob Gibson, a shattered Steve Blass) to reconnect him with the game.

Angell's 1975 profile of Blass remains one of the definitive treatments of the myth of heroes. Blass, a pitcher for the Pirates and star of the 1971 World Series, after having had his best season in the majors the following year, collapsed into "two years of pitching wildness—a sudden, near-total inability to throw strikes [and] no one, including Blass himself, [could] cure or explain [it]." What made Blass's slump so "frustrating" and "bewildering" was that he seemed to have all his stuff, at least when he was not facing batters; he had no injuries; and he received nothing but patience and support from his coaches, the front office, and the fans, who deluged him "with unsolicited therapies, overnight cures, naturopathies, exorcisms, theologies, and amulets." Nothing helped— not additional starting assignments, not a bullpen stint, not something called "optometherapy," not hypnotism, and not rehabilitation with the Charleston Charlies.

Angell discusses with Blass all the possible reasons for his "unique" slump. No other pitcher has "lost his form in such a sudden and devastating fashion and been totally unable to recover." Angell brings in the testimony of baseball experts and analyzes the most prevalent "theories," from Blass's unconscious fear of hitting a batter to his distress over the death of Roberto Clemente, feelings whose "Oedipal elements . . . are attractive to those who incline in such a direction."

The mystery of Blass remains unsolved, and as Blass himself suggests, it might be nothing more than that his control has simply disappeared. The ambiguity of the title "Gone for Good" suggests that Angell himself might believe as much. But in Blass's disintegration, Angell sees something "deeper within us," something more emblematic of baseball, almost a corruption of the myth of America. Its rumblings had begun in the sixties (when Blass was still a boy), but it grew in the fans' despair that "the heart of the game is not physical but financial," that the old ballgame is also gone for good. We forget too easily that "the man out there is no longer just another great athlete, an idealized hero, but only a man—only ourself." In this light, the theories of Blass's demise mean absolutely nothing if baseball can no longer be "a release from the harsh everyday American business world but its continuation and apotheosis."

The essay ends with Angell and Blass playing a mental game of baseball in which there are "no control problems." Blass gets through the tough top of the Cincinnati order, giving up a couple of hits. The game beckons memory of a simpler, perhaps more ideal, form of baseball in which an imaginary game can be as satisfying as the World Series.

Twenty years later, Angell continues to dwell in the myth of the best game, often writing about what players actually do on the field. "Trying to learn the game . . . protects us from its overattachments and repeated buffetings, and for me, as years go by, this has become almost the best part of baseball."

More Scholars on the Mound

The late A. Bartlett Giamatti, a Renaissance scholar, attempted to put baseball's myths of timelessness (it is an illusion, for all games must stop) and memory (but it is a necessary illusion) into euphuistic prose in his 1977 essay "The Green Fields of the Mind." The result was, like much of his writing, pretentious. Giamatti may well be baseball's Euphues ("Be valiant, but not too venturous. Let thy attire be comely, but not costly") when he intones, "New England exulted in its blessedness, and roared its thanks for all good things, for [Jim] Rice and for a summer stretching halfway through October."

Michael Novak, one of the world's leading religious scholars, found the myth of America in *The Joy of Sports* (1976). Novak labels baseball "The Rural Anglo-American Myth." The game begins in ritual and "rural religion": "entering the stadium, one's children in tow, is like walking, almost, through some ancient catacomb"; players "waiting like the Israelites in the desert for the return of a fruitful rain of hits" or the umpire's dusting "off the sacred 'home,' starting place, keystone, source and touchstone of triumph" is (to borrow the book's subtitle) "the Consecration of the American Spirit." In a subsequent essay in *The Joy of Sports*, called "The Dodgers, The Bums," Novak recalls how he once halted his lecture on *The Nichomachean Ethics* to let his class listen to Sandy Koufax pitch in the 1965 World Series, demonstrating perhaps better than he could "Aristotle's conception of the highest moral habit of mind, *phronesis*, the skill of 'hitting the mark' at every moment."

Novak writes in brief epigrammatic bursts, Emersonian in style. Yet baseball is not a game that preaches self-reliance in Emerson's sense that nothing is at last sacred but the integrity of your own mind. Baseball, rather, perfects the design of law and society in terms of its "close liturgical enactment of the white Anglo-Saxon Protestant myth." Baseball is almost a textbook study of the great American experiment: it is "Lockean," "designed like the federal system of checks and balances," a game of "rural cunning," and "an antidote to the national passion for bigness." And because of, rather than in spite of, its myth, baseball is accessible to *all* peoples. Non-WASPs play baseball and share in its riches. Baseball, hence, is a means of "Americanization." Its constant is individualism: a team is "an association of individuals," and teamwork resembles "public-spiritedness." All sports represent some vision of America, but only baseball gets close to its core of "equality" and "fairness."

A Poet on the Mound

Of all the American poets who have written about baseball, from Rolfe Humphries and Marianne Moore to Richard Hugo, William Stafford, and Tom Clark in recent times, none has been more prolific than Donald Hall (b. 1928), the poet and critic whose baseball essays include one about his aborted "tryout" with the Pittsburgh Pirates (when he was forty-something and out of shape). Hall repeatedly discovers the perfect harmonies of the national pastime in the relationship between metaphor and the myth of memory. The theme of memory is best expressed through intimate connections with the images and icons of the past: fathers playing catch with sons, old-timers' games, Fenway Park. Protected by the rhythm of the seasons and the myth of timelessness, baseball absorbs and repels all inevitable changes (players retire), as well as superficial ones (the whims of moguls), for "inside the ball, be it horsehide or cowhide, the universe remains unaltered."

Hall's "The Country of Baseball" (which doubles as the first chapter from his collaborative book *Dock Ellis in the Country of Baseball* [1976]) belongs most of all to the players. What begins with games of street ball or "cowpasture ball" culminates in afternoon bus rides to minor league parks, before one becomes a full-fledged citizen of the major leagues. Within this "polyglot" of citizens, there is room for the flakes and misfits (like Ellis) who embody baseball's free-spirited nature. Though the country of baseball grows "paler and fainter," it never wholly vanishes, even when players must eventually make a life outside its boundaries. There exists, if not in reality, "a crepuscular duplicate of their old country." The Ted Williams who fishes and listens to Red Sox games is one with the "ghostly" Williams whose "flat-swing meets the ball in 1939, in 1948, in 1960." The defiantly racist player who refused to play with a colored man finds himself doing just that in an old-timers' game. "Dixie Walker flies out to Willie Mays," and the past and the present flow into one.

The strains of melancholy that accompany Hall's familiar essays on other subjects can be heard at times in baseball's passing seasons. Rookies barely able to shave when you are in elementary school become "grizzled veterans" by the time you are out of high school: "In a few years the green shoot becomes the withered stalk, and you learn the shape of the hill all beings travel down." Baseball is not the meaning of life, Hall writes, but those aspects of baseball that "organize and formal-ize" the game also uncover the myths from which the meaning of life emerges.

In other essays published in various books, journals, and magazines and later collected in *Fathers Playing Catch with Sons* (1985), Hall finds in baseball all the rich themes, from Yankee individualism and male-bond-ing to the virtues of the American melting pot. Writing about baseball allowed him entry into its deeper world. He got as close as one could to his subject with his book on the maverick Ellis, shifting seamlessly from present to past, contrasting the country of baseball with the country outside of baseball, which shaped Ellis the man and ballplayer. The book is, unintentionally perhaps, a reflection on the destructive black militan-cy and separatism and black rage rationalizations of the sixties, especial-ly as Hall discusses Ellis's aggression in hitting batters and his refusal to "sit in the bullpen for a spell" when he seemed to have lost his fastball. But Hall gives his subject free rein—lets him speak accurately and faith-fully, give his side of the stories, and clear up any misunderstandings cre-ated by the press, even though Ellis can be as vague and contradictory as "the newspaper flap." Ellis "exercises his life in the pursuit of freedom." Hall shows Ellis's deep "resolve," his "pride in his blackness," and his desire, above everything else, to pitch.

Hall's own love of baseball suffuses his prose and the pleasure he takes in telling a good anecdote. His essays paint word-pictures of New England in the manner of Thoreau and others. Hall's memories come not from ballparks and sandlots but from radio and television, which he listens to and watches on the New Hampshire farm where he lives. Baseball, in fact, reappears, like an old friend, in Hall's memoir, *Life Work* (1993), a long, thoughtful, and moving essay on the relationship between one's life and work, made all the more poignant by Hall's discovery while writing the essay that he had liver cancer. With a satellite dish installed at Eagle Pond Farm, "the Red Sox arrive at the tube from outer space," sometimes occupying his attention, other times providing background music to his work. On the work ethic, Hall happily finds ballplayers evenly divided: some play for fun, and some arrive "in excellent physical shape and then [step] up [their] preparations."

Relying on the baseball books he has read and reviewed and on his own personal experiences, Hall writes essays about all of baseball's "peripheries": the weighty timelessness of an old-timers' game, his belated acceptance of the message board in Fenway Park, and the austere dignity of "Crackerjack and peanuts and Schlitz and hot dogs." Hall included several more baseball essays in *Principal Products of Portugal* (1995), in which "by baseball, and not by another American sport, memories bronze themselves." Hall recalls Dennis "Oil Can" Boyd, Carlton Fisk, and Ted Williams, whose swing reminds him of the old Duke Ellington song ("It Don't Mean A Thing If It Ain't Got That Swing"), both of which "seemed as natural as leaves to the tree"; but his finest moment is saved for the World Series of 1968, in which centerfielder Mickey Stanley of Detroit, who, when much needed in a pinch, became "an amateur shortstop" and "saved the day." Stanley handled double plays, tagged base stealers, and took twenty-nine chances to finish the Series with only two errors on balls hit deep in the hole, both errors questionable." Hall sees it as "the great moment of Mickey Stanley's baseball life; and it was virtually the last moment, although he played ten posthumous years in the major leagues."

Report Card

By mid-decade Roger Kahn had taken to the road to assess the state of baseball in America in light of all the changes that had taken place in the game and in the nation. Kahn was animated by his journalistic curiosity, but also by his firm faith in the myth of America. Whatever baseball was or is, "its inherent rhythm, minutes and minutes of passivity erupting into seconds of frenzied action, matches an attribute of the American character." Though few critics thought so, *A Season in the Sun* (1977) is a better baseball book than *The Boys of Summer*.

For one thing, the book is not confined to the major leagues. Kahn shows how much its ancillary baseball worlds are a part of baseball, from a game of catch with his two sons to the college team of the former major leaguer Wally Moon at John Brown University in Siloam Springs, Arkansas. These are the vantage points of the country game and its pastoral myths, where the ballfield is a "mystic creation, the Stonehenge of America."

Kahn visits the baseball of the front offices: the prosperous Dodgers are "a cohesive organization . . . like IBM . . . [in which] Dodger officials follow a company line," in contrast to the anemic, debt-ridden Houston Astros organization, which despite a rich Texas history filled with a century of baseball lore and names like Hornsby, Speaker, and Dean (who came out of Houston's baseball past), is on the verge of bankruptcy. In *A Season in the Sun*, Kahn returns to his roots as a journalist, demonstrating his keen ability at interviewing and passing down great anecdotes. He integrates his quotes masterfully, moving effortlessly from one subject to another.

But the focus of the book is not the changes in baseball but the constants. While Kahn's trip to the Eastern League centers on the president of the league and a manager of a double-A team, the reader nonetheless feels the presence of minor leaguers playing ball, "hard by the Housatonic River, in the old New England valley town called Pittsfield." Few will make the majors (none of Moon's charges ever do); they take from the game only its earliest codes of conduct and discipline.

In the shadow of this "Country of the Poor," the forgotten minor leagues, Kahn is one of only 200 spectators at "the most exciting game I'd seen on any level all year." Between the pitches, when the great conversation becomes most alive, Kahn recalls his youthful days at the progressive Camp Robinson Crusoe, his Elysian Fields, "in the idylls of those summers," where "we wanted to play baseball and . . . we did play baseball every summer day." These minor league and summer camp games stay etched in his memory, as will that day's 135-foot home run, which should have been a foul out. Upon these subaltern diamonds, baseball flourishes through acts of faith, kindness, and generosity.

Kahn witnesses moments in different places touched in different ways by baseball. Three different "boys of summer" summon up memory and anecdote: the former black star Artie Wilson, now a car salesman, whose "big league career was a brevity of pathos"; Wilson looks back on the game, despite its racial injustices, "with a warmth that others focus on distant, old romances." Stan Musial, substantially wealthy now, "knows just who he is. Stan Musial, Hall-of-Fame, great batsman and, thirteen years after he racked his last double to right center field, still an American hero." Early Wynn, one of baseball's "bolsheviks" (troublemakers), works for a boat company. There is now, as in his pitching days, "nothing bland . . . nothing subdued, nothing cautious," about him. A later visit to Chicago White Sox owner Bill Veeck, for whom baseball "was entertainment, just like the circus," is illuminated by the image of the ageless Minnie Minoso (53 years old perhaps) lining a single to left field, "the oldest man ever to make a major league hit."

The dreams baseball inspires are universal. In Puerto Rico, "The Children of Roberto" (Clemente) "play baseball now because they love the game. It is their national fanaticism." The narrative ends, of course, at the World Series ("quite beyond forgetting"), where Kahn watches the great Johnny Bench, in the throes of an ugly divorce and an off year, "salvage his season and wrest his career from decline—and his face, his face frozen into inexpressible joy."

The end of any season, particularly one in the sun, is filled with mixed emotions of pain and joy. In the "Epilogue after a Chilly Autumn," Kahn, like Heraclitus, rediscovers the significance of his season in the sun: "A man resists season change as he resists the passage of time. Nothing is stable. All is in flux. And one grows older. Today is the first day of winter, and all summers, even last summer, are locked into history with Tyre."

Content to let the "mysteries alone" in *A Season in the Sun*, Kahn delves deeper into the mysteries of the minor leagues in his account of the year he owned a franchise, the 1983 Utica Blue Sox, the only unaffiliated minor league team. *Good Enough to Dream* (1985) is about a different group of boys of summer and their memorable season in the class A New York–Penn League, in which they went from being "Diamonds in the Rough" to "invincible Olympians," amassing a wide lead at the beginning of the season, watching that lead dwindle during "the dog-day nights," and finally capturing the division title and league championship. Though the book does not hold the reader's interest for the entire 351 pages, the final moments of the season are rendered in sanguine prose: "Seen from within, lived from within, a pennant race that slashes about you like the boiling, misty river under Niagara Falls, where everyone wants to win and only a few can be winners, is something else."

The book contains many of Kahn's familiar themes and techniques: realistic dialogue; excellent character studies, particularly of the volatile but earnest manager Jim Gattis; romanticism ("I don't like to be informed on what a great catch or a .380 batting average is worth in cash . . . ; the last romantic moment may be a high line drive to left"); familial remembrances and relationships (Kahn's father and his adolescent daughter, who works for him and learns to contend with "Utica lust"); thoughts about the inside game; anecdotes about players and managers and sportswriters and old teams; and pithy observations: "For all its glories, baseball is a brutal business."

The "new journalistic" conceit of the book is familiar: the narrator functions not only as a journalist but as an inside participant on a completely different level than he has ever experienced before. Bill Veeck had taken us inside the workings of a ball club before when, "in 1951, in a moment of madness, [he] became owner and operator of a collection of old rags and tags known to baseball historians as the St. Louis Browns." But Veeck had been an iconoclast. Kahn is consumed by the game, and the minor leagues become a world with dreams of its own. "Beyond reason, the team becomes an extension of your essence, your values, your competence, your very manhood."

The book begins, as all Kahn's books seem to, when he was a "Nine Year Old Right Fielder," and "the first dream, full of innocence and sunlight, is to play the game." Elysian Fields can be "Reton, Washington, . . . West Arthur Street, Chicago, . . . or Camp Robinson Crusoe." But "the death of the baseball dream, with all its innocence and sunlight, comes early to most." He works the metaphor of the dream throughout the book, reawakening it in himself and in his players. Kahn, to whom "the ball games were so much more interesting than the business side that I never took the business very seriously," played a part in the team's success by implementing many commonsense practices into the franchise operation. The players will not get major league offers or even calls from farm teams higher up the ladder; their success and the satisfaction they derive from the season are rooted solely in their ability to play, their pure professionalism. The team represents nothing so much as a tiny version of America: "That is, to be sure, the sum of the individual ball players, the solid citizens, the drinkers, the chasers, the loud and the silent, but it is more than that as well. . . . In short, a baseball team is various, affected by victories and losses, wives and girlfriends, hangovers, the schedule, the press, the management and the weather."

The owner recognizes his own place in such a democracy, which also depends upon "the response of the ball players to authority." In defeat as well as victory, "the thrall of baseball" affects everyone "in ways that [are] powerful and relentless."

The seventies were a time of reflection and reconsideration. At the age of 89, the sportswriter Fred Lieb covered nearly an entire century of baseball, from Cobb to Nolan Ryan, in *Baseball As I Have Known It* (1977), which, surprisingly, voiced enthusiastic support for the way the game had evolved. Philip Roth, writing in the *New York Times* on opening day 1973, returned, as he often did in his fiction, to his boyhood baseball days in Newark. "My Baseball Years" recalls the era when baseball was a childhood preoccupation, and "news of . . . cataclysmic . . . events . . . reached me while I was out playing ball." The myth of America exceeded any hope he had of becoming great at the game: "Baseball was a kind of secular church that reached into every class and region of the nation and bound millions upon millions of us together in common concerns, loyalties, rituals, enthusiasms, and antagonisms." Roth learned the geography of the nation as he followed the major and minor league teams in the *Sporting News*. Cities that he learned about in history class began to assume real life only when he connected them with baseball. Not until he got to college and fell in love with literature did he realize that baseball had been his introduction to literature in the way it transformed small details—a player's batting stance or way of running around the bases—into brief bursts of delight. Even "The Star-Spangled Banner" was far less stirring for him at school than at a ballpark, where it touched all "our inimical countrymen," including "out in the Africa of the bleachers, Newark's Negroes."

The old Negro leagues, long ignored like the players themselves, had finally gained recognition in literature during this period, though the sportswriters for the venerable black newspapers have yet to gain the accolades they deserve. It had been almost half a century since Damon Runyon ruefully walked away from a story on the legendary Smokey Joe Williams because "the idea of a black baseball player was too alien to him and, he figured, to his readers." Oral histories such as *Voices from the Great Black Baseball Leagues* (1975) and full-length studies like *Only the Ball Was White* (1970) ensured that the stories were told and helped open the floodgates to later research on the Negro leagues. The books were also instrumental in helping more black stars gain admittance into the Hall of Fame. Satchel Paige's *Maybe I'll Pitch Forever* (1962) received renewed interest. Beyond the famous folksy wisdom of a man who "could nip frosting off a cake" with his fastball lies the story of one of baseball's greatest players, the "Black Matty" whose greatest disappointment would come in not being the first African American to shatter the dehumanizing color barrier. As for contemporary black players, Charles Einstein's *Willie's Time* (1979) was an attempt at a biography of Mays on the order of John Dos Passos's *U.S.A.* (1930–36). Though the focus is Mays's uncontentious role in the civil rights movement during the five presidencies under which he played, Einstein never loses sight of Mays's great accomplishments and image as a baseball icon.

The new economic realities of baseball would make the changes in the game even more distressing. Using the Boston Red Sox as a microcosm, the sportswriter Peter Gammons saw the sixth game of the 1975

World Series as closure to a period when "what was different about running a baseball team was that the executives were out in the open market like any other business executives." The final game of that World
Series would be "the last one played under the old rules." Commenting
on the "restless mobility of 'free agent' superstars," who were becoming
ubiquitous by 1977, George Will, the political conservative, noted that
"baseball capitalism that respects only market forces is profoundly
destructive because it dissolves the glue of sentiment that binds fans to
teams."

Until 1973, baseball had changed only in increments—the dead
ball had died; a quarter of a century later the color line had been broken;
and a decade or so after that the 16 long-time franchises would disperse
as the leagues expanded. But the designated hitter rule of 1973 was only
the first of several coming assaults on tradition.

Writers in the twilight era (the current state of descending darkness,
ambiguity, insensibility in baseball) nonetheless have attempted to keep
alive baseball's continuities. (In 1994 Dave Anderson of the *New York
Times* published a book recounting the 15 greatest pennant races
between 1908 and 1993, perhaps to remind us, with the coming of
wild-card playoffs, of just what we will be missing.) These writers, some
old, some new, return again and again to history and myths, without
which there would be no enduring baseball literature—and very little
passion for the game itself.

CHAPTER 12

The Twilight Era

Since the late 1980s, there has been a resurgence in the writing of baseball history and biography as well as a proliferation of interesting (if bland) speculative statistical studies, pioneered by Bill James and other writers, and numerous volumes on the business and political sides of baseball, made all the more relevant by the ominous 1994 season-ending player strike. (Whether the 1994 season, like wartime baseball, becomes simply another tale in baseball lore remains to be seen.) To be sure, business and legal maneuverings, like gambling, have been longtime neighbors of baseball in the sporting world; but writers in the past dealt with them less seriously, either in a condescending way (especially if writers were chummy with team owners and front office men), or, in Rube-like fashion, with understated humor. As J. Roy Stockton observed about the Philadelphia Phillies organization of the 1940s, which managed to stay in the black, only barely, by selling its promising players to wealthier teams year after year, "Where other clubs would send green players to minor leagues for seasoning, the Phillies season them in Philly uniforms. And if a young man has talent, he develops it more rapidly with the Phils, because he learns under major-league conditions. The Phillies have that as an argument, if they meet sales resistance."

The thrust of books about baseball lives now falls within the spectrum of old-fashioned hagiography, psychobiography and pure expose, and social commentary. Thus, we have books on the cultural impact of players as marketable commodities, the various pathologies of recent and deceased players, as well as, on the other hand, inspirational works (like Dave Dravecky's *Comeback* [1990] and *When You Can't Come Back* [1992]) and scholarly assessments, many of which do not seem to be about baseball at all. Nicholas Dawidoff's masterful biography of Moe Berg, *The Catcher Was a Spy* (1994), explores the life of one of baseball's most fascinating characters, whose off-the-field exploits (as a linguist, espionage

173

agent, middle-age freeloader, and would-be autobiographer) have been
of great interest to baseball fans since Berg's erudite persona first entered
baseball lore. Berg himself had written a 1941 essay for *Atlantic Monthly*
(replete with French and Latin phrases) in which he quipped, "Good
fielding and pitching, without hitting, or vice versa, is like Ben
Franklin's half a pair of scissors—ineffectual."

Though they are enlightening and make for good reading, few of
these books are prose masterpieces, and even the better ones could have
benefited from more careful editing and shorter length. One exception is
Mark Winegardner's Boswellian *Prophet of the Sandlots* (1990), his year-
long account of his travels with legendary Cubs and Phillies scout Tony
Lucadello. Winegardner's book is a human drama, and he skillfully uses
the by-now-familiar techniques of the nonfiction novel. Unlike other
scouts, Lucadello was an iconoclast who picked prospects (51 of whom
became major leaguers) and conceived of training them by two unique
systems (the "eight sides" approach for scouting and the "Lucadello wall"
for teaching), although he was never fully confident in his ideas or his
abilities. We see an often maligned and misunderstood man who had
become a baseball anachronism long before he became an acknowl-
edged, if still unsung, baseball genius. He was shamefully underpaid,
but so in love with what he did that the labor of it caused him to "driv[e]
leased cars 2.3 million miles down the back roads of nine states and
three Canadian provinces, roads which led him to hundreds of thousands
of ball players. . . ." Winegardner finds a place for him nonetheless in the
myth of heroes. Without warning, Lucadello wrote the ending of the
book himself by committing suicide on the pitcher's mound of a ballfield
in his hometown. Yet the tortured psyche had been there all along, and
the violent nature of his death came as no surprise, even to
Winegardner, who mutes the tragedy and puts it firmly in perspective.
"The constant for Tony ha[d] been baseball," but *organized* baseball had,
in its own way, abandoned and betrayed him. The wealth of anecdotes
Winegardner drew out of Lucadello ("'You can't have been around baseball as long as I have without having stories'") does less to swell the
myth of timelessness than to chip away at the myth of the best game, by
which he lived and worked. What troubled Lucadello were not only the
rampant changes of modern society facing any 75-year-old scout, but
also, the worst sin of all for a purist like him, "the trend toward signing
good athletes in the absence of complete ball players." The tragedy of his
death, like the almost-tragedy of George Bailey in Frank Capra's film *It's
a Wonderful Life* (1947), as well as the meaning of his life, is that he "had
his hands in a lot of lives, more than anyone he knew."

An intriguing long profile is Richard Ben Cramer's *The Seasons of the Kid* (1991), originally published in a shorter version in *Esquire* in 1986 and one of several books on Ted Williams in the last few years. It represents a turning point (some would say low point) in sports new journalism. Not content just to push point-of-view to the edges, as older literary journalists (like Joan Didion and Dominick Dunne) have continued to do in other fields, Cramer lets his subject dictate the nature of the essay. The idea of late "new journalism" is to follow a subject around, then watch and wait for the right (usually sensational) angle or image to reveal itself to the writer (as Tony Kornheiser would do in writing about Mike Schmidt, and Pat Jordan in writing about Steve Carlton and others). In Cramer's hands the aged Williams is the same cantankerous Williams of youth, swearing at passing motorists, "hurling out ugly words at his vision of pain," or yelling at Cramer for not coming prepared to the interview by having read Williams's *My Turn at Bat* (1969). Cramer also provides to great effect familiar Williamsesque anecdotes and background (emphasizing the controversial ones); but he can be appreciative when borrowing memory about a Williams Cramer had never seen play: "There was a special sound from a crowd when Ted got his pitch, turned on the ball, whipped his bat in that perfect arc—and missed. It was a murmurous rustle, as thousands at once let breath escape, gathered themselves, and leaned forward again. To see Ted suffer a *third* strike was an event four times more rare, and more remarkable, than seeing him get a hit." Though some readers will view Williams merely as a misanthrope and Cramer the poor, abused journalist, it is Williams who manages, oddly, to come across as sympathetic: we admire his taking no guff from anyone, his being wise to what the reporter is up to, his evading the questions about his personal life, and his reminding us who he was and what he had accomplished in the field. *The Seasons of the Kid* is a riveting piece of writing, all the more so because its hero-subject emerges unscathed, and the journalist has the courage at least to let the chips fall where they may. As Williams tells Cramer, "'I haven't got my whole career to screw around with you, bush!'"

As for autobiography, the most compelling item since Jimmy Piersall's cathartic account of his nervous breakdown, *Fear Strikes Out* (1955), and Ty Cobb's *My Life in Baseball*—and a fitting contrast to the Cobb—is Bob Gibson's *Stranger to the Game* (1994). Fulfilling all the essential ingredients of the genre, including baseball lore and 20/20 hindsight, the book has the added dimension of addressing racial issues as they pertain to a great pitcher and extraordinary individual whose ferocious brushback pitch in the heady days of baseball in the sixties was far more intimidating mainly because he *happened to be black*. In a review of Gibson's book, the scholar Gerald Early compared Gibson's earlier *From Ghetto to Glory* (1967), in which Gibson "celebrates . . . not the fact that he won but his nearly palpable and visceral *will* to win," to the later book, in which "the will to win [is] a manifestation of the integrity of the game of baseball itself." Gibson dislikes the modern game and dwells throughout the book in the myth of timelessness. Perhaps, as Early suggests, the myth is dishonest and the changes in the game, as they were for players of the 30s and 40s who lived into the next generation of baseball and voiced their own complaints, are irrevocable. Indeed, they are irrevocable; but that fact alone cannot dislodge a myth that even Gibson has come to believe. As Donald Hall wrote, "Baseball carries its own time, its own motion and stillness; baseball runs counterclockwise."

In social history, three recent works demonstrate literary craftmanship as well as scholarship. Bruce Kuklick's *To Every Thing a Season* (1991) examines Shibe Park in Philadelphia through the lives of different "people insofar as their stories intersected with the park." These stories belong not just to owners and players but to "neighbors . . . employees, fans, real estate speculators, . . . local politicians, . . . novelists, baseball businessmen in other cities, architects, engineers, presidents of the United States." The ballpark is seen as the hub of the city, reflecting the changing cultural milieu of Philadelphia and, by extension, "urban America." David Halberstam's *Summer of '49* is a trip back to a time when "the fever was in the streets" and "Charlie Silvera, a young catcher just brought up from the minor leagues, saw the streets outside the hotel jammed with excited Boston fans [and] felt like a Christian on his way to the Coliseum." A season that everyone believed "would belong to Boston" had again "ended up with nothing" for Boston.

In addition to using anecdotes and capsule biographies and all facets of the great conversation, Halberstam relies heavily on the "new journalistic" technique of bending points of view. With economy and empathy, he captures the tortured psyche of the old pro Don Newcombe in his 1949 World Series loss to the Yankees: "As soon as Henrich hit it, Newcombe knew it was a home run. One pitch, he thought, all it takes is one pitch. As quickly as he could he tucked his glove into his hand and walked off the mound. Often pitchers are stunned and wait on the mound long enough to survey the damage. Not Newcombe. He never looked around. He was in the dugout before Henrich reached the plate."

Halberstam's *October 1964* (1994) is much like *Summer of '49* in style, but different in motif. *October 1964* is about baseball in a different age—

one of lessening, if still precarious, racial tensions (Cardinal players and their families, black and white, roomed and partied together at the same Florida hotel). If anything, generational tensions were becoming far worse. By 1964 the second generation of black players—Bob Gibson, Curt Flood, Lou Brock (many of them scouted by old Negro League greats like Buck O'Neil)—had come of age. The New York Yankees, still mostly a white, power-hitting team, were in irreversible decline, while St. Louis represented the new breed of ball clubs: fast, tough, and integrated. Perhaps no anecdote Halberstam tells better demonstrates how far baseball had come since Jackie Robinson than the following about Bill White, a black player, and Harry Walker, once one of the most racist:

> Harry Walker remained fond of Bill White, and when Bill White was made president of the National League, Harry Walker was delighted. One day in 1990 Harry Walker, by then living in Leeds, Alabama, called up White and said that he would like to visit him at his home in Pennsylvania. White said that Harry Walker ought to know that he was divorced now and that the woman he was living with was not black. Walker laughed and said, "Bill, that stuff doesn't bother me anymore—I'm way past that." So he came up to visit White, and his visit became something of an annual trip. White was touched by how much one man had changed over the years.

It was left to Roger Kahn, however, to write the best social history of baseball, and his most popular book since *The Boys of Summer*. After a sentimental book on DiMaggio and Marilyn Monroe and a disastrous collaboration with Pete Rose, Kahn took heart again in the myth of memory. *The Era* (1993) spans the years 1947–57, "When the Yankees, the Giants, and the Dodgers Ruled the World." It is a pure baseball book, romantic, pleasurable, reluctant to let any world besides baseball into its pages and keeping references to the present to a minimum. The book is filled with light essays, familiar anecdotes, firsthand reportage, narrative history, player profiles, statistical arguments (such as "the relative performance measure" of Joe DiMaggio), and hot-stove controversy: Stan Musial, "slope-shouldered, balanced, taut as the bow of a stout archer" as he "coils at home plate," Kahn believes, was the finest hitter of the era, perhaps of all time, for he had to hit against black pitchers while Ruth and Cobb did not.

Wrapped up in the early years of the era, Kahn must compress the last six years into a single chapter, "Recessional." As always, he relies on his own memories as a young *Herald Tribune* reporter as well as on reliable press accounts of the day; but he quotes from players and reporters still living, adding new revelations and truths, some of which were off the record at the time (such as facts about the Brooklyn Dodgers' often misdiagnosed financial health). He does so in his own quirky and informal style, as though the book were a long letter to a friend. Yet he emphasizes aspects of the era that, though already noted in other books, still have not been given full consideration. One such subject is, again, race relations, which Kahn dwells on at great length, devoting much attention to incidents surrounding Jackie Robinson and other black ballplayers. Kahn provides new insights on the threatened St. Louis player strike (which his mentor, Stanley Woodward, scooped) and recounts—perhaps more thoroughly than anyone else—the ugly epithet-spewing incident involving the Phillies' Ben Chapman and Jackie Robinson. The racial theme recurs in every year of the era, from Robinson's first game to his sale by the Dodgers to the Giants: "Walter [O'Malley] liked blacks docile. He preferred Pullman porters to Jackie Robinson." Without sermonizing on the subject of racism (Kahn quotes the St. Louis newsman Bob Broeg calling Woodward's article "barnyard journalism"), Kahn nonetheless shows how history has been downplayed by a few white players' "*Bunkum americanus.*"

Kahn tries to show in one self-contained essay why "The Era was the greatest age in baseball history." In the era, "baseball was every athlete's first choice" (even Jim Thorpe wanted to play it but "could not hit a major league curve ball"). "The ballplayers were godlike. The managers were giants in the earth." He also remembers the era in sights and sounds, such as watching Willie Mays at spring training in Phoenix in 1954: "That springtime forty years ago comes back in a whispering rush and I see Arizona again, the wide pellucid sky, and the baked hills wanting grass, and the desert winds blowing whorls of sand. Strange country to one used to the Berkshire hills, strange and lonely. But not when Willie was playing ball on scruffy, alkaline soil."

The Era celebrates not only a time but memory itself, which "revives the vanished ballfields." The "ordeals" and "passions" of the men of the era might seem primary, Kahn notes, but "without second base, without the ballfield in the background," none of the stories "could ever have played out." Whatever may have been happening in the outside world, there was always baseball. In an era of "'mock nuclear attack[s]' on Manhattan" staged by the civilian defense office, baseball was America's bomb shelter.

Writers at Work

One noticeable change in writers of the twilight era has been their willingness to incorporate greater scientific measures (sabermetrics, total average, relative performance measure) into the fabric of their prose. The paleontologist Stephen Jay Gould, who annually reviews baseball books in the *New York Review of Books*, contemplated "the extinction of the .400 hitter" in a *Vanity Fair* article. The gradual disappearance of .400 hitters reflects the homeostasis that systems undergo when they normalize. Thus, dead-ball era hitters could rule the day because no one had learned how to stop their progress. "Wee Willie Keeler could hit 'em where they ain't [and compile a .432 average in 1897] because fielders didn't yet know where they should be." As a result, "a game unmatched for style and detail has simply become more balanced and beautiful." Gould's baseball essays are much like his writings on other subjects—dogmatic, breezily analytical, didactic, and filled with literary allusions to Omar Khayyám, Isaiah, or Ecclesiastes.

Science and baseball may complement each other, but as Gould admits, "we need myths so badly." His best essay, "The Streak of Streaks" (1989), argues that Joe DiMaggio's 56-game hitting streak was the greatest single accomplishment in the world of sports. It "sits on the shoulders of two bearers—mythology and science." Streaks and slumps, Gould notes, ought not to occur "above and beyond the frequency predicted by coin-tossing models." One cannot criticize DiMaggio's streak for its moments of fortuitousness because streaks are, point-blank, "a matter of extraordinary luck imposed upon great skill." What was incredible about the streak was that "DiMaggio accomplished what no other ball player has done. He beat the hardest taskmaster of all, a woman who makes Nolan Ryan's fastball look like a cantaloupe in slow motion—Lady Luck." In the realm of mathematical probabilities, the streak was the closest a mortal might ever come to eluding death, "at least for awhile." Still, the valor and heroism DiMaggio demonstrated during the streak mean nothing to Gould compared with the time DiMaggio sent the young Gould an autographed baseball in a box marked "insured."

George Will (b. 1941), the political commentator and essayist, attempted to give the game a greater sense of austerity (others thought positivism). Will substituted empirical data for references to primordial epic struggles. His underlying theme is (as Gould also contends) that baseball is played better today than it has ever been played before.

Will's earliest baseball essays were routinely about the longtime suf-ferings of Chicago Cub fans, for whom baseball's pastoral myths are bogus. The pained Cubs team itself has a special place in baseball lore, characterized by Warren Brown in *The Chicago Cubs* (1946) as the "dull, sickening thud . . . accompanying a plunge to baseball's depths." While April brings renewal to other teams, "spring is the winter of the Cub fan's soul." For Will, there is no Elysian Fields, for only "weeds . . . reclaim the trellis of my life." Such moments are motifs in various Will essays. In "The Chicago Cubs, Overdue" (1974), he writes: "Spring, earth's renewal, a season of hope for the rest of mankind, became for me an experience comparable to being slapped around the mouth with a damp carp. Summer was like being bashed across the bridge of the nose with a crowbar—ninety times. My youth was like a long rainy Monday in Bayonne, New Jersey."

Emerging from these early pieces was Will's familiar style—fiercely intellectual, with a rich store of historical and literary allusions and fewer anecdotes than he would employ in later writings. What Kahn sees as romantic, Will views as a matter of tradition intended to ward off the "unromantic baseball news" of the day. The perennial afflictions of the Cubs are character-building: "Have you ever known a Yankee fan with real character?" Growing up with the Cubs made Will a conservative; to him, the world looks something like the forest in Hawthorne's "Young Goodman Brown": "a dark and forbidding place where most new knowledge is false." When the Cubs begin inevitably to snatch defeat from the jaws of victory, Will urges Cub fans to "rage, rage against the blasting of our hopes."

Will is an ardent traditionalist, but also a pragmatist. He advocated the building of better stadiums, insisting in "Take Me Out to a Night Game" (1988) that "real baseball purists want to see the game played well." He welcomed night games in Wrigley Field (the last stadium to install lights, in 1988), noting that the people doing the most complain-ing were the ones who rarely went to ball games: "If all the sentimental-ists . . . had really passed through the Ebbets Field turnstiles a tenth as often as they say, the Dodgers would still be in Brooklyn."

The conflict between tradition and modernity often ends up for Will in a "metaphysical puzzle." When baseball expanded its league champi-onship series from five games to seven, Will wrote in an essay called "Don't Beep in My Outfield" (1985): "This puts in conflict two princi-ples that are moral absolutes. One is: the more baseball the better. The other is: everywhere, but especially in baseball, change is deplorable.

Well, some absolutes are more absolute than others, and the former principle is absoluter." On the subject of aluminum bats, however, Will is a strict constructionist of the pastoral myth. The one-of-a-kind Louisville Slugger (unlike mass-produced wood-lathe bats) is a sign from the deity. A product of nature, of a special tree, "grown straight toward sunlight" and shielded by other less important trees, even "Thomas Aquinas . . . neglected to mention the ash tree . . . when he was ginning up proofs of God's existence." Similarly, the Louisville Slugger is a product of middle-American exactitude, a sort of folk art. Using anecdotes about great hitters like Orlando Cepeda and Ted Williams, Will bemoans the coming of aluminum bats, popular for their longevity: "Immortality is not a virtue in things that should not exist at all." He portends changes in the record book introduced "after baseball became subservient to the science of metallurgy." If tradition fails to persuade, he will appeal to aesthetics: "If the sound of an aluminum bat were food, it would be lima beans." The crack of the bat becomes the "ping" of the bat, and gone is that heavenly occupation of "working amidst ash chips, which smell better than bacon in the morning."

In the late eighties, Will began focusing his attention on the nature of professionalism in baseball, reshaping the myth of heroes. He admires the Baltimore catcher Jamie Quirk's "exacting standards of craftsmanship and accountability" in assuming responsibility for a costly run in a crucial game. Furthermore, Quirk "did a manly thing in trying to block blame from reaching a 22-year-old pitcher." All in all, Quirk's actions "vivify the axiom that sport reveals as well as builds character." In praising Wade Boggs in 1986 and later Pete Rose, "who competed simultaneously against the other team and his own high standards," Will discovers why baseball "can be an exciting and elevating school" (and why he lets his children take off from school on opening day): "Acquisition of particular skills leads to appreciation of all skills. To learn a sport is to learn what mastery means, even if you fall short of it. Playing a sport, and appreciating the play of a Rose, is an apprenticeship in craftsmanship."

Will would expand upon the theme of craftsmanship in baseball in his full-length study of the game, *Men at Work* (1990). Will's workingmen win games "by small things executed in a professional manner" and by their painstaking attention to detail, a resolute attitude that minimizes reliance on luck, and a desire to practice and to reap advantages when the other guy fails. Mind over body is the essential craft of baseball. Because modern technologies can better process information, the player and managers who access and interpret information win more ball games.

Men at Work, however, is no mere compilation of statistical analyses. Dipping into the great conversation, Will concludes that "baseball has become a science in the sense that it emphasizes repetitious precision in the execution of its component actions." For the fans, too, "baseball is a game that most rewards attention to detail." As for great hitters, success has to do with "breaking the problem down into small component parts and mastering them, one at a time."

Will posits his thesis through four thoughtful profiles of a manager, pitcher, hitter, and shortstop (that is, a defensive player). The selection of these men, all at the top of their profession at the time of writing, is arguable, but they serve as fixed reference points in a much larger picture.

Will manages to hold the reader's interest by using the familiar devices of baseball prose writing: puns ("About one thing Karl Marx, a lefty, was right") and anecdotes ("The 1962 pennant race may have been decided by a groundskeeper"). In addition, Will uses numerous literary and historical allusions. Commenting on Bill James's quip that Napoleon invented relief pitching, Will responds, "Right. And Wellington won at Waterloo because he had what every team needs, a closer. His closer was Blucher's Prussians." Will, however, primarily relies on detailed analyses to show why certain defensive greats belong in the Hall of Fame or why good leadoff batters "combine power and speed and a discriminating eye that enables them to receive a lot of walks, thereby further fattening their on-base percentage."

The quality of both play and individual players, Will asserts, is getting better continually. He calls the age of heroes "piffle," preferring assets like discipline, moral integrity, and intelligence and men who "demonstrate an admirable seriousness about their capabilities." Players thought to possess only natural ability are more often among the most intelligent of ballplayers. But his main argument concerns the development of the individual skills necessary for the modern game. Baseball is work and craft; only after those disciplines are mastered is it a game that grownups play. The nature of this craft shapes Will's version of the myth of America: "I believe that America's real problem is individual under-stretch, a tendency of Americans to demand too little of themselves, at their lathes, their desks, their computer terminals. . . . If Americans made goods and services the way [Cal] Ripken makes double plays, [Tony] Gwynn makes hits, [Orel] Hershiser makes pitches, and [Tony] La Russa makes decisions, you would hear no more about the nation's trajectory having passed its apogee." The myth of heroes belongs not to men of brawn but to men of brains. In another respect, Will's vision of the game is even more conservative, reaching back to the dead-ball era of speed, toughness, and fundamentals.

Donald Kagan, former dean of Yale College and Colgate Professor of History and Classics at Yale, engaged Will in a friendly, old-fashioned hot-stove debate in the pages of *The Public Interest* in 1990. Kagan faulted Will for reneging on his conservative credentials: "An admirer of a nobler time should look askance at the use of the designated hitter and other specialists who demean the all-roundedness esteemed by both the principle of aristocracy and liberal education." Kagan criticizes baseball, as he feels Will does not, for its aesthetic decline, its lethargy and mediocrity. Baseball in the fifties was for Will "insufficiently entertaining because it was not sufficiently intelligent"; for Kagan, "all the thrills offered by baseball were present in abundance." It was "a time of heroic greatness and consistent excellence, when dynasties were challenged by other dynasties," *and* shorter games.

Kagan blames the fall of baseball on the American "Götterdämmerung" of the post-1960s, and Will's cloudy thinking on the "lengthy frustration" of so many Cub-less pennants. He also faults Will's reasoning when it comes to the role of hitters, who generally do what is best for themselves rather than risk rising above an occasion. The great hitters of the past had a measure of selflessness, as well as braggadocio. Heroes often must do what those who look up to and depend upon them expect them to do. Ruth at his pinnacle typified the baseball hero. "If Mighty Casey came to bat at a crucial moment today," writes Kagan, "George Will would want him to punch a grounder through the right side to move the runner to third and leave things up to the next batter."

Will responded to Kagan point by point. He asserts, for instance, that games have been lengthened not by boredom but by an increased dependence on strategies, such as relief pitching and base stealing, "which result in repeated throws over to first base and other disruptions of the pitcher's concentration"; if "Mighty Casey, instead of swinging for the fences and striking out, had moved the runner along, he would have earned no praise from Kagan. But there might have been joy in Mudville."

Will pays homage to the statistical verities and the myth of the best game handed down to us in its natural state and embellished by strong, competitive men:

I wrote *Men at Work* . . . to rescue baseball from the fell clutches of a
certain kind of person who writes about it. . . . That person loves baseball in his fashion, but does not really think that baseball is enough.
Enough, that is, to hold his attention, deserve his admiration, and sat-
isfy his desire for entertainment that is elegant, beautiful, and inspir-
iting. Sooner or later such a person gets down to his real business,
which is loading the game with the freight of theory, until what is a
nice sport staggers under the weight of significance. Make that
Significance.

Will wanted to get closer to the source of the myths: "Baseball was
evolving from lower forms of activity at about the time the Colonies
were evolving into a nation, and baseball became a mode of work—as
distinct from a mere pastime—remarkably soon after the nation got
going." The myth of timelessness exists for both Kagan and Will, locked
into patterns of renewal by the efforts of "all the baseball people who
transmit the game, remarkably intact, through the whirl of American
change." Both men interpret the myth of heroes in the Greek sense: for
Kagan, heroes are Olympians who display "a natural excellence that we
ourselves can achieve only in dreams"; for Will, "seeing people compete
courageously and fairly helps emancipate the individual by educating his
passions."

In some ways, Will and Kagan were debating all over again the old
question of whether or not baseball is chiefly American in origin. That
debate, too, had been about a kind of purity. Like Spalding long before
him, Kagan is very much the romantic. Will stands in for Chadwick,
exulting in the "remarkable exhibitions of skill in playing." But the
argument itself is as old as the hills, as old as ballparks. In the twilight
era, the great conversation is still very much alive.

Whistling Through Their Teeth

The twilight era has also seen the emergence of more women writers on
the subject of baseball. Female reporters did not enter the sports scene
until the seventies, though baseball wives, from Laraine Day (Leo
Durocher's ex-wife) in 1952 to coauthors Bobbie Bouton and Nancy
Marshall in 1983, have written revealing books about their experiences
with baseball men.

Allison Gordon, the best female beat writer, described her five years
covering the Toronto Blue Jays in *Foul Ball!* (1984), and Doris Kearns
Goodwin's essay "From Father, With Love" (1986) relates how baseball

had been passed down through the generations in her family. Even Gordon sees beyond gender as she observes:

> Baseball is as eternal as green grass and blue sky, and has been passed down through the generations, both on the diamond and in the stands. There are Ty Cobb and Babe Ruth, shagging flies in the out-field. Jackie Robinson, Honus Wagner, and Lou Gehrig take infield practice with Willie Upshaw, Alfredo Griffin, and Damaso Garcia. Cy Young leans against the bull-pen fence while Dave Steib warms up before a game. And every fan in the stands carries a memory of a father or a grandfather who took him to his first game, and the line goes back for more than a century.

Several women authors appear in Ron Fimrite's anthology *Birth of a Fan* (1993), though none of their essays is particularly memorable. A few histories have been published on women in baseball and on the All-American Girls Professional Baseball League, which existed between 1943 and 1954 (and was the subject of the popular movie *A League of Their Own* [1992]). Glenn Stout, reviewing a flawed collection of women writers on baseball, notes, "The question has yet to be answered: well, what about women writing on baseball? Do women have a different per-spective? Do they write about baseball differently from men?"

As Carol Iannone observes, "The most feminine of writing is per-haps the romance novel, and the most masculine, the Mike Hammer series." To be sure, male and female baseball writers have followed this stereotype. It is no doubt what prompts Danielle Torrez to sound like Danielle Steele, upon Torrez's autographing a baseball that has also been signed by her ballplaying husband, whom she will shortly divorce: "I crossed my T with Mike's on purpose. I was touching him, this time, forever. I held onto the ball for a moment, just savoring. I could not sim-ply let go of this last piece of my life all by myself." Suffice it to say, whether the baseball writer is male or female, as Iannone writes, "the greater the writer, the greater the capacity to transcend particularities."

The rich and generous baseball passages from Annie Dillard's mem-oir of the fifties, *An American Childhood* (1987), may serve as a standard. Good enough to play baseball with the boys, the young Dillard sets up a pitching target in her garage, trains hard, and learns to play a "two-handed baseball game" that "required . . . accuracy . . . and honor." Baseball is Dillard's way of entering the secret fraternity of the opposite sex. She is not allowed to play in the all-boys little league in her native Pittsburgh, only "dumb softball" at school with other girls, who don't care about the game. She hates the bogus game, which makes her long for the "just so" feel of a real baseball: "when you hit it with a bat it cracked—and your heart cracked, too, at the sound of it." At home, her father listens to the Pirates, who were perennially in the cellar, as her mother comments on the syllabic music of baseball talk: "That's marvelous," Mother said. "Terwilliger bunts one. No wonder you listen to baseball. Terwilliger bunts one." Later in the narrative, the "fragments of Biblical language" Dillard learns at Presbyterian church camp become her own "Terwilliger bunts one," just as when she was younger she learned to draw by sketching her baseball mitt: its "gesture—its tense repose, its expectancy, which ran up the hollows like a hand." Baseball's myth of memory fits neatly into Dillard's theme of topology, "the dreaming memory of land as it lay this way and that." The Pirates are not a team but a place that she returns to in her topology of the mind, and she recalls moments with vivid clarity: "Clemente had thrown from right field to the plate, as apparently easily as a wheel spins. The ball seemed not to arc at all; the throw caught the runner from third. You could watch this man at inning's end lope from right field to the dugout, and you'd weep—at the way his joints moved, and the ease and power in his spine."

The hot-stove league can handle the argument of whether women will ever play in the major leagues (as they have in little league, in college, and, most recently, on the lower professional level). Women writers are no less enamored than men with baseball's ability to bind them with the past, with thoughts of girlhood heroes and ritual celebrations in American life as well as memories of parents, families, and first loves. And for more than a few, the game itself keeps them in its grip.

Baseball Boy

If one writer alone speaks for the eighties and nineties, it is the Amherst College graduate and *Washington Post* sportswriter-essayist Thomas Boswell (b. 1947), for whom baseball is far more elitist than democratic. The ghosts of Pegler and Smith and the old wordsmiths make Boswell the spokesman for baseball at twilight, when "the emptier the park became, the more beautiful it seemed." Boswell understands that while Americans now share a certain passion for all sports, baseball remains supreme. Writing about sports means dealing with "the commonsense ethics of everyday life."

"Baseball," Boswell says, echoing his favorite poet, Emily Dickinson, "is one of our many doors out of the house of grief." Thus, it speaks to

the most extraordinary moments in life, such as the devastating earthquake that occurred at the start of the 1989 World Series in San
Francisco. That year, after all, had "been baseball's saddest season since
1919." Bart Giamatti died in the wake of the scandal over the gambling
adventures of "the scoundrel" Pete Rose. Donnie Moore, the goat of the
previous year's American League playoffs, committed suicide in despair.
Dave Dravecky, who bounced back after a cancer operation, broke his
arm and doomed it to amputation. Though there were a few shining
moments, the earthquake put things back into grim perspective.
Nonetheless, the World Series remained the one place where baseball
fans could experience the "need for ritual and manageable meaning" and
remember "how to meet the road erect." Boswell's metaphors can be far-
reaching, dizzying, and deceptive. He mixes close reportage (conversation and mood pieces like Frank Graham's) with allusions to baseball
lore, which he picked up from the books he read at the Library of
Congress, where his father worked. The mix is satisfying enough, intelligent and often heartfelt. If the style sometimes overwhelms, the substance rarely misses its mark. Describing the middle-aged Sandy Koufax,
he writes: "That central inviolate self remains as untouchable as a
Koufax fastball, as admirable as a Koufax curve," thus turning baseball
metaphor in on itself to explain itself.

His prose, like the titles of his books, *How Life Imitates the World
Series* and *Why Time Begins on Opening Day* (1984), is emphatic and self-
assured. The pennant-deciding playoff game between Boston and New
York in 1978 was "The Greatest Game Ever Played" because of its
"beautiful ambivalence"; the 1951 playoff between the Giants and
Dodgers "was the epitome of baseball's age of innocence."

Boswell sees the myth of the best game in its most concrete terms.
Ballplayers are men who "are of normal size, speak in a normal tone of
voice, and, both up to and after the first pitch, act like sensible men."
Baseball is the best game, not because it is larger than life (it is not)
or the vessel of some larger Truth, but because it is "a slice of our reality
. . . , a vast serendipity."

He is fond of the aphorism and the quote, local color ("canvases for a
lifetime"), history, and his own invention of "total average" (total bases
divided by total outs), which motivates his selection of greatest players
(Babe Ruth comes first, Hank Aaron is twentieth). With all the force of
the hot-stove league, Boswell takes issue with Ted Williams's rule of
never swinging at the first pitch: "Who'd have guessed that Williams
was dead wrong? Who'd have imagined that, in fact, his idea was exactly backward? Who'd have believed that with this one perverse idea,

Williams could have damaged a quarter century's worth of hitters and hurt the entire sport?"

Boswell goes wherever baseball goes. In winter baseball ("beisbol"), he discovers "A Country for Old Pitchers" (1980). San Juan is an Eden for the handful of American players allowed to play on one of three teams, and it is homecoming for the natives. Winter ball is a proving ground, a training school, and an old-age home for Latino stars, attended to with its own customs and superstitions—religious and otherwise. Boswell circumnavigates baseball's geography of the imagination, encompassing Cuban ball as well as rookie ball in the Appalachian Leagues ("a place for major league bodies and high school minds") and little leagues where the kids toe the rubber, mimicking major leaguers while the coaches (parents) pretend to be Earl Weaver.

The essays collected in *How Life Imitates the World Series* progress through baseball's seasons. After winter ball there is spring training, "baseball's annual idyll to indolence," where the Dodgers have urbanized what is left of the pastoral myth. Boswell posits his theory of the "big inning" to show that "pennants are won in March," when teams are practicing the fundamentals that will "minimize [their] opponents' big innings, while maximizing [their] own." Knowing baseball lets us "get so close to the game's skin that we can hear it breathing."

Boswell can turn from Rube to Matty in a single essay. He describes Ted Williams's annual visit to the Louisville factory to "pick . . . out the chunks of ash from which his splendid splinters would be doweled." He writes eloquently of sore-armed pitchers, minor league promoters, spitballs and scuffed balls, and batting practice—"the Rosetta Stone that unlocks many of the game's hieroglyphics." He introduces us to fathers who start a sandlot team so their sons can play after them; former prospects who travel 100 miles to play a couple of games, unable to relinquish their dreams; and the peculiar baseball notion of "veteran fortitude": aging players prevailing over the effects of time, just as the game itself does, when the deterioration of their skills is accompanied by strength, character, and resolve, with which they manage to develop or adjust to new skills. Boswell's titles, on the other hand, are witty and punning, never losing sight of the fun to be had on ball fields: "Glove's Labor Lost" (1980) is about buying his first glove, "Arms and the Men" (1980) about sore-armed pitchers, and "Hustling to Tie Cobb" (1980) about Pete Rose's assault on the all-time hit record.

The essays in *Why Time Begins on Opening Day* pick up where the previous collection leaves off. Boswell, notebook in hand, wanders about ballparks looking for the sweet spots in each one. The truest parks, the

Parthenons of baseball, change "their identities every day, depending on the direction and force of the wind," while modern parks betray baseball's pastoral myth with false winds and grass. Newer parks have subtracted the marvelous element of distance, removed the epic *"upper deck"* home run, "the over-the-roof and the (hold your breath) tape-measure home run." Boswell writes that the joy of following a single team keeps one from flitting after mere victories, in contrast to Sheed, who advocates "adopting various teams for a few years, like an uncle taking a niece to tea at the Plaza."

His tone often varies from essay to essay. He presents a long disabuse of umpires: "That baseball has not had one crooked-ump scandal in a century may be an unmerited divine inspiration." In another piece, he inquires into the efficacy of starting rotations, which, sharing a metaphor with Angell, Boswell calls "the Rubik's Cube of baseball." In depicting the 1981 season—the year of the split-season and George Steinbrenner and team rancor and drugs and baseball in wintry Montreal and free-agent grabbing—Boswell found that baseball's "wonderful lack of seriousness" had been replaced "with gravity, with a foolish seriousness" redeemed only by the World Series, which the winning team "would play for fun—just as baseball always has been played."

He goes around the bases, from home plate, where the catcher squats "like a beached crustacean," back to the dugout, where "Smoky's Children" (1982), the pinch hitters, sit on the bench, "waiting for their fleeting two-minute chuck of failure-filled piecework." He visits baseball in the bushes, the colleges, and the living rooms, where grown men play a card and dice form of baseball in their own organized league.

And he returns to his youth, where he preferred "the world of disorganized baseball" to seven-inning, organized little league ball, in which one batted "only" three times. Boswell recalls those "days with a kind of freedom different from anything since," as well as "the maze of streets, all the secret personal fields that others simply call urban decay."

His most recent essays find him catching up with old heroes, laying out his all-star lineups, detailing recent changes in the game, doing some further ballpark wandering, checking in with his beloved Orioles, summing up the great managers, regarding players on their way up or way down, and contemplating the various economic realities of the game in the corporate age. He imagines what he would do if he were baseball commissioner, an adult fantasy comparable to a kid's dream of playing major league ball: he would install the DH in both leagues, institute interleague play, abolish the all-star game, and eliminate balks. "Opening Day will be a national holiday. For children. Like us."

"99 Reasons Why Baseball Is Better than Football" (1987) pokes great fun at the hot-stove theme, baseball's statistical rage, and its rivalry with football. Readers can choose their favorites ("Best book for a lifetime on a desert island: *The Baseball Encyclopedia*") and discover where Boswell is wrong ("Football worships the specialists. Baseball worships the generalists") or shortsighted ("Baseball has no 'wild cards'"). Though mostly intended to be humorous ("Baseball means Spring's Here. Football means Winter's Coming"), Boswell searches for what sets baseball apart: "Baseball has no penalties at all. A home run is a home run. You cheer. In football, on a score, you look for flags. If there's one, who's on it? When can we cheer? Football acts can all be repealed. Baseball acts stand forever." Thus, "if [the umpire] Don Denkinger screws up in a split-second of Series tension, it's instant lore."

But finally, it is in the familiar essays on baseball that Boswell is at his best. In them, all the myths and themes remain strong and whole. Each collection of Boswell's is anchored by one or two of these essays that attempt to answer, not the question "What is baseball?" but the question "Why baseball?"

In "How Life Imitates the World Series" (1980), Boswell sees baseball's pastoral myth as reflecting the dual tenors of life: leisure and pressure. The calm "Summer Game" is the "pastime of our national mythology." The "Autumn Game"—the pennant races down to the wire, the playoffs and World Series—"is not so gentle": players who excel during the year fall short during postseason play, and vice versa.

"The Fourth Dimension: Baseball Memory" (1984) explains the lure of the old-timers' game and the Hall of Fame for players and for fans: they constitute "one long communal rejoicing at all our commonly held memories"—an oddity in the twilight era, when, as Will notes, players are "present oriented, uninterested in baseball history." "Why Time Begins on Opening Day" (1984) demonstrates how contemporary writers keep baseball's pastoral myth alive: "Why, awakened at dawn on a winter morning by rowdy starlings, do we catch ourselves thinking of Florida? Has baseball set its roots so firmly that, even asleep, the sound of birds means spring and spring means spring training and that means Florida?"

The game's literary dimension, which "enriches language and imagination at almost every point of contact," shows up also in "the diamonds of our minds" from earliest youth. Borrowed memory lets us put the game "back together an hour or a century later with almost no loss of detail or drama."

The myth of America is yet another link in our national spirit, guarded by our communal ballparks: "In few of our public places do our differences of age, race, and the rest give way so readily to our common tastes." The myth of timelessness is also on loan to us at these parks: "Even moments that happened fifty years before our birth have an almost tangible reality for us. The foul lines never move, the bases stay ninety feet apart and a windblown pop-up drifts today just as it did when Rabbit Maranville made his first basket catch."

Boswell's heroes are everywhere, but they are best exemplified by men like Mike Schmidt ("He did what so many great athletes have failed to do; he left us wanting more") and Roy Sievers, his boyhood idol, who many years later taught Boswell "that heroes fail . . . that they fall from public favor while they are still in yours."

The great conversation makes philosophers, statisticians, theorists, managers, naysayers, do-gooders, and crack reporters of us all. Those who look at baseball and opening day as something of a one-night stand never put baseball "on the same high shelf with our most entrenched emotions." Those of us who frequent ballparks or wash our cars on a hot Sunday afternoon while listening to a game on the radio allow ourselves to flow effortlessly into the "baseball continuum."

In "The Grip of the Game" (1987), written after the birth of his son, the meaning of the sport comes home to Boswell in a personal way. He returns to a theme discussed in an early essay, "Where Did You Go? Out. What Did You Do? Baseball" (1980). The responsibilities of fatherhood compel him to remember that baseball, in its purest form, ought to be anarchic and frivolous, "a wonderful waste of time, a raspberry in the face of authority." The Boswell of the nineties is more mature and contrite (he admits now that Nolan Ryan *is* a great pitcher) but continues, like Angell, to have many unanswered practical questions: "How do you pitch when you get in trouble with runners in scoring position? How do you pitch late in the game when you're tired?" Statistics still intrigue him, but he is much more inclined to see the game as the old Rubes did, with "appetite and laughter and a wayward nonchalance that would be self destructive in the lives of most of us."

Whatever befalls it, baseball adapts and endures. "The game is our excuse to talk," to "spend an hour figuring out some new angle on the game." Boswell gives us the definitive, concluding image for baseball in the twilight era: that of the fan sitting in the stands "until the last out, not really knowing why."

Conclusion

There is perhaps no better argument for or against "the death of base-ball" than the amount of "serious" academic scholarship that has been devoted to baseball and baseball literature in the last quarter-century. I have attempted to demonstrate the small but significant contribution baseball literature has made to American literature in general and the effect baseball has had in drawing so many authors to its mysteries, plea-sures, and myths. Omissions of certain texts or scholarly concerns reflect either my ignorance of them or my critical bias that a common sport ought to have a common literature.

As noted earlier, I do not believe that baseball—even with all its tumultuous changes—cannot endure as the best game: it will adapt; orthodox fans will cleave to it no matter what; and it will continue to grow in organized little leagues and in minor league towns. Major League baseball will have its moments of greatness yet, even as it falls out of favor with the general public from time to time—or forever, for that matter. The worst that can happen is that baseball *will* become just another game. What made baseball the national pastime long ago was that everybody could and did play it—it was what the novelist Alan Lelchuck described as the "perfect rounding out of the day." Now every-one plays basketball and even soccer (a truly immigrant sport), though neither sport has entrenched itself in the national consciousness (as base-ball once did), nor is it ever likely to do so.

Baseball *writing* (the great conversation), on the other hand, linked as it is to the old traditions and myths, stands to lose much of its power and distinctness if people begin to lose faith and belief in the *idea* of a national game. Mike Sowell in *One Pitch Away* (1995) infers as much from his analysis of the fatal home run pitch Donnie Moore threw to Dave Henderson in the 1986 American League Championship Series. Moore later attempted to kill his wife and then killed himself after sev-eral manic depressive years that followed the crucial event. The modern baseball audience could not interpret the game Moore lost anything remotely like the baseball audiences who witnessed or inherited Merkle, Snodgrass, Owen, and Buckner. They savaged and humiliated Moore, and their hostility was not the cartoonish rowdyism of an earlier era, but genuine hostility born of meanness and envy—people angered by big-salaried ballplayers who do not produce up to their expectations. We seem to have lost sight of the myth of heroes at this point in the second baseball millennium, Sowell seems to be saying, if "people are so quick to blame someone. After that pitch, Donnie couldn't go onto the field without the fans booing him. He couldn't hold his head up high. He tried, but they wouldn't let him." But there is hope yet that the message of baseball will not be separated from the messenger—the great game itself.

During the 1993 League Championship Series between the Phillies and the Braves, I let my six-year-old son stay up to watch the games past midnight; when I was his age, World Series games were played in the afternoon and I will never forget rushing home from school to watch Jim Lonborg's one-hitter for Boston against St. Louis in 1967 on TV. In the game my son and I watched together, the Phillies' third baseman made a costly error to send the game into extra innings—only to get the game-winning hit in the bottom of the tenth. His teammates carried this goat-turned-hero off on their shoulders. My son had not seen anything like that, and there was a little lesson to be learned in it (about baseball, not life) that was worth having him stay up late for. As Curt Smith noted, with the advent of night World Series games, kids cannot identify with the most important ritual in all of baseball if they have to go to bed. We have come, unfortunately, a long way from the day when a father would pull his son out of school to hear "what Don Larsen is doing to the Dodgers."

Baseball is not a religion, of course, but it sometimes acts like one. People who do not understand why so many Americans invest so much of their time watching, playing, writing about, or *believing* in this "game of inches" might consider something G. K. Chesterton said about the early councils that debated the doctrines of Christian belief: "It is so inexplicable to all the modern critics of the history of Christianity. I mean, the monstrous wars about the small points of theology; the earth-quakes of emotion about a gesture or a word. It was only the matter of an inch, but an inch is everything."

Notes and
References

Line numbers refer to the line on which a citation or quotation begins; every line with text on it (i.e., including headings) is counted as a line.

Introduction

Page	Line	Source
xi	1	Thomas Boswell, *How Life Imitates the World Series* (Garden City, N.Y.: Doubleday, 1982), 113.
xi	18	Quoted in Roger Kahn, *The Boys of Summer* (New York: Harper & Row, 1972), 339.
xi	25	James T. Farrell, *My Baseball Diary* (New York: A. S. Barnes, 1957), 19–21.
xii	3	Lawrence Ritter, *The Glory of Their Times*, rev. ed. (New York: William Morrow, 1984), 118.
xii	7	Harold Seymour, *Baseball: The People's Game* (New York: Oxford University Press, 1990), 18.
xii	14	F. O. Matthiessen, *The American Renaissance* (New York: Oxford University Press, 1941), xv.
xii	20	A. Bartlett Giamatti, *Take Time for Paradise: Americans and Their Games* (New York: Summit Books, 1989), 90.
xii	25	Philip Roth, *Portnoy's Complaint* (New York: Random House, 1969), 69.
xii	29	Donald Hall, *Fathers Playing Catch with Sons* (San Francisco: North Point Press, 1985), 30.
xii	31	Roger Kahn, *A Season in the Sun* (New York: Harper & Row, 1977), 5.
xii	35	Roger Angell, "Early Innings," in *Birth of a Fan*, ed. Ron Fimrite (New York: Macmillan, 1993), 19.
xii	38	Roy Blount, "Baseball in My Blood," in Fimrite, *Birth of a Fan*, 27.
xii	41	Doris Kearns Goodwin, "From Father with Love," in *The Red Sox Reader*, ed. Dan Riley (Boston: Houghton Mifflin, 1991), 11.
xiii	3	Charles Krauthammer, "A Bad Year for Baseball," *Philadelphia Inquirer*, 8 October 1994.
xiii	15	Jerry Klinkowitz, *Writing Baseball* (Urbana and Chicago: University of Illinois Press, 1991), 7.
xiii	20	Quoted in Roger Kahn, *The Era, 1947–1957: When the Yankees,*

the Giants, and the Dodgers Ruled the World (New York: Ticknor & Fields, 1993), 159.

xiii   22   Roger Angell, *The Summer Game* (New York: Viking, 1972), 4–5.

xiii   29   Mark Harris, *Diamond* (New York: Donald I. Fine, 1994), 134.

xiv   1   Thomas Wolfe, *You Can't Go Home Again* (New York: Harper Brothers, 1940), 69.

xiv   5   William Zinsser, *On Writing Well*, 4th ed. (New York: Harper Perennial, 1990), 57.

xiv   11   David Sanders, "The Field of Play," *The National Pastime* ([premier issue] 1982), 13.

xiv   13   Thomas McGuane, "Introduction" to *Best American Sportswriting 1992*, ed. Glenn Stout (Boston: Houghton Mifflin, 1993), xvi–xvii.

xiv   15   Nickname for *The Baseball Encyclopedia*; Macmillan published the ninth edition in 1993. Originally published in 1969; Joseph Reichler edited the first six editions.

xiv   18   Luke Salisbury, "On Baseball Books," *Cooperstown Review* ([premier issue] 1993), 96.

xiv   21   Arthur Daley, *Times at Bat: A Half Century of Baseball* (New York: Random House, 1950), 286.

xiv   27   T. Coraghessan Boyle, "The Hector Quesadilla Story," in *Greasy Lake and Other Stories* (New York: Viking Penguin, 1985), 95.

xiv   32   Tristram P. Coffin, *The Old Ball Game* (New York: Herder and Herder, 1971), 13–14; Robert W. Creamer, *Baseball in '41* (New York: Viking, 1991), 11.

xv   2   David Halberstam et al., "How the Game Has Changed," *Newsweek*, 22 August 1994, 56.

xv   16   Kahn, *The Era*, 9.

xv   18   Robert M. Hutchins, *The Great Conversation: The Substance of a Liberal Education* (Chicago: Encyclopedia Britannica, 1952), 86.

xv   25   John Gross, ed., "Introduction" to *The Oxford Book of Essays* (New York: Oxford University Press, 1991), xix, xxii.

xv   39   A. J. Liebling, *The Telephone Booth Indian* (San Francisco: North Point Press, 1990), 24.

xvi   13   Charles Einstein, "Preface" to *The Fireside Book of Baseball* (New York: Simon & Schuster, 1956), xix.

xvi   17   David Halberstam, *October 1964* (New York: Villard Books, 1994), 175.

xvi   19   Hall, *Fathers Playing Catch*, 128.

xvi   21   Angell, *Summer Game*, 4.

xvi   31   C. S. Lewis, *The Screwtape Letters* (New York: Macmillan, 1943), 127–28.

xvi   40   Wilfrid Sheed, *Baseball and Lesser Sports* (New York: HarperCollins, 1991), 11.

xvii   3   Stephen Jay Gould, "The Virtues of Nakedness," *New York Review of Books*, 11 October 1990, 4.

xvii   11   Gene Lees, *Singers and the Songs* (New York: Oxford University Press, 1987), 70–71.

Chapter 1

Page	Line	Source

1   3   William Zinsser, *Spring Training* (New York: Harper & Row, 1989), 4.

1   9   *The International Directory of Little Magazines and Small Presses: 1992–1993*, 28th ed., ed. Len Fulton (Paradise, Calif.: Dustbooks, 1992), 60.

1   14   Angell, *Summer Game*, x.

1   15   Stanley Woodward, *Sports Page* (New York: Simon & Schuster, 1949), 146.

1   21   Ring Lardner, *Some Champions*, ed. Matthew J. Bruccoli and Richard Layman (New York: Scribner's, 1976), 63.

1   23   Roger Kahn, *Good Enough to Dream* (New York: Doubleday, 1985), 139.

2   5   Tom Clark, *The World of Damon Runyon* (New York: Harper & Row, 1978), 44.

2   8   Boswell, *World Series*, 3.

2   20   Quoted in David Plaut, *Speaking of Baseball* (Philadelphia: Running Press, 1993), 211.

2   23   Lee Allen, *The Hot Stove League* (New York: A. S. Barnes, 1955), v.

2   36   Jack Kavanaugh, letter to the author, 19 November 1993.

2   40   Warren Brown, from "Don't Believe Everything You Read," in *The Second Fireside Book of Baseball*, ed. Charles Einstein (New York: Simon & Schuster, 1958), 61.

3   5   George W. Daley, "The Merkle 'Boner'—or Was It O'Day's?" in *Greatest Sports Stories from the* New York Times, ed. Allison Danzig and Peter Brandwein (New York: A. S. Barnes, 1951), 73.

3   28   Quoted in Joseph Wallace, ed., *The Baseball Anthology* (New York: Harry N. Abrams, 1994), 158.

3   39   Hall, *Fathers Playing Catch*, 128–29.

4   7   Marvin Cohen, *Baseball the Beautiful* (New York: Links Books, 1974), 2–3, 72–73, 117.

4   11   Hall, *Fathers Playing Catch*, 67.

4   12   Bruce Catton, "The Great American Game," in *The Third Fireside Book of Baseball*, ed. Charles Einstein (New York: Simon & Schuster, 1968), 91.

4	13	Merritt Clifton, "Baseball and American Manhood," in *Baseball and the Game of Ideas: Essays for the Serious Fan*, ed. Peter C. Bjarkman (Delhi, N.Y.: Birch Brook Press, 1993), 147.
4	15	Einstein, *Fireside Book of Baseball 1*, 183.
4	17	Garrison Keilor, "What Did We Do Wrong," in *We Are Still Married* (New York: Viking, 1989), 281; W. P. Kinsella, *Shoeless Joe* (Boston: Houghton Mifflin, 1982), 85.
4	21	Bob Feller, with Bill Gilbert, *Now Pitching* (New York: Birch Lane Press, 1990), 223; Eric Rolfe Greenberg, *The Celebrant* (New York: Everest House, 1983), 86.
4	26	Michael Oriard, *Reading Football: How the Popular Press Created an American Spectacle* (Chapel Hill: University of North Carolina Press, 1993), 23.
4	31	Marianne Moore, *The Complete Poems,* (New York: Macmillan and Viking, 1967), 221–23.
4	35	Max Apple, *Houston Post*, 24 June 1987, reprinted in Paul Dickson, *Baseball's Greatest Quotations* (New York: HarperCollins, 1991), 24.
5	1	Zinsser, *Spring Training*, 8.
5	4	Sheed, *Baseball and Lesser Sports*, 8.
5	5	George Will, *Men at Work* (New York: Macmillan, 1990), 5.
5	6	Klinkowitz, *Writing Baseball*, 26.
5	6	Stephen Jay Gould, "The Creation Myths of Cooperstown," *Natural History*, November 1969, reprinted in Klinkowitz, *Writing Baseball*, 23–34.
5	14	Stephen Jay Gould, "The Extinction of the .400 Hitter," in *The Armchair Book of Baseball*, ed. John Thorn (New York: Scribner's, 1985), 148.
5	15	Will, *Men at Work*, 206.
5	17	Hall, *Fathers Playing Catch*, 129.
5	27	Einstein, *Third Fireside Book*, 502–3.
5	34	William Least Heat Moon, *Blue Highways: A Journey into America* (Boston: Atlantic/Little, Brown, 1982), 278–81.
6	4	"Interview with Baseball Manager Frankie Papp," *Classic Bob and Ray*, vol. 2 (New York: Radioart, 1991), audiotape.
6	10	Will, *Men at Work*, 172.
6	16	Joseph Epstein, "Merely Anecdotal," *American Scholar*, Spring 1992, 175.
6	26	Allen, *Hot Stove League*, 22.
6	37	Einstein, *Fireside Book of Baseball 1*, 216.
7	4	Hall, *Fathers Playing Catch*, 67.
7	6	Robert Lipsyte, "The Long Road to Broken Dreams," in *Great Sports Reporting*, ed. Allen Kirschner (New York: Dell, 1969), 61.
7	23	Donald Elder, *Ring Lardner* (Garden City, N.Y.: Doubleday, 1956), 118.

7	38	Louis D. Rubin, Jr. quoted in "The Essential Baseball Library," ed. Paul D. Adomites, *SABR Review of Books* 2, no. 1 (1987): 13.
7	40	Ritter, *Glory of Their Times*, xvii.
8	8	Paul Dickson, *Baseball's Greatest Quotations* (New York: HarperCollins, 1991), xi.
8	13	Quoted in Jimmy Breslin, *Can't Anybody Here Play This Game?* (New York: Viking, 1963), 15.
8	14	Marianne Moore, foreword to *A Marianne Moore Reader* (New York: Viking, 1961, 1965), xv (xiii–xviii).

Chapter 2

Page	Line	Source
9	4	Lloyd Lewis, "The Prince of Pitchers," *Chicago Daily News*, 23 January 1943, reprinted in *Sports Extra*, ed. Stanley Frank (New York: A. S. Barnes, 1944), 273.
9	12	John Kieran, "Pitcher Cullop Shapes up as Baseball Jack-of-all-Trades," in *Wake up the Echoes: From the Sports Pages of the* New York Herald Tribune, ed. Bob Cooke (Garden City, N.Y.: Hanover House, 1956), 215.
9	24	James Crusinberry, "Carbon-Copy No Hitters," in *The Greatest Sports Stories from the* Chicago Tribune, ed. Arch Ward (New York: A. S. Barnes, 1953), 143.
10	3	Charles Fountain, *Sportswriter: The Life and Times of Grantland Rice* (New York: Oxford University Press, 1993), 3.
10	12	Grantland Rice, "It Was Johnson's Day at Last," in Grantland Rice and Harford Powel, eds., *The Omnibus of Sport* (New York: Harper Brothers, 1932), 156.
10	18	Stanley Walker, *City Editor* (New York: Frederick A. Stokes, 1934), 120.
10	21	Einstein, *Second Fireside Book*, 272.
10	24	Hall, *Fathers Playing Catch*, 114.
10	40	Donald Honig, *Baseball America* (New York: Macmillan, 1985), 44.
11	8	Arthur "Bugs" Baer, "The Crambury Tiger," in Collier's *Greatest Sports Stories*, ed. Tom Meany (New York: A. S. Barnes, 1955), 189.
11	18	Einstein, *Fireside Book of Baseball 1*, 236.
11	34	Cooke, *Wake up the Echoes*, 70–71, 230.
12	12	Ward, *Stories from the* Chicago Tribune, 120.
12	29	Thorn, *Armchair Book of Baseball*, 307.
12	39	Joseph Epstein, *Partial Payments* (New York: W. W. Norton, 1989), 259–60.
13	8	Bob Considine, "Fall Guys of Baseball," in *Best Sports Stories 1950*, ed. Irving T. Marsh and Edward Ehre (New York: E. P. Dutton, 1951), 80.

13	15	Daley, *Times at Bat*, 8–9.
13	33	Stanley Woodward, "One Strike Is Out," in *Best Sports Stories: 1948 Edition*, ed. Irving T. Marsh and Edward Ehre (New York: E. P. Dutton, 1948), 24.
14	1	Woodward, *Sports Page*, 206.
14	15	Dick Young, "Dodgers on the Rocks," in *Best Sports Stories: 1955 Edition*, ed. Irving T. Marsh and Edward Ehre (New York: E. P. Dutton, 1955), 75.
14	25	Kahn, *The Era*, 128.
14	37	Tom Wolfe and E. W. Johnson, eds., *The New Journalism* (New York: Harper & Row, 1973), 65.
15	1	Quoted in James D. Hart, *The Oxford Companion to American Literature*, 5th ed. (New York: Oxford University Press, 1983), 759.
15	7	Thorn, *Armchair Book of Baseball*, 268.

Chapter 3

Page	Line	Source
16	12	Gould, "Creation Myths," 27.
16	17	Sheed, *Baseball and Lesser Sports*, 59.
16	23	No one has put the idea more succinctly or eloquently, which is why Barzun's fugitive sentence from *God's Country and Mine* (Boston: Atlantic/Little, Brown, 1954) has been quoted so widely, even as it has been taken out of context.
17	5	George Will, "Baseball's Woes—and Ours," *Newsweek*, 21 September 1992, 92.
17	25	Jeffrey Hart, "Can Cal Ripken Save The Game of Baseball?," *Conservative Chronicles* 10, no. 38 (20 September 1995): 5.
17	27	Cal Thomas, "Packwood and Ripken: Virtueless and Virtuous," *Conservative Chronicles* 10, no. 38 (20 September 1995): 13.
17	38	A. Bartlett Giamatti, "Baseball and the American Character," in *The Baseball Chronicles*, ed. David Gallen (New York: Carroll & Graf, 1991), 357.
18	5	Lesley Hazelton, [untitled "Hers" column], *New York Times Magazine*, 22 May 1986, reprinted in *The Yankees Reader*, ed. Miro Weinberger and Dan Riley (Boston: Houghton Mifflin, 1991), 4.
18	12	Zinsser, *Spring Training*, 8.
18	17	David Lamb, *The Stolen Season* (New York: Random House, 1991), 107.
18	23	John O'Sullivan, "Nationhood: An American Activity," *National Review*, 21 February 1994, 38.
18	30	Francis Trevelyan Miller, "Introduction" to Connie Mack, *My 66 Years in the Big Leagues* (Philadelphia: John C. Winston, 1950), iii–iv.
18	36	Harris, *Diamond*, 10.

19	2	Robert Lipsyte, "The Dying Game," *Esquire*, April 1993, 103, 105.
19	8	Zinsser, *Spring Training*, 5.
19	10	Farrell, *My Baseball Diary*, 82.
19	12	Rice, *Omnibus of Sport*, 188.
19	20	Brian Boyd, *Vladimir Nabokov: The American Years* (Princeton, N.J.: Princeton University Press, 1991), 4.
19	29	Hall, *Fathers Playing Catch*, 129.
19	34	Zinsser, *Spring Training*, 145, 151.
20	5	Richard Hugo, "The Anxious Fields of Play," in *Into the Temple of Baseball*, ed. Richard Grossinger and Kevin Kerrane (Berkeley, Calif.: Celestial Arts, 1990), 222.
20	18	Daniel Okrent, "Endless Summer," in *Summer*, ed. Alice Gordon and Vincent Viga (Reading, Mass.: Addison-Wesley, 1990), 39.
21	13	Roger Angell, *Five Seasons* (New York: Simon & Schuster, 1977), 22.
21	23	Quoted in Michael Gershman, *Diamonds: The Evolution of the Ballpark* (Boston: Houghton Mifflin, 1993), 7.
21	30	Ted Solotaroff, "Green and Spacious, Played in Clockless Time," *New York Times Book Review*, 11 June 1972, 1.
21	40	Zinsser, *Spring Training*, 7.
22	11	Art Hill, *I Don't Care If I Never Come Back: A Baseball Fan and His Game* (New York: Simon & Schuster, 1980), 15.
22	19	Sheed, *Baseball and Lesser Sports*, 93, 95.
22	26	Wilfrid Sheed, *My Life as a Fan: A Memoir* (New York: Simon & Schuster, 1993), 15.
22	31	Floyd Skloot, "Trivia Tea: Baseball as Balm," *Gettysburg Review*, Summer 1992, 377–88, reprinted in *The Best American Essays 1993*, ed. Joseph Epstein (New York: Ticknor & Fields, 1993), 332, 327.
23	10	Nicholas Dawidoff, *The Catcher Was a Spy: The Mysterious Life of Moe Berg*, (New York: Pantheon Books, 1994).
23	18	Coffin, *Old Ball Game*, 103.
23	24	Leigh Montville, "Citizen Ryan," in *Sports Illustrated Baseball* (Birmingham: Oxmoor House, 1993), 121.
23	37	Jonathan Yardley, "The Real Frank Merriwell," in *The Ultimate Baseball Book*, ed. Daniel Okrent and Harris Lewine (Boston: Houghton Mifflin, 1979), 70.
24	6	Sheed, *Baseball and Lesser Sports*, 146.
24	14	Michael Seidel, *Streak: Joe DiMaggio and the Summer of '41* (New York: McGraw-Hill, 1988), 3, xi.
24	23	Florence King, *With Charity Toward None: A Fond Look at Misanthropy* (New York: St. Martin's Press, 1992), 8, 146.
24	30	Stephen Jay Gould, "Good Sports and Bad," *New York Review of Books*, 2 March 1995, 24.

25	8	Donald Barthelme, "The Art of Baseball," in *The Spirit of Sport*, ed. Constance Sullivan (Boston: Little, Brown/New York Graphics Society, 1985), 53.
25	16	John Updike, "Hub Fans Bid Kid Adieu," *The New Yorker*, 22 October 1960, reprinted in *Assorted Prose* (New York: Alfred A. Knopf, 1965), 134.
25	22	Harris, *Diamond*, 234.

Chapter 4

Page	Line	Source
26	4	Coffin, *Old Ball Game*, 9.
26	9	Harold Seymour, *Baseball: The Early Years*, rev. ed. (1960; New York: Oxford University Press, 1989), 41.
26	20	Quoted in Seymour, *Early Years*, 41.
26	27	Quoted in Edwin McDowell, "The Literati's Appreciation for Baseball," *New York Times*, 8 April 1981.
27	10	Jack Lang, "Baseball Reporting," in *Total Baseball* (second edition), John Thorn and Peter Palmer, eds. (New York: Warner Books, 1991), 648.
27	20	Henry Chadwick, "From the Game of Base Ball: How to Learn It, How to Play It, and How to Teach It," in *Baseball: A Treasury of Art and Literature*, ed. Michael Ruscoe (New York: Hugh Lauter Levin Associates, 1993), 33.
27	22	Charles Alexander, *Our Game* (New York: Henry Holt, 1991), 22–23.
27	28	Walt Whitman, "On Baseball, 1858," in *The Armchair Book of Baseball II*, ed. John Thorn (New York: Scribner's, 1987), 417–18.
27	35	Quoted in Douglass Wallop, *Baseball: An Informal History* (New York: W. W. Norton, 1969), 119–20.
27	40	*New York Times*, [editorial], reprinted in *Low and Inside*, ed. Ira L. Smith and H. Allen Smith (Garden City, N.Y.: Doubleday, 1949), 136, 140.
28	7	Dickson, *Baseball's Greatest Quotations*, 445.
28	7	Twain had given a banquet speech at Delmonico's Restaurant in New York on 8 April 1889, toasting "the boys who ploughed a new equator round the globe stealing bases on their bellies"—a reference to the recent worldwide baseball tour undertaken by A. G. Spalding and others.
28	10	See Darryl Brock, "Mark Twain and the Great Base Ball Match," *The National Pastime*, no. 14 (1994): 55.
28	15	R. W. Stallman, *Stephen Crane: A Biography*, rev. ed. (New York: George Braziller, 1973), 19–29.
28	23	R. W. Stallman and E. R. Hagemann, *The New York Sketches of*

		Stephen Crane and Related Pieces (New York: New York University Press, 1966), x (fn).
28	32	Stephen Crane, *The Monster and Other Stories* (New York: Harper Brothers, 1899), 36.
29	5	Quoted in Seymour, *People's Game*, 574.
29	7	Rube Foster, called "The Father of Black Baseball," created (in 1920) and presided over the Negro National League, having once been a star pitcher himself. A writer from *The Crisis* (perhaps Du Bois himself) wrote these words for an advertisement when Foster was managing his own team, the great Chicago National Giants.
29	10	Ruscoe, *Baseball Treasury*, 34.
29	16	Einstein, *Fireside Book of Baseball 1*, 46.
29	23	Ruscoe, *Baseball Treasury*, 31–32.
29	33	Ruscoe, *Baseball Treasury*, 49.
29	40	Ruscoe, *Baseball Treasury*, 32.
30	10	Wallace, *Baseball Anthology*, 86.
30	24	Benjamin G. Rader, foreword to Albert G. Spalding, *America's National Game: Historic Facts Concerning the Beginning, Evolution, Development, and Popularity of Base Ball* (Lincoln: University of Nebraska Press, 1992), xiii.
30	36	Spalding, *America's National Game*, 6.
31	1	Spalding, *America's National Game*, 14.
31	3	Spalding, *America's National Game*, 4.
31	26	Meany, Collier's *Greatest*, 103.
31	39	Ruscoe, *Baseball Treasury*, 50.
32	8	Einstein, *Old Ball Game*, 9.
32	18	Seymour, *Early Years*, 17.
32	26	Hugh Fullerton, "The Fellows Who Made the Game," *Saturday Evening Post*, 21 April 1928, 18.
32	33	Warren Brown, *The Chicago Cubs* (New York: Putnam, 1946), 12.
32	38	See Tom Nawrocki, "The Chicago School of Baseball Writing," *The National Pastime* 13 (1993): 86.
33	8	Einstein, *Third Fireside Book*, 487–88.
33	23	Fullerton, "Fellows Who Made the Game," 184.
33	31	Red Smith, "Introduction" to Christy Mathewson, *Pitching in a Pinch* (1912; New York: Stein & Day, 1977), ix.
34	1	Mathewson, *Pitching in a Pinch*, 184.
34	14	Mathewson, *Pitching in a Pinch*, 187.
34	20	Kahn, *Boys of Summer*, 23.
34	26	Mark Harris, *The Southpaw* (New York: Bobbs-Merrill, 1953), 147.
34	37	Wallace, *Baseball Anthology*, 119.
35	16	Charles Dryden, "Phillies Lost Before Record Breaking Crowd," *Philadelphia North American*, 25 April 1905.
35	33	Fullerton, "Fellows Who Made the Game," 188.

35	34	Charles Dryden, "Runs and Money Not for Phillies on Same Day," *Philadelphia North American*, 29 April 1905.
36	20	Charles Dryden, "Rainy Day Interview, No. 1," *Philadelphia North American*, 6 April 1905.
36	22	Ward, *Stories from the* Chicago Tribune, 77.
36	25	Ward, *Stories from the* Chicago Tribune, 90–92.
36	29	Einstein, *Fireside Book of Baseball 1*, 102.
36	41	Charles Dryden, "Phillies Fell Back into Their Old Ways," *Philadelphia North American*, 7 July 1904.
37	5	Ward, *Stories from the* Chicago Tribune, 63.
37	11	Ward, *Stories from the* Chicago Tribune, 79.
37	27	Frank, *Sports Extra*, 20.
37	33	Elder, *Ring Lardner*, 46.

Chapter 5

Page	Line	Source
38	5	Frederick Lewis Allen, *The Big Change: America Transforms Itself, 1900–1950* (New York: Harper Brothers, 1952), 132–33.
38	12	Julian Symons, *Makers of the New: The Revolution in Literature, 1912–1939* (New York: Random House, 1987), 9, 121.
38	18	Don Marquis (1878–1937) was a humorist and dramatist. Archy was a cockroach, and mehitabel a cat. Because of his size, archy, who occupied Marquis's typewriter after Marquis had left the office for the day, tapped out his columns with his head and so could not depress the shift key.
39	2	Symons, *Makers of the New*, 122.
39	4	I do not mean that Crane himself would have thought to use a ballpark, but am rather referring to Crane's use of the bridge as a symbol for the myth of America, or what he called (in a letter to Gorham Munson) a "mystical synthesis of 'America.'" (Quoted in a new edition of *The Bridge* [New York: The Limited Editions Club, 1981], ix.)
39	13	Quoted in Charles Molesworth, *Marianne Moore: A Literary Life* (New York: Atheneum, 1990), 166–67. The incident is also discussed by Donald Hall in *Fathers Playing Catch with Sons*.
39	30	Lardner, *Some Champions*, 21.
39	32	Jimmy Breslin, *A Life of Damon Runyon* (New York: Ticknor & Fields, 1991), 208.
39	39	David Quentin Voigt, *American Baseball: From the Commissioners to Continental Expansion*, vol. 2 (University Park: Pennsylvania State University Press, 1983), 234.
40	4	Danzig, *Stories from the* New York Times, 85.
40	17	Allen, *Hot Stove League*, 10.

40	20	Ring Lardner, *Ring Around the Bases: The Complete Baseball Stories of Ring Lardner*, ed. Matthew J. Bruccoli (New York: Scribner's, 1992), xi–xii.
40	30	Elder, *Ring Lardner*, 141–42.
41	3	Ring Lardner, "I'm Forever Blowing Ball Games," in Meany, Collier's *Greatest*, 101.
41	15	Coffin, *Old Ball Game*, 169.
41	19	Lardner, *Some Champions*, 62.
41	26	Gallen, *Baseball Chronicles*, 47, 50.
41	40	Ward, *Stories from the* Chicago Tribune, 132–33.
42	22	Quoted in Jonathan Yardley, *Ring: A Biography of Ring Lardner* (New York: Random House, 1977), 102.
42	39	Yardley, *Ring*, 133.
43	11	Ward, *Stories from the* Chicago Tribune, 145.
43	33	Elder, *Ring Lardner*, 85.
44	11	Van Loan recommended to *Post* editor George Horace Lormier that he publish Lardner's first installments of *A Busher's Letters Home*.
44	24	Asinof, *Eight Men Out*, 58
44	34	Frederick G. Lieb, "Lardner, Gifted Press-Box Wit, Chosen Winner of Spink Award," *The Sporting News*, 2 November 1963, 10.
45	11	Lardner, *Ring Around the Bases*, 580.
45	18	Lardner, *Ring Around the Bases*, 579.
45	21	Lardner, *Ring Around the Bases*, 585.
45	22	Lardner, *Ring Around the Bases*, 596.
45	29	Lardner, *Ring Around the Bases*, 590.
45	33	Lardner, *Ring Around the Bases*, 592.
45	38	Lardner, *Ring Around the Bases*, 595.
46	5	Lardner, *Ring Around the Bases*, 599.
46	8	Lardner, *Ring Around the Bases*, 606.
46	15	Lardner, *Ring Around the Bases*, 609.
46	22	Yardley, *Ring*, 216.
46	29	Einstein, *Third Fireside Book*, 253.
47	7	Einstein, *Third Fireside Book*, 256.
47	13	Einstein, *Third Fireside Book*, 257.
47	18	Lardner, *Ring Around the Bases*, 569.
47	20	Lardner, *Ring Around the Bases*, 575.
47	28	Lardner, *Some Champions*, 63.
47	33	Lardner, *Some Champions*, 65.
47	36	Lardner, *Some Champions*, 63.
48	11	George Herman Ruth, *Babe Ruth's Own Book of Baseball* (New York: Putnam, 1928), 3.
48	28	Lardner, *Some Champions*, 55.
48	33	Lardner, *Some Champions*, 79.

48	36	Lardner, *Some Champions*, 79.
49	2	Lardner, *Some Champions*, 79.
49	4	Lardner, *Some Champions*, 80.
49	8	Lardner, *Some Champions*, 80.
49	11	Lardner, *Some Champions*, 81.
49	14	Lardner, *Some Champions*, 82.
49	26	Virginia Woolf, "American Fiction," in *The Moment and Other Essays* (New York: Harcourt, Brace, Jovanovich, 1974), 123.
49	35	Dickson, *Baseball's Greatest Quotations*, 239.

Chapter 6

Page	Line	Source
50	5	Breslin, *Life of Damon Runyon*, 208.
50	8	Creamer, *Baseball in '41*, 25–26.
50	16	John Lardner, *It Beats Working* (Philadelphia: Lippincott, 1947), 52.
50	19	Thorn, *Armchair Book II*, 234.
50	21	Quoted in Asinof, *Eight Men Out*, 139.
51	2	Cooke, *Wake up the Echoes*, 46.
51	5	Marshall Smelser, *The Life That Ruth Built* (Lincoln: University of Nebraska Press, 1993), 73–74.
51	10	Fullerton, "Fellows Who Made the Game," 18.
51	19	Hugh Fullerton, *Jimmy Kirkland and the Plot for the Pennant* (Philadelphia: Winston, 1915).
51	22	Kahn, *The Era*, 71.
51	37	Einstein, *Fireside Book of Baseball 1*, 235–36.
52	6	Einstein, *Fireside Book of Baseball 1*, 235.
52	9	Einstein, *Fireside Book of Baseball 1*, 236.
52	16	Einstein, *Fireside Book of Baseball 1*, 236.
52	34	Ward, *Stories from the* Chicago Tribune, 303.
52	39	Ward, *Stories from the* Chicago Tribune, 303.
53	3	Ward, *Stories from the* Chicago Tribune, 305.
53	22	Ward, *Stories from the* Chicago Tribune, 260.
53	30	Ward, *Stories from the* Chicago Tribune, 238–39
53	37	Einstein, *Fireside Book of Baseball 1*, 263.
54	15	Lardner, *It Beats Working*, 73.
54	24	Daley, *Times at Bat*, 295, 391.
54	29	Daley, *Times at Bat*, 391.
54	31	Daley, *Times at Bat*, 295.
54	40	Daley, *Times at Bat*, 393–94.
55	5	Cooke, *Wake up the Echoes*, 155.
55	11	Quoted in Jerome Holtzman, *No Cheering in the Press Box* (New York: Holt, Rinehart, & Winston, 1974), 40.
55	37	Red Smith, *To Absent Friends* (New York: Atheneum, 1982), 370.

56	5	Damon Runyon, "The Snatching of Bookie Bob," in *A Treasury of Damon Runyon*, Clark Kinnaird, ed. (New York: Modern Library, 1958), 100.
56	9	Damon Runyon, "Baseball Hattie," in *The Fireside Book of Baseball*, vol. 4, ed. Charles Einstein (New York: Simon & Schuster, 1987), 328.
56	16	Quoted in Asinof, *Eight Men Out*, 108–9.
56	23	Quoted in Clark, *World of Damon Runyon*, 101.
56	32	Quoted in Asinof, *Eight Men Out*, 3.
57	17	Quoted in Clark, *World of Damon Runyon*, 91.
57	22	Einstein, *Fireside Book of Baseball 1*, 280.
57	37	Einstein, *Fireside Book of Baseball 1*, 282.
57	39	Einstein, *Fireside Book of Baseball 1*, 281.
58	1	Einstein, *Fireside Book of Baseball 1*, 281.
58	4	Breslin, *Life of Damon Runyon*, 211.
58	7	Robert W. Creamer, *Stengel: His Life and Times* (New York: Simon & Schuster, 1984), 11.
58	13	Breslin, *Life of Damon Runyon*, 213.
58	16	Breslin, *Life of Damon Runyon*, 213.
58	19	Breslin, *Life of Damon Runyon*, 214.
58	21	"Yankee Holiday," in *Fifty Famous Sports Stories*, ed. Caswell Adams (New York: Stamford House, 1946), 193.
58	24	Adams, "Yankee Holiday," 194.
58	27	Adams, "Yankee Holiday," 193.
58	36	Damon Runyon, "The Main Event," in *A Treasury of Damon Runyon*, 415–18.
59	16	Heywood Hale Broun, *Whose Little Boy Are You? A Memoir of the Broun Family* (New York: St. Martin's/Marek, 1983), 56–57.
59	32	Cooke, *Wake up the Echoes*, 219.
60	5	Heywood Broun, *Collected Edition of Heywood Broun*, comp. Heywood Hale Broun (New York: Harcourt Brace and Co., 1941), 66.
60	17	Einstein, *Fireside Book of Baseball 1*, 35–37.
60	34	Broun, *Heywood Broun*, 355.
60	39	Broun, *Heywood Broun*, 356–57.
61	10	Broun, *Heywood Broun*, 489–90.
61	27	Broun, *Heywood Broun*, 490–91.
62	7	Paul Gallico, "Saint Bambino," in *Great Baseball Stories*, ed. Jerry D. Lewis (New York: Tempo Books, 1979), 39.
62	10	Holtzman, *No Cheering*, 71.
62	19	Paul Gallico, *A Farewell to Sports* (New York: Alfred A. Knopf, 1938), 288.
62	32	Jimmy Cannon, *Nobody Asked Me, But . . . The World of Jimmy Cannon*, ed. Jack Cannon and Tom Cannon (New York: Holt, Rinehart, & Winston, 1978), 29.
62	35	Gallico, *Farewell to Sports*, 32.

62	40	Gallico, *Farewell to Sports*, 33.
63	8	Gallico, *Farewell to Sports*, 40.
63	18	Gallico, *Farewell to Sports*, 44.
63	24	Gallico, *Farewell to Sports*, 42.
63	26	Gallico, *Farewell to Sports*, 40–41.
64	2	Gallico, *Farewell to Sports*, 123.
64	6	Gallico, *Farewell to Sports*, 129.
64	8	Gallico, *Farewell to Sports*, 134.
64	13	Gallico, *Farewell to Sports*, 126.
64	14	Gallico, *Farewell to Sports*, 124.
64	16	Gallico, *Farewell to Sports*, 127.
64	21	Gallico, *Farewell to Sports*, 129.
64	24	Gallico, *Farewell to Sports*, 132.
64	25	Gallico, *Farewell to Sports*, 133.
64	28	Gallico, *Farewell to Sports*, 134.
64	29	Gallico, *Farewell to Sports*, 135.
64	30	Gallico, *Farewell to Sports*, 135–36.
64	34	Gallico, *Farewell to Sports*, 124.
64	36	Gallico, *Farewell to Sports*, 132.
64	37	Gallico, *Farewell to Sports*, 132.
64	40	Holtzman, *No Cheering*, 70.
65	13	Grantland Rice, *The Tumult and the Shouting* (New York: A. S. Barnes, 1954), 9.
65	15	Fountain, *Sportswriter*, 102.
65	22	Rice, *Tumult and the Shouting*, 7.
66	1	Frank, *Sports Extra*, 96.
66	3	Charles C. Alexander, *Ty Cobb* (New York: Oxford University Press, 1984), 236.
66	5	Rice, *Tumult and the Shouting*, 29.
66	7	Grantland Rice, "Game Called," in *Best Sports Stories: 1949 Edition*, Irving T. Marsh and Edward Ehre, eds. (New York: E. P. Dutton, 1949), 39.
66	15	Wallace, *Baseball Anthology*, 158–62.
66	29	Walker, *City Editor*, 124.
66	34	Grantland Rice, "Open Letter to Ted Williams," in *The Ted Williams Reader*, ed. Lawrence Baldassaro (New York: Simon & Schuster/Fireside, 1991), 70–75.
66	40	Grantland Rice, "Reg'lar Fellers," in *Best Sports Stories: 1947 Edition*, ed. Irving T. Marsh and Edward Ehre (New York: E. P. Dutton, 1947), 90.
67	4	Weinberger, *Yankees Reader*, 14.
67	11	Rice, *Tumult and the Shouting*, 101–15.
67	22	Plutarch, *The Lives of the Noble Grecians and Romans* (Dryden translation) in *Great Books of the Western World* 14, Robert Maynard Hutchins, ed. (Chicago: Encyclopedia Britannica, Inc., 1952), 390.

67	32	Rice, *Tumult and the Shouting*, 352.
67	35	Dickson, *Baseball's Greatest Quotations*, 351.
68	6	Jim Reisler, *Black Writers/Black Baseball: An Anthology of Articles from Black Sportswriters Who Covered the Negro Leagues* (Jefferson, N.C.: McFarland & Co., 1994), 6.
68	13	Reisler, *Black Writers*, 37.
68	16	Reisler, *Black Writers*, 118.
68	23	Reisler, *Black Writers*, 97.
68	34	Reisler, *Black Writers*, 81.
68	41	Reisler, *Black Writers*, 37.
69	6	Reisler, *Black Writers*, 109.
69	12	Reisler, *Black Writers*, 142.

Chapter 7

Page	Line	Source
70	22	Cannon, *Nobody Asked Me, But*, 68–69.
71	2	Cannon, *Nobody Asked Me, But*, 25.
71	8	Cannon, *Nobody Asked Me, But*, 27.
71	17	Cannon, *Nobody Asked Me, But*, 70.
71	20	Cannon, *Nobody Asked Me, But*, 28, 35.
71	22	Sheed, *Baseball and Lesser Sports*, 200.
71	30	Cannon, *Nobody Asked Me, But*, 72–73.
72	3	Cannon, *Nobody Asked Me, But*, 54.
72	6	Holtzman, *No Cheering*, 276.
72	20	Cannon, *Nobody Asked Me, But*, 50.
72	20	Cannon, *Nobody Asked Me, But*, 45.
72	21	Jimmy Cannon, *Who Struck John?* (New York: Dial, 1956), 153.
72	23	Cannon, *Nobody Asked Me, But*, 36.
72	26	Cannon, *Nobody Asked Me, But*, 72.
72	30	Einstein, *Fireside Book of Baseball 1*, 43–44.
72	35	Fimrite, *Birth of a Fan*, 136.
73	2	Joe Williams, *The Joe Williams Baseball Reader*, ed. Peter Williams (Chapel Hill, N.C.: Algonquin Books of Chapel Hill, 1989), 203.
73	5	Jules Tygiel, *Baseball's Great Experiment: Jackie Robinson and His Legacy* (New York: Oxford University Press, 1983), 306.
73	12	Cannon, *Who Struck John?*, 238.
73	18	Einstein, *Second Fireside Book*, 76.
73	24	Cannon, *Nobody Asked Me, But*, 41.
73	26	Baldassaro, *Ted Williams Reader*, 262.
73	29	Cannon, *Who Struck John?*, 27.
73	32	Cannon, *Nobody Asked Me, But*, 62.
73	34	Quoted in Plaut, *Speaking of Baseball*, 385.
74	4	Cannon, *Who Struck John?*, 135.
74	7	Cannon, *Who Struck John?*, 95–96.

74	9	Holtzman, *No Cheering*, 276–77.
74	25	Quoted in Dickson, *Baseball's Greatest Quotations*, 401.
74	32	Williams, *Williams Baseball Reader*, 12, 42, 94.
75	5	E. B. White, *Essays of E. B. White* (New York: Harper & Row, 1977), viii.
75	12	Holtzman, *No Cheering*, 245.
75	24	Red Smith, *The Red Smith Reader*, ed. David Anderson (New York: Random House, 1982), 130.
75	33	Einstein, *Second Fireside Book*, 343–44.
75	41	Smith, *To Absent Friends*, viii.
76	5	Smith, *To Absent Friends*, 25.
76	9	Smith, *Red Smith Reader*, 160.
76	16	George Plimpton, ed., *The Norton Book of Sports* (New York: W. W. Norton, 1992), 21.
76	27	Smith, *Red Smith Reader*, 120.
76	33	Quoted in Dickson, *Baseball's Greatest Quotations*, 343.
76	40	Smith, *Red Smith Reader*, 121.
77	2	Smith, *Red Smith Reader*, 121–22.
77	18	Smith, *Red Smith Reader*, 122.
77	24	Smith, *Red Smith Reader*, 122.
77	40	Hall, *Fathers Playing Catch*, 133.
78	2	Red Smith, *The Best of Red Smith* (New York: Franklin Watts, 1963), 12–14.
78	12	Ira Berkow, *Red: A Biography of Red Smith* (New York: Times Books, 1986), 157.
78	18	Smith, *Red Smith Reader*, 141.
78	21	Smith, *Best of Red Smith*, 84.
78	24	Smith, *Best of Red Smith*, 134.
78	25	Pat Jordan, *The Suitors of Spring* (New York: Dodd, Mead, 1973), 94.
78	30	Smith, *Red Smith Reader*, 137.
78	34	Smith, *Red Smith Reader*, 130.
78	38	Smith, *Red Smith Reader*, 154.
79	9	Red Smith, *Strawberries in the Wintertime* (New York: Quadrangle/New York Times, 1974), 26.
79	18	Smith, *To Absent Friends*, 208, 158, 446.
79	27	Holtzman, *No Cheering*, 247.
80	17	Lardner, *It Beats Working*, 42.
80	25	Einstein, *Second Fireside Book*, 222.
80	35	Einstein, *Second Fireside Book*, 222–29.
81	19	John Lardner, *The World of John Lardner*, ed. Roger Kahn (New York: Simon & Schuster, 1961), 153–61.
81	32	Woodward, *Sports Writer*, 201.
81	38	Lardner, *It Beats Working*, 53–54.
82	10	Smith, *To Absent Friends*, 366.

82	15	Einstein, *Fireside Book of Baseball 1*, 216.
82	19	Roger Kahn, *Games We Used to Play* (New York: Ticknor & Fields, 1992), 69.
82	21	Kahn, *Games We Used to Play*, 69.
82	24	John Lardner, "Advisor to Presidents," in *I Managed Good, but Boy Did They Play Bad*, ed. Jim Bouton and Neil Offen (New York: Playboy Press, 1973), 208.
82	26	Lardner, *It Beats Working*, 209.
82	27	Lardner, *It Beats Working*, 204.
82	34	John Lardner, "Mr. Henderson and the Cooperstown Myth," in *Thirty Years of Best Sports Stories*, ed. Irving T. Marsh and Edward Ehre (New York: E. P. Dutton, 1975), 54.
82	38	Thorn, *Armchair Book of Baseball*, 233.
83	7	Thorn, *Armchair Book of Baseball*, 238.
83	9	Thorn, *Armchair Book of Baseball*, 242.
83	11	Thorn, *Armchair Book of Baseball*, 242.
83	13	Thorn, *Armchair Book of Baseball*, 243.
83	16	Thorn, *Armchair Book of Baseball*, 243.
83	18	Thorn, *Armchair Book of Baseball*, 233.
83	22	Thorn, *Armchair Book of Baseball*, 234.
83	28	Lardner, *World of John Lardner*, 125–33.
83	34	Lardner, *World of John Lardner*, 126–27.
84	3	Lardner, *World of John Lardner*, 132–33.
84	12	Einstein, *Third Fireside Book*, 248–50.
84	26	Einstein, *Third Fireside Book*, 250.
84	30	Einstein, *Third Fireside Book*, 250.
84	33	Einstein, *Third Fireside Book*, 252.
84	39	George Plimpton, ed., *The Norton Book of Sports* (New York: W. W. Norton, 1992), 17.

Chapter 8

Page	Line	Source
85	20	David Halberstam, *Summer of '49* (New York: William Morrow, 1989), 19.
86	4	Mark Harris, *Short Work of It* (Pittsburgh: University of Pittsburgh Press, 1979), 3–4.
86	30	Einstein, *Fireside Book of Baseball 1*, 2.
86	34	Nelson Algren, "So Long, Swede Risberg," originally printed in *Chicago Magazine*, July 1981, 138–41, 158; reprinted in *Best Sports Stories: 1982 Edition*, ed. Edward Ehre (New York: E. P. Dutton, 1982), 51.
87	4	Ehre, *Best Sports Stories 1982*, 49, 46.
87	15	Ehre, *Best Sports Stories 1982*, 53–54.
87	33	Einstein, *Fireside Book of Baseball 1*, 3.

87	35	Einstein, *Fireside Book of Baseball 1*, 3–4.
88	1	Einstein, *Fireside Book of Baseball 1*, 2–5.
88	10	David Sanders, "Farrell as Fan," *The National Pastime*, Spring 1985, 85.
88	23	Farrell, *My Baseball Diary*, 257.
88	27	Farrell, *My Baseball Diary*, 259.
88	33	Farrell, *My Baseball Diary*, 238.
88	36	Farrell, *My Baseball Diary*, 108.
88	40	Farrell, *My Baseball Diary*, 176.
89	1	Farrell, *My Baseball Diary*, 114, 187.
89	4	Farrell, *My Baseball Diary*, 233.
89	6	Farrell, *My Baseball Diary*, 155.
89	13	Farrell, *My Baseball Diary*, 187.
89	18	Farrell, *My Baseball Diary*, 145.
89	23	Farrell, *My Baseball Diary*, 41.
89	27	Farrell, *My Baseball Diary*, 132.
89	32	Farrell, *My Baseball Diary*, 236.
90	1	*Sports Illustrated Baseball*, 284.
90	5	*Sports Illustrated Baseball*, 285.
90	14	*Sports Illustrated Baseball*, 286.
90	16	*Sports Illustrated Baseball*, 285.
90	17	*Sports Illustrated Baseball*, 284.
90	19	Lipsyte, "Dying Game," 105.
90	23	*Sports Illustrated Baseball*, 286, 284, 286.
90	30	*Sports Illustrated Baseball*, 258.
90	33	*Sports Illustrated Baseball*, 259–60.
90	40	*Sports Illustrated Baseball*, 260
91	2	*Sports Illustrated Baseball*, 258.
91	6	*Sports Illustrated Baseball*, 260.
91	8	*Sports Illustrated Baseball*, 261.
91	10	*Sports Illustrated Baseball*, 258.
91	12	*Sports Illustrated Baseball*, 261.
91	14	*Sports Illustrated Baseball*, 259.
91	16	*Sports Illustrated Baseball*, 258.
91	17	*Sports Illustrated Baseball*, 261.
91	21	Seymour, *People's Game*, 128.
91	30	Allen, *Big Change*, 24.
92	2	Shirley Jackson, *Raising Demons*, in *The Magic of Shirley Jackson*, Stanley Edgar Hyman, ed. (New York: Farrar, Straus, and Giroux, 1966), 679.
92	6	Jackson, *Raising Demons*, 676.
92	8	Jackson, *Raising Demons*, 679.
92	11	Jackson, *Raising Demons*, 680.
92	13	Jackson, *Raising Demons*, 683.
92	16	Lonnie Wheeler, *Bleachers: A Summer in Wrigley Field* (Chicago: Contemporary Books, 1988), 3.

92	19	Jackson, *Raising Demons*, 681.
92	23	Jackson, *Raising Demons*, 682.
92	25	Jackson, *Raising Demons*, 677.
92	26	Jackson, *Raising Demons*, 684.
92	27	Jackson, *Raising Demons*, 686.
92	30	Jackson, *Raising Demons*, 684–87.

93 5 Jacques Barzun, [excerpt] "From God's Country and Mine," reprinted in Charles Einstein, ed., *The Second Fireside Book of Baseball*, from which all quotations are made.

93 5 Einstein, *Second Fireside Book*, 20.

93 9 Einstein, *Second Fireside Book*, 21.

93 15 Einstein, *Second Fireside Book*, 20.

93 17 Einstein, *Second Fireside Book*, 20–21.

93 24 Einstein, *Second Fireside Book*, 20.

93 28 Einstein, *Second Fireside Book*, 20–21.

94 7 Roger Kahn, *How the Weather Was* (New York: Harper & Row, 1973), 80.

94 22 Kahn, *Games We Used to Play*, 60.

94 28 Kahn, *Games We Used to Play*, 82.

94 30 Kahn, *Games We Used to Play*, 74.

94 32 Kahn, *Games We Used to Play*, 75.

94 35 Quoted in Irving T. Marsh and Edward Ehre, eds., "Preface" to *Best Sports Stories: 1960 Edition* (New York: E. P. Dutton, 1960), 19.

94 40 Kahn, *How the Weather Was*, 26.

95 4 Roger Kahn, "Where Have All Our Heroes Gone," in Irving T. Marsh and Edward Ehre, eds., *Best Sports Stories 1975* (New York: E. P. Dutton, 1975), 255.

95 8 Kahn, "Where Have All Our Heroes Gone," 256.

95 9 Kahn, "Where Have All Our Heroes Gone," 256.

95 11 Kahn, "Where Have All Our Heroes Gone," 257.

95 16 Kahn, "Where Have All Our Heroes Gone," 264.

95 19 Kahn, "Where Have All Our Heroes Gone," 259.

95 21 Kahn, "Where Have All Our Heroes Gone," 264.

95 29 Kahn, *How the Weather Was*, 27–37.

96 2 Kahn, *Games We Used to Play*, 34–35.

96 13 Kahn, *Games We Used to Play*, 32–35.

97 6 Seymour Krim, *"Shake It for the World, Smartass"* (New York: Delta, 1970), 344–45.

97 16 Einstein, *Second Fireside Book*, 190.

97 29 Einstein, *Second Fireside Book*, 198.

97 37 Einstein, *Second Fireside Book*, 192.

98 8 Wolfe and Johnson, *New Journalism*, 51.

98 15 W. C. Heinz, *Once They Heard the Cheers* (New York: Doubleday, 1979), 227.

98 18 Einstein, *Fireside Book of Baseball 1*, 185.

98	31	Roger Kahn, "Introduction" to Arnold Hano, *A Day in the Bleachers* (1955; New York: Da Capo Press, 1982), vi.
99	5	Some 30 years later, Daniel Okrent took to the bleachers in a book that recalled Hano's in that it covered a single game. *Nine Innings* (New York: McGraw-Hill, 1983) detailed a regular-season game between the Brewers and the Orioles in 1982. Okrent's implication was that any random game during the season might have significant consequences by the end of the season. In *Nine Innings*, the game itself is text. Underlying it are numerous subtexts: the design of County Stadium; the trades that occurred at the winter meetings; spring training; player biographies; a look inside a player's locker; baseball news and history and other contemporary baseball lore.
99	8	Hano, *Day in the Bleachers*, 20.
99	14	Hano, *Day in the Bleachers*, 27.
99	17	Hano, *Day in the Bleachers*, 1, 4–5.
99	22	Allen, *Hot Stove League*, 225.
99	27	Hano, *Day in the Bleachers*, 2.
100	5	Hano, *Day in the Bleachers*, 55.
100	6	Hano, *Day in the Bleachers*, 132.
100	11	Hano, *Day in the Bleachers*, 4.
100	13	Hano, *Day in the Bleachers*, 83.
100	17	Hano, *Day in the Bleachers*, 109.
100	22	Hano, *Day in the Bleachers*, 109.
100	30	Hano, *Day in the Bleachers*, 124.
100	35	Hano, *Day in the Bleachers*, 125.
101	5	Hano, *Day in the Bleachers*, 123–24.
101	9	Hano, *Day in the Bleachers*, 123.
101	13	Hano, *Day in the Bleachers*, 141.
101	17	Hano, *Day in the Bleachers*, 153.
101	24	Hano, *Day in the Bleachers*, 106.

Chapter 9

Page	Line	Source
102	5	Harold Kaese and R. G. Lynch, *The Milwaukee Braves* (New York: Putnam, 1954), 286.
102	7	Tom Meany, *Mostly Baseball* (New York: A. S. Barnes, 1958), 314.
103	8	Updike, *Assorted Prose*, 128.
103	13	Updike, *Assorted Prose*, 128.
103	17	Updike, *Assorted Prose*, 128.
103	19	Updike, *Assorted Prose*, 127.
103	27	Updike, *Assorted Prose*, 128–32.
104	5	Updike, *Assorted Prose*, 133–34.

104   10   Updike, *Assorted Prose*, 137.
104   23   Updike, *Assorted Prose*, 143–44.
104   29   Updike, *Assorted Prose*, 137.
104   31   Updike, *Assorted Prose*, 145–47.
105   2   Updike, *Assorted Prose*, 147.
105   7   Einstein, *Third Fireside Book*, 465.
105   10   Updike, *Assorted Prose*, 147.
105   13   Kahn, *The Era*, 84.
105   16   Updike, *Assorted Prose*, 133.
105   22   Ed Linn, "The Kid's Last Game," *Sport*, February 1961, most recently reprinted (the piece has been widely anthologized) in Lawrence Baldassaro, ed., *Ted Williams Reader*, 222–55.
105   28   Baldassaro, *Ted Williams Reader*, 222–23.
105   41   Baldassaro, *Ted Williams Reader*, 230–32.
106   12   Baldassaro, *Ted Williams Reader*, 249.
106   15   Baldassaro, *Ted Williams Reader*, 243.
106   24   Baldassaro, *Ted Williams Reader*, 252.
106   27   Baldassaro, *Ted Williams Reader*, 254.
106   31   Updike, *Assorted Prose*, 134.
106   33   W. C. Heinz, "Stan Musial's Last Day," in *Best Sports Stories: 1964 Edition*, ed. Irving T. Marsh and Edward Ehre (New York: E. P. Dutton, 1964), 71.
107   2   Heinz, *Sports Stories 1964*, 74–75.
107   14   Heinz, *Sports Stories 1964*, 74.
107   16   Heinz, *Sports Stories 1964*, 78.
107   20   Arnold Hano, "Stan Musial's Last Game," in *The Best of Sport, 1946–1971*, ed. Al Silverman (New York: Viking, 1972), 302.
108   12   Quoted in Mike Shannon, *Baseball: The Writers' Game* (South Bend, Ind.: Diamond Communications, 1992), 22.
108   32   Jim Brosnan, *The Long Season* (New York: Harper Brothers, 1960; New York: Penguin Books, 1983), vi.
109   8   Brosnan, *Long Season*, 5.
109   22   Brosnan, *Long Season*, 4–5.
109   35   Brosnan, *Long Season*, 37.
110   1   Brosnan, *Long Season*, vi–vii.
110   5   Brosnan, *Long Season*, 29.
110   9   Brosnan, *Long Season*, 27.
110   11   Brosnan, *Long Season*, 135.
110   28   Brosnan, *Long Season*, 54.
110   31   Brosnan, *Long Season*, 56.
110   34   Brosnan, *Long Season*, 60.
111   4   Brosnan, *Long Season*, 72.
111   7   Brosnan, *Long Season*, 89.
111   13   Brosnan, *Long Season*, 70.
111   18   Brosnan, *Long Season*, 91.

111   18   Brosnan, *Long Season*, 90.
111   24   Brosnan, *Long Season*, 99, 131, 220.
111   28   Brosnan, *Long Season*, 103.
111   34   Brosnan, *Long Season*, 186.
112   2   Brosnan, *Long Season*, 160.
112   6   Brosnan, *Long Season*, 162.
112   21   Brosnan, *Long Season*, 244.
112   22   Brosnan, *Long Season*, 205.
112   24   Brosnan, *Long Season*, 145.
112   26   Brosnan, *Long Season*, 236.
112   28   Brosnan, *Long Season*, 74.
112   31   Brosnan, *Long Season*, 260.
112   38   Brosnan, *Long Season*, 259.
113   9   Brosnan, *Long Season*, 267.
113   18   Jim Brosnan, *Pennant Race* (New York: Harper Brothers, 1962),
              195.
113   34   George Plimpton, *Out of My League* (New York: Harper & Row,
              1961; New York: Penguin Books, 1983), ix.
114   5   Plimpton, *Out of My League*, 3, 7.
114   22   Plimpton, *Out of My League*, 12.
114   31   Plimpton, *Out of My League*, 21.
114   39   Plimpton, *Out of My League*, 26–27.
115   9   Plimpton, *Out of My League*, 33.
115   14   Plimpton, *Out of My League*, 43.
115   16   Plimpton, *Out of My League*, 41.
115   19   Marianne Moore, "A Poet on the Mound," *New York Herald
              Tribune Lively Arts*, 23 April 1961, reprinted in *A Marianne Moore
              Reader* (New York: Viking, 1965), 244.
115   22   Plimpton, *Out of My League*, 46.
115   25   Plimpton, *Out of My League*, 49.
115   33   Plimpton, *Out of My League*, 66–67.
115   40   Plimpton, *Out of My League*, 79.
116   8   Plimpton, *Out of My League*, 90.
116   27   Plimpton, *Out of My League*, 95.
117   13   Plimpton, *Out of My League*, 101.
117   15   Plimpton, *Out of My League*, 104.
117   22   Plimpton, *Out of My League*, 105.
117   37   Plimpton, *Out of My League*, 122.
118   6   Plimpton, *Out of My League*, 138.
118   9   Plimpton, *Out of My League*, 141.
118   12   Plimpton, *Out of My League*, 142–43.
118   20   Angell, *Five Seasons*, 305.
118   32   Plimpton, *Out of My League*, 127.
118   39   Plimpton, *Out of My League*, 144–45.
119   4   Plimpton, *Out of My League*, 147.

119	10	Plimpton, *Out of My League*, 149.
119	13	Angell, *Five Seasons*, 294.
119	25	Silverman, *Best of* Sport, 203.
119	31	Jimmy Breslin, "Last of the Old Pros," in *Best Sports Stories: 1959 Edition*, ed. Irving T. Marsh and Edward Ehre (New York: E. P. Dutton, 1959), 73–74.
119	38	Holtzman, *No Cheering*, 280.
120	5	Breslin, *Can't Anybody Here*, 17–18.
120	11	Breslin, *Can't Anybody Here*, 16.
120	12	Breslin, *Can't Anybody Here*, 47.
120	19	Breslin, *Can't Anybody Here*, 19.
120	22	Breslin, *Can't Anybody Here*, 67.
120	27	Breslin, *Can't Anybody Here*, 25.
120	34	Williams, *Williams Baseball Reader*, 171.
121	1	Breslin, *Can't Anybody Here*, 62.
121	7	Breslin, *Can't Anybody Here*, 33.
121	11	Breslin, *Can't Anybody Here*, 64–65.
121	22	Breslin, *Can't Anybody Here*, 75.
121	29	Breslin, *Can't Anybody Here*, 110.
121	31	Breslin, *Can't Anybody Here*, 111.
121	33	Breslin, *Can't Anybody Here*, 112.
121	35	Breslin, *Can't Anybody Here*, 115.
121	37	Breslin, *Can't Anybody Here*, 110.
122	1	Breslin, *Can't Anybody Here*, 75.
122	13	Breslin, *Can't Anybody Here*, 54.
122	19	Andy McCue, *Baseball by the Books* (Dubuque: William C. Brown, 1991), 8.
122	28	Einstein, *Third Fireside Book*, 326.
123	8	Wolfe and Johnson, *New Journalism*, 46.
123	10	Charles Alexander, "Introduction" to Ty Cobb with Al Stump, *My Life in Baseball: The True Record* (1961; Lincoln: University of Nebraska Press, 1993), xi–xii.
123	13	Einstein, *Third Fireside Book*, 441.
123	21	Einstein, *Third Fireside Book*, 442.
123	26	Einstein, *Third Fireside Book*, 451.
123	31	Einstein, *Third Fireside Book*, 443.
123	33	Einstein, *Third Fireside Book*, 441.
123	35	Einstein, *Third Fireside Book*, 444.
124	8	Einstein, *Third Fireside Book*, 446.
124	14	Einstein, *Third Fireside Book*, 451.
124	18	Einstein, *Third Fireside Book*, 447.
124	21	Einstein, *Third Fireside Book*, 441.
124	26	Einstein, *Third Fireside Book*, 448.
124	32	Einstein, *Third Fireside Book*, 451.
124	35	Einstein, *Third Fireside Book*, 448.

124	35	Einstein, *Third Fireside Book*, 451.
125	1	Einstein, *Third Fireside Book*, 452.
125	9	Quoted in Yardley, *Ultimate Baseball Book*, 82.
125	12	Einstein, *Third Fireside Book*, 449.
125	20	Einstein, *Third Fireside Book*, 452.
125	28	Ruscoe, *Baseball Treasury*, 184.
125	31	Breslin, *Sports Stories 1959*, 113.
126	2	Irwin Shaw, *Voices of a Summer's Day* (New York: Delacorte Press, 1965), 12.
126	5	Shaw, *Voices of a Summer's Day*, 7
126	13	Gay Talese, "The Silent Season of the Hero," in *Best Sports Stories: 1967 Edition*, ed. Irving T. Marsh and Edward Ehre (New York: E. P. Dutton, 1967), 31.
126	23	Talese, *Sports Stories 1967*, 49.
126	26	Talese, *Sports Stories 1967*, 40.
126	30	Talese, *Sports Stories 1967*, 44.
126	33	Talese, *Sports Stories 1967*, 40, 33, 43.
127	2	Talese, *Sports Stories 1967*, 47.
127	10	Talese, *Sports Stories 1967*, 45.
127	12	Talese, *Sports Stories 1967*, 41.
127	16	Talese, *Sports Stories 1967*, 32.
127	23	Talese, *Sports Stories 1967*, 38–39.
127	34	Talese, *Sports Stories 1967*, 50.
128	8	Dick Johnson, "A Conversation with Roger Angell," *SABR Review of Books* 3 (1988): 48.
128	14	Angell, *Summer Game*, 3.
128	15	Angell, *Five Seasons*, 410.
128	17	See James A. Memmott, "Wordsworth in the Bleachers: The Baseball Essays of Roger Angell," *Journal of American Culture*, Summer 1982, 42–51.
128	30	Angell, *Summer Game*, 196.
128	34	Angell, *Summer Game*, x.
128	39	Angell, *Summer Game*, 137, 281, 93, 254, 131.
129	9	Edward Hoagland, "A Fan's Notes," *Harper's*, July 1977, 76.
129	20	Angell, *Summer Game*, 17.
129	23	Angell, *Summer Game*, 41.
129	29	Angell, *Summer Game*, 83.
129	32	Angell, *Summer Game*, 103–4.
129	38	Angell, *Summer Game*, 143–44.
130	2	Angell, *Summer Game*, 180.
130	7	Angell, *Summer Game*, 186, 196.
130	14	Angell, *Summer Game*, 202, 205.
130	29	Angell, *Summer Game*, 199–200.
130	37	Angell, *Summer Game*, 214.
130	2	Angell, *Summer Game*, 3.

131	7	Angell, *Summer Game*, 292.
131	15	Angell, *Summer Game*, 292.
131	23	Angell, *Summer Game*, 293.
131	25	Angell, *Summer Game*, 294.
131	27	Angell, *Summer Game*, 303.
131	29	Angell, *Summer Game*, 294.
131	31	Angell, *Summer Game*, 297.
131	36	Angell, *Summer Game*, 303.
131	39	Angell, *Summer Game*, 303, 296.
132	2	Thorn, *Armchair Book of Baseball*, 267.
132	29	George Plimpton, "Letter from an October Afternoon," *Harper's*, October 1964, 52, 51.
132	35	"Letter," 52.
133	2	"Letter," 55.
133	5	"Letter," 55.
133	9	"Letter," 53.
133	16	"Letter," 54.
133	20	"Letter," 56.
133	28	"Letter," 55.
133	35	"Letter," 55.
134	2	Marianne Moore, "One Poet's Pitch for the Cardinals to Win the Series," *New York Times*, 28 September 1968.
134	10	"Letter," 57.
134	16	"Letter," 58.
134	21	"Letter," 52.
134	26	Marianne Moore, "Ten Answers: Letter from an October Afternoon, Part II," *Harper's*, November 1964, 94–98.
135	14	Willie Morris, *North Toward Home* (Boston: Houghton Mifflin, 1967).
135	15	Morris, *North Toward Home*, 102.
135	20	Morris, *North Toward Home*, 104.
135	26	Morris, *North Toward Home*, 106.
135	36	Morris, *North Toward Home*, 107.
136	5	Morris, *North Toward Home*, 108, 112.
136	18	Morris, *North Toward Home*, 116, 117, 119.
136	30	Morris, *North Toward Home*, 119.
136	38	Morris, *North Toward Home*, 121, 122.
137	7	Morris, *North Toward Home*, 123.
138	6	Jim Bouton, *I'm Glad You Didn't Take It Personally* (New York: William Morrow, 1971), 81.
138	12	Jim Bouton and Leonard Shecter, *Ball Four* (New York: World Publishing, 1970), 38.
138	15	Bouton and Shecter, *Ball Four*, 155.
138	16	Bouton and Shecter, *Ball Four*, 260.
138	18	Bouton and Shecter, *Ball Four*, ix.

138	18	Belinsky, baseball's quintessential playboy, realizing his mistake, later became the subject of Maury Allen's *Bo: Pitching and Wooing* (New York: Dial Press, 1973), written with Belinsky's "uncensored cooperation." His famous summation of his affair with the actress Mamie Van Doren was: "She gained some things from being with me and I gained some things from being with her. Isn't that the way it's supposed to be with a girl?" (150).
138	23	Quoted in Bouton, *Take It Personally*, 145.
138	32	Bouton and Shecter, *Ball Four*, 258.
138	37	Bouton and Shecter, *Ball Four*, 17.
139	4	Bouton and Shecter, *Ball Four*, xiii.
139	7	Roger Angell, review of *Ball Four* in *New Yorker*, 25 July 1970, 79.
139	10	Bouton and Shecter, *Ball Four*, 225.
139	13	Bouton and Shecter, *Ball Four*, 59.
139	13	Bouton and Shecter, *Ball Four*, 64.
139	14	Bouton and Shecter, *Ball Four*, 325.
139	30	Bouton and Shecter, *Ball Four*, 351.
139	39	Bouton and Shecter, *Ball Four*, 198.
140	9	Bouton and Shecter, *Ball Four*, 76.
140	12	Bouton and Shecter, *Ball Four*, 123.
140	16	Bouton and Shecter, *Ball Four*, 145.
140	18	Bouton and Shecter, *Ball Four*, 120–22.
140	25	Bouton and Shecter, *Ball Four*, 113.
140	28	Bouton and Shecter, *Ball Four*, 117–23.
140	37	Bouton and Shecter, *Ball Four*, 275.
141	2	Bouton and Shecter, *Ball Four*, 9.
141	5	Bouton and Shecter, *Ball Four*, 179.
141	14	Bouton and Shecter, *Ball Four*, 398.
141	23	Bouton, *Take It Personally*, 65.
141	28	Bouton, *Take It Personally*, 93.

Chapter 10

Page	Line	Source
142	16	Pat Jordan, *A False Spring* (New York: Dodd, Mead, 1975), 11.
142	18	Jordan, *False Spring*, 32.
142	22	Jordan, *False Spring*, 18.
143	11	Jordan, *False Spring*, 36.
143	32	White, *Essays of E. B. White*, 121.
142	37	Darrell Berger, "Revealing a Larger Truth," *SABR Review of Books* ([premier issue] 1986), 74.
144	6	Jordan, *False Spring*, 240–41.
144	10	Jordan, *False Spring*, 50.
144	18	Jordan, *False Spring*, 52.

144	22	Kahn, *Season in the Sun*, 46.
144	33	Jordan, *False Spring*, 63.
144	40	Jordan, *False Spring*, 79.
145	7	Jordan, *False Spring*, 90.
145	13	Jordan, *False Spring*, 132.
145	14	Jordan, *False Spring*, 129.
145	18	Jordan, *False Spring*, 131.
145	23	Jordan, *False Spring*, 124.
145	26	Jordan, *False Spring*, 132–33.
145	35	Jordan, *False Spring*, 145.
145	38	Jordan, *False Spring*, 149.
145	41	Jordan, *False Spring*, 156.
146	14	Jordan, *False Spring*, 157.
146	24	Jordan, *False Spring*, 166.
146	31	Jordan, *False Spring*, 167.
146	33	Jordan, *False Spring*, 178.
146	38	Jordan, *False Spring*, 194.
147	10	Jordan, *False Spring*, 214.
147	18	Jordan, *False Spring*, 227.
147	28	Jordan, *False Spring*, 237.
147	33	Jordan, *False Spring*, 263–64.
147	38	Jordan, *False Spring*, 268.
148	4	Jordan, *False Spring*, 275.
148	7	Jordan, *False Spring*, 277.
148	17	Shannon, *Writers' Game*, 144.
148	33	Jordan, *Suitors of Spring*, 13.
148	36	Jordan, *Suitors of Spring*, 29–30.
149	9	Jordan, *Suitors of Spring*, 92.
149	27	Jordan, *Suitors of Spring*, 115.
149	31	Jordan, *Suitors of Spring*, 122.
149	34	Jordan, *Suitors of Spring*, 121–22.
150	4	Jordan, *Suitors of Spring*, 133.
150	7	Jordan, *Suitors of Spring*, 139.
150	9	Jordan, *Suitors of Spring*, 146.
150	14	Jordan, *Suitors of Spring*, 178.
150	19	Jordan, *Suitors of Spring*, 203.
150	31	Jordan, *Suitors of Spring*, 141.
151	2	Harris, *Diamond*, 272.
151	3	Harris, *Diamond*, 274.
151	11	Harris, *Diamond*, 276.
151	14	Harris, *Diamond*, 153.
151	18	Harris, *Diamond*, 154.
151	29	Harris, *Short Work of It*, 122.
151	31	Harris, *Short Work of It*, 123.
151	36	Harris, *Short Work of It*, 123.

151	38	Harris, *Short Work of It*, 127.
151	39	Harris, *Short Work of It*, 126.
151	41	Harris, *Short Work of It*, 122.
152	2	Harris, *Short Work of It*, 123.
152	6	Harris, *Short Work of It*, 127.
152	10	Harris, *Diamond*, 152.
152	14	Okrent, *Ultimate Baseball Book*, 315.
152	21	Kahn, *Boys of Summer*, 18.
152	26	Kahn, *Boys of Summer*, 323.
153	9	Kahn, *Boys of Summer*, 174.
153	11	Kahn, *Boys of Summer*, 135–36.
153	15	Kahn, *Boys of Summer*, 311.
153	16	Kahn, *Boys of Summer*, 279.
153	18	Kahn, *Boys of Summer*, 287.
153	20	Kahn, *Boys of Summer*, 278.
153	22	Kahn, *Boys of Summer*, 402.
153	28	Kahn, *Boys of Summer*, 125.
153	29	Kahn, *Boys of Summer*, 205–6.
153	39	Kahn, *Boys of Summer*, 23.
154	1	Kahn, *Boys of Summer*, 22.
154	12	Kahn, *Boys of Summer*, 396.
154	23	Kahn, *Boys of Summer*, 56.
154	27	Kahn, *Boys of Summer*, 125.
154	32	Kahn, *Boys of Summer*, 194.
155	6	Kahn, *Boys of Summer*, 204.
155	10	Kahn, *Boys of Summer*, xiii.
155	17	Kahn, *Boys of Summer*, 210.
155	23	Kahn, *Boys of Summer*, 327.
155	24	Kahn, *Boys of Summer*, 385.
155	25	Kahn, *Boys of Summer*, 270.
155	30	Kahn, *Boys of Summer*, 311.
155	33	Kahn, *Boys of Summer*, 365–66.
155	36	Kahn, *Boys of Summer*, 386.
155	38	Kahn, *Boys of Summer*, 402.
156	1	Kahn, *Boys of Summer*, 423.
156	6	Kahn, *Boys of Summer*, 438.
156	8	Bouton, *Take It Personally*, 204.

Chapter 11

Page	Line	Source
157	4	Thorn, *Armchair Book of Baseball*, 222.
157	22	Grossinger, *Temple of Baseball*, xiii.
158	4	Grossinger, *Temple of Baseball*, 151.
158	11	Grossinger, *Temple of Baseball*, 84.

| 158 | 28 | Cohen, *Baseball the Beautiful*, 120. |

158 28 Cohen, *Baseball the Beautiful*, 120.

158 39 Quote appeared originally in Catalogue 33/Baseball, Archer's Used and Rare Books (Kent, Ohio, 1995), page 8, and reprinted here by permission of Paul Bauer.

159 17 Jim Brosnan, "The Short Season," in *Best Sports Stories: 1977 Edition*, ed. Irving T. Marsh and Edward Ehre (New York: E. P. Dutton, 1977), 131.

159 27 Robert W. Creamer, *Babe: The Legend Comes to Life* (New York: Simon & Schuster, 1974), 185.

159 32 Creamer, *Babe*, 204.

160 9 George Plimpton, *One for the Record* (New York: Harper & Row, 1974), 43–44.

160 17 Plimpton, *One for the Record*, 108.

160 20 Plimpton, *One for the Record*, 8.

160 32 Hank Aaron and Lonnie Wheeler, *I Had a Hammer* (New York: HarperCollins, 1991), 149.

160 40 Harris, *Diamond*, 163.

161 1 Kahn, *Games We Used to Play*, 151.

161 3 Kahn, *Games We Used to Play*, 154.

161 5 Kahn, *Games We Used to Play*, 155.

161 14 Angell, *Five Seasons*, 303.

161 19 Angell, *Five Seasons*, 303.

161 22 Angell, *Five Seasons*, 304.

161 26 Angell, *Five Seasons*, 305.

161 35 Angell, *Five Seasons*, 306.

161 39 Angell, *Five Seasons*, 306.

162 3 Angell, *Five Seasons*, 306.

162 11 Roger Angell, *Once More Around the Park* (New York: Ballantine Books, 1990), 186.

162 22 Angell, *Once More*, 146.

162 27 Angell, *Once More*, 153, 161.

162 35 Angell, *Five Seasons*, 19.

162 37 Angell, *Once More*, 207, 268.

163 2 Angell, *Summer Game*, x.

163 3 Johnson, "Conversation with Roger Angell," 48.

163 14 Angell, *Five Seasons*, 224, 226.

163 16 Angell, *Five Seasons*, 245.

163 23 Angell, *Five Seasons*, 249.

163 28 Angell, *Five Seasons*, 252.

163 36 Angell, *Five Seasons*, 250–51.

164 11 Angell, *Once More*, 263.

164 20 Thorn, *Armchair Book of Baseball*, 143.

164 25 Michael Novak, *The Joy of Sports* (New York: Basic Books, 1976), 56–69.

164 28 Novak, *Joy of Sports*, 68, 57.

164	37	Novak, *Joy of Sports*, 74.
165	5	Novak, *Joy of Sports*, 58.
165	7	Novak, *Joy of Sports*, 59, 63.
165	8	Novak, *Joy of Sports*, 67, 69.
165	11	Novak, *Joy of Sports*, 61.
165	12	Novak, *Joy of Sports*, 69, 66.
165	14	Novak, *Joy of Sports*, 64, 65.
165	29	Hall, *Fathers Playing Catch*, 51.
165	34	Hall, *Fathers Playing Catch*, 69.
165	36	Hall, *Fathers Playing Catch*, 68, 70.
166	1	Hall, *Fathers Playing Catch*, 70.
166	3	Hall, *Fathers Playing Catch*, 75.
166	5	Hall, *Fathers Playing Catch*, 75.
166	10	Hall, *Fathers Playing Catch*, 50.
166	13	Hall, *Fathers Playing Catch*, 50–51.
166	27	Hall, *Fathers Playing Catch*, 104.
166	31	Hall, *Fathers Playing Catch*, 106.
166	31	Hall, *Fathers Playing Catch*, 81.
166	32	Hall, *Fathers Playing Catch*, 96, 97.
167	2	Donald Hall, *Life Work* (Boston: Beacon Press, 1993), 46, 38.
167	9	Hall, *Fathers Playing Catch*, 48.
167	13	Donald Hall, *Principal Products of Portugal: Prose Pieces* (Boston: Beacon Press, 1995), 212.
167	17	Hall, *Principal Products*, 222.
167	20	Hall, *Principal Products*, 199.
167	31	Kahn, *Season in the Sun*, 8.
168	1	Kahn, *Season in the Sun*, 7.
168	4	Kahn, *Season in the Sun*, 38.
168	16	Kahn, *Season in the Sun*, 81.
168	21	Kahn, *Season in the Sun*, 81.
168	24	Kahn, *Season in the Sun*, 69, 68.
168	33	Kahn, *Season in the Sun*, 83, 85.
168	36	Kahn, *Season in the Sun*, 94.
168	40	Kahn, *Season in the Sun*, 107.
169	1	Kahn, *Season in the Sun*, 134.
169	3	Kahn, *Season in the Sun*, 142.
169	4	Kahn, *Season in the Sun*, 120.
169	7	Kahn, *Season in the Sun*, 170.
169	14	Kahn, *Season in the Sun*, 171.
169	18	Kahn, *Season in the Sun*, 151, 205.
169	29	Kahn, *Good Enough to Dream*, 294–95.
169	34	Kahn, *Good Enough to Dream*, 71.
169	38	Kahn, *Good Enough to Dream*, 302.
169	40	Kahn, *Good Enough to Dream*, 295.
170	4	Bill Veeck and Ed Linn, *Veeck as in Wreck* (New York: Putnam, 1962), 11.

170	8	Kahn, *Good Enough to Dream*, 105.
170	11	Kahn, *Good Enough to Dream*, 3, 5.
170	15	Kahn, *Good Enough to Dream*, 11.
170	18	Kahn, *Good Enough to Dream*, 71.
170	25	Kahn, *Good Enough to Dream*, 155.
170	31	Kahn, *Good Enough to Dream*, 155.
170	32	Kahn, *Good Enough to Dream*, 85.
171	1	Thorn, *Armchair Book of Baseball*, 265.
171	3	Thorn, *Armchair Book of Baseball*, 266.
171	15	Thorn, *Armchair Book of Baseball*, 265.
171	17	See my forthcoming volume, *Twentieth Century Sportswriters*, in the Dictionary of Literary Biography series (Gale Research, Inc., 1996) for essays.
171	22	Breslin, *Life of Damon Runyon*, 226.
171	26	Leroy "Satchel" Paige with David Lipman, *Maybe I'll Pitch Forever* (1962; Lincoln: University of Nebraska Press, 1993).
172	1	Peter Gammons, *Beyond the Sixth Game* (Boston: Houghton Mifflin, 1985), 269, 272.
172	5	George Will, *The Pursuit of Happiness and Other Sobering Thoughts* (New York: Harper & Row, 1978), 313.

Chapter 12

Page	Line	Source
173	15	J. Roy Stockton, "Them Phillies—Or How to Make Failure Pay," *Saturday Evening Post*, 4 October 1941, 48.
174	4	Thorn, *Armchair Book of Baseball*, 35.
174	16	Mark Winegardner, *Prophet of the Sandlots: Journeys With a Major League Scout* (New York: The Atlantic Monthly Press, 1990), 70.
174	30	Winegardner, *Prophet of the Sandlots*, 3.
174	32	Winegardner, *Prophet of the Sandlots*, 13.
174	37	Winegardner, *Prophet of the Sandlots*, 101.
174	41	Winegardner, *Prophet of the Sandlots*, 273.
175	13	Richard Ben Cramer, *The Season of the Kid* (New York: Prentice Hall, 1991), 65.
175	19	Cramer, *Seasons of the Kid*, 3.
175	32	Cramer, *Seasons of the Kid*, 15.
176	3	Gerald Early, review of Bob Gibson with Lonnie Wheeler, *Stranger to the Game: The Autobiography of Bob Gibson* (New York: Viking Press, 1994) in *Nine: A Journal of Baseball History and Social Policy Perspectives* 4, no. 1 (Fall 1995): 112, 113.
176	13	Hall, *Principal Products*, 206.
176	17	Bruce Kuklick, *To Every Thing a Season: Shibe Park and Urban Philadelphia, 1909–1976* (Princeton, N.J.: Princeton University Press, 1991), 6.
176	24	Halberstam, *Summer of '49*, 11.

176	28	Halberstam, *Summer of '49*, 18.
176	28	Halberstam, *Summer of '49*, 250.
176	34	Halberstam, *Summer of '49*, 257–58.
177	13	Halberstam, *October 1964*, 359.
177	27	Kahn, *The Era*, 9.
178	16	Kahn, *The Era*, 327.
178	19	Kahn, *The Era*, 342.
178	22	Kahn, *The Era*, 286.
178	23	Kahn, *The Era*, 283, 286.
178	28	Kahn, *The Era*, 318.
178	33	Kahn, *The Era*, 10.
178	38	Kahn, *The Era*, 305.
179	5	Stephen Jay Gould, "Losing the Edge: The Extinction of the .400 Hitter," *Vanity Fair*, March 1983, 120, 264–78.
179	17	Giamatti, *Baseball Chronicles*, 294.
179	17	Originally published in *Chance: New Directions in Statistics and Computing*, November 1989.
179	33	Giamatti, *Baseball Chronicles*, 291.
180	4	Brown, *Chicago Cubs*, 4.
180	6	Will, *Pursuit of Happiness*, 311.
180	7	Will, *Pursuit of Happiness*, 310.
180	9	Will, *Pursuit of Happiness*, 309.
180	19	Will, *Pursuit of Happiness*, 312.
180	20	Will, *Pursuit of Happiness*, 313.
180	23	Will, *Pursuit of Happiness*, 308.
180	25	Will, *Pursuit of Happiness*, 309.
180	29	George Will, *Suddenly: The American Idea Abroad and At Home, 1986–1990* (New York: The Free Press, 1990), 380.
180	32	Will, *Suddenly*, 381.
180	39	Thorn, *Armchair Book II*, 421.
181	5	Einstein, *Fireside Book 4*, 424.
181	22	Will, *Suddenly*, 24.
181	27	Will, *Suddenly*, 399.
181	37	Will, *Men at Work*, 7.
182	4	Will, *Men at Work*, 318.
182	8	George F. Will, "The Pursuit of Excellence," *Boston Globe*, 16 October 1986, reprinted in *The Red Sox Reader*, ed. Dan Riley (Boston: Houghton Mifflin, 1991), 117.
182	15	Will, *Men at Work*, 195.
182	16	Will, *Men at Work*, 267.
182	19	Will, *Men at Work*, 131.
182	23	Will, *Men at Work*, 171.
182	27	Will, *Men at Work*, 322.
182	35	Will, *Men at Work*, 322.
183	8	Donald Kagan, "George Will's Baseball—A Conservative Critique," *The Public Interest* 101 (Fall 1990): 6.

| 183 | 13 | Will, *Men at Work*, 33. |

183 13   Will, *Men at Work*, 33.
183 14   Kagan, "George Will's Baseball," 8.
183 15   Kagan, "George Will's Baseball," 9.
183 19   Kagan, "George Will's Baseball," 16.
183 33   George Will, "The Romantic Fallacy in Baseball—A Reply," *The Public Interest* 101 (Fall 1990): 23, 26.
184 1   Will, "Romantic Fallacy in Baseball," 21.
184 10   Will, *Men at Work*, 294.
184 15   Will, *Men at Work*, 6.
184 18   Kagan, "George Will's Baseball," 4.
184 19   Will, *Men at Work*, 6.
185 3   Allison Gordon, *Foul Ball! Five Years in the American League* (New York: Dodd Mead, 1984), 11–12.
185 18   Glenn Stout, "What Do Women Think?" in *Cooperstown Review* 2 (1994): 199. Stout was reviewing *Diamonds Are a Girl's Best Friend*, ed. Elinor Nauen (New York: Faber and Faber, 1994).
185 21   Carol Iannone, "Is There a Women's Perspective in Literature?" *Academic Questions* 7, no. 1 (Winter 1993–94): 66.
185 26   Danielle Gagnon Torrez and Ken Lizotte, *High Inside: Memoirs of a Baseball Wife* (New York: Putnam, 1983), 235–36.
185 30   Iannone, "Women's Perspective in Literature," 66.
185 35   Annie Dillard, *An American Childhood* (New York: Harper & Row, 1987), 97–100.
186 5   Dillard, *American Childhood*, 110.
186 7   Dillard, *American Childhood*, 132.
186 10   Dillard, *American Childhood*, 78.
186 12   Dillard, *American Childhood*, 3.
186 15   Dillard, *American Childhood*, 221.
186 33   Thomas Boswell, *Cracking the Show* (New York: Doubleday, 1994), xi.
186 36   Thomas Boswell, *Game Day: Sports Writings* (New York: Doubleday, 1990), xi.
186 38   Boswell, *Game Day*, 368.
187 3   Boswell, *Game Day*, 369.
187 5   Boswell, *Game Day*, 368, 370.
187 19   Boswell, *World Series*, 55.
187 25   Boswell, *World Series*, 14, 24.
187 27   Boswell, *World Series*, 15.
187 29   Boswell, *World Series*, 6.
187 32   Boswell, *World Series*, 13.
187 34   Boswell, *World Series*, 30.
187 39   Boswell, *Cracking the Show*, 295.
188 11   Boswell, *World Series*, 120.
188 16   Boswell, *World Series*, 44.
188 17   Boswell, *World Series*, 61.
188 20   Boswell, *World Series*, 78.

188	23	Boswell, *World Series*, 169.
188	26	Boswell, *World Series*, 170.
188	30	Boswell, *World Series*,253.
189	1	Thomas Boswell, *Why Time Begins on Opening Day* (New York: Doubleday, 1984), 13.
189	4	Boswell, *Why Time Begins*, 14.
189	8	Sheed, *My Life as a Fan*, 216.
189	11	Boswell, *Why Time Begins*, 115.
189	14	Boswell, *Why Time Begins*, 275, 286.
189	22	Boswell, *Why Time Begins*, 160.
189	22	Boswell, *Why Time Begins*, 202.
189	27	Boswell, *Why Time Begins*, 114.
189	28	Boswell, *Why Time Begins*, 115.
189	41	Thomas Boswell, *The Heart of the Order* (New York: Doubleday, 1989), 38–47.
190	3	Boswell, *Heart of the Order*, 29–37.
190	21	Boswell, *World Series*, 247.
190	27	Boswell, *Why Time Begins*, 261.
190	29	George Will, "The Phillies' Mr. Start-Me-Up," *Newsweek*, 4 April 1994, 70.
190	31	Boswell, *Why Time Begins*, 247.
190	36	Boswell, *Heart of the Order*, 35.
190	39	Boswell, *Why Time Begins*, 248.
191	2	Boswell, *Why Time Begins*, 250.
191	5	Boswell, *Why Time Begins*, 249.
191	10	Boswell, *Cracking the Show*, 276.
191	12	Boswell, *Game Day*, 339.
191	17	Boswell, *Why Time Begins*, 287.
191	20	Boswell, *World Series*, 298.
191	26	Boswell, *Heart of the Order*, 362.
191	30	Boswell, *Cracking the Show*, 107.
191	33	Boswell, *Heart of the Order*, 363.
191	36	Boswell, *Cracking the Show*, ix–x.
191	39	Boswell, *Cracking the Show*, xii.
192	19	Alan Lelchuck, "Softball Season," in *The Temple of Baseball*, ed. Richard Grossinger (Berkeley: North Atlantic Books, 1985), 85.
192	38	Mike Sowell, *One Pitch Away: The Players' Stories of the 1986 League Championships and World Series* (New York: Macmillan, 1995), 106.
193	19	Curt Smith, "Where Have All the Children Gone," *Reader's Digest*, October 1993, 61–63.

Selected
Bibliography

Primary Works

Angell, Roger. *The Summer Game*. New York: Viking, 1972.

————. *Five Seasons: A Baseball Companion*. New York: Simon & Schuster, 1977.

————. *Late Innings: A Baseball Companion*. New York: Simon & Schuster, 1982. Angell was jolted by the 1981 player strike. Includes an in-depth portrait of Bob Gibson and scathing attacks on what Angell calls baseball's "corporate masochism."

————. *Season Ticket: A Baseball Companion*. Boston: Houghton Mifflin, 1988. In these essays, Angell becomes "more engrossed in the craft and techniques of the game." He was forced to deal with his dual partisanship during the Mets–Red Sox 1986 World Series.

————. *Once More Around the Park: A Baseball Reader*. New York: Ballantine Books, 1990.

Boswell, Thomas. *How Life Imitates the World Series*. Garden City, N.Y.: Doubleday, 1982.

————. *Why Time Begins on Opening Day*. New York: Doubleday, 1984.

————. *The Heart of the Order*. New York: Doubleday, 1989.

————. *Game Day: Sports Writings*. New York: Doubleday, 1990.

————. *Cracking the Show*. New York: Doubleday, 1994.

Bouton, Jim, and Leonard Shecter. *Ball Four: My Life and Hard Times Throwing the Knuckleball in the Big Leagues*. New York: World Publishing, 1970.

————. *I'm Glad You Didn't Take It Personally*. New York: William Morrow, 1971. Bouton's sequel to *Ball Four*.

Breslin, Jimmy. *Can't Anybody Here Play This Game?* New York: Viking, 1963.

Brosnan, Jim. *The Long Season*. New York: Harper Brothers, 1960. Reprint, New York: Penguin Books, 1983.

————. *Pennant Race*. New York: Harper Brothers, 1962.

Broun, Heywood. *Collected Edition of Heywood Broun*. Compiled by Heywood Hale Broun. New York: Harcourt, Brace and Co., 1941.

Cannon, Jimmy. *Nobody Asked Me, But . . . The World of Jimmy Cannon*. Edited by Jack Cannon and Tom Cannon. New York: Holt, Rinehart, & Winston, 1978.

————. *Who Struck John?* New York: Dial, 1956.

Farrell, James T. *My Baseball Diary*. New York: A. S. Barnes, 1957.

Gallico, Paul. *Farewell to Sport*. New York: Alfred A. Knopf, 1938.

Halberstam, David. *Summer of '49*. New York: William Morrow, 1989.

———. *October 1964*. New York: Villard Books, 1994.

Hall, Donald. *Fathers Playing Catch with Sons: Essays on Sport {Mostly Baseball}*. San Francisco: North Point Press, 1985.

Hano, Arnold. *A Day in the Bleachers*. New York: Thomas Y. Crowell Co., 1955. Reprint, New York: Da Capo Press, 1982.

Harris, Mark. *Short Work of It*. Pittsburgh: University of Pittsburgh Press, 1979.

———. *Diamond: Baseball Writings of Mark Harris*. New York: Donald I. Fine, 1994.

Jordan, Pat. *The Suitors of Spring*. New York: Dodd, Mead, 1973.

———. *A False Spring*. New York: Dodd, Mead, 1975.

Kahn, Roger. *The Boys of Summer*. New York: Harper & Row, 1972.

———. *How the Weather Was*. New York: Harper & Row, 1973.

———. *A Season in the Sun*. New York: Harper & Row, 1977.

———. *Good Enough to Dream*. New York: Doubleday, 1985.

———. *Games We Used to Play: A Lover's Quarrel with the World of Sports*. New York: Ticknor & Fields, 1992.

———. *The Era, 1947–1957: When the Yankees, the Giants, and the Dodgers Ruled the World*. New York: Ticknor & Fields, 1993.

Lardner, John. *It Beats Working*. Philadelphia: Lippincott, 1947.

———. *Strong Cigars and Lovely Women*. New York: Funk & Wagnalls, 1951.

———. *The World of John Lardner*. Edited by Roger Kahn. New York: Simon & Schuster, 1961.

Lardner, Ring. *Some Champions: Sketches and Fiction*. Edited by Matthew J. Bruccoli and Richard Layman. New York: Scribner's, 1976.

———. *Ring Around the Bases: The Complete Baseball Stories of Ring Lardner*. Edited by Matthew J. Bruccoli. New York: Scribner's, 1992.

Mathewson, Christy. *Pitching in a Pinch*. New York: Putnam, 1912. Reprint, New York: Stein & Day, 1977.

Plimpton, George. *Out of My League*. New York: Harper & Row, 1961.

———. *One for the Record: The Inside Story of Hank Aaron's Chase for the Home-Run Record*. New York: Harper & Row, 1974.

Rice, Grantland. *The Tumult and the Shouting*. New York: A. S. Barnes, 1954.

Sheed, Wilfrid. *Baseball and Lesser Sports*. New York: HarperCollins, 1991.

———. *My Life as a Fan*. New York: Simon & Schuster, 1993.

Smith, Red. *Views of Sport*. New York: Alfred A. Knopf, 1954.

———. *The Best of Red Smith*. New York: Franklin Watts, 1963.

———. *Strawberries in the Wintertime: The Sporting World of Red Smith*. New York: Quadrangle/New York Times, 1974.

———. *The Red Smith Reader*. Edited by David Anderson. New York: Random House, 1982.

———. *To Absent Friends*. New York: Atheneum, 1982.

Spalding, Albert G. *America's National Game: Historic Facts Concerning the Beginning, Evolution, Development and Popularity of Base Ball*. New York:

American Sports Publishing Company, 1911. Reprint, Lincoln: University of Nebraska Press, 1992.

Will, George F. *The Pursuit of Happiness and Other Sobering Thoughts*. New York: Harper & Row, 1978.

———. *Men at Work*. New York: Macmillan, 1990.

Winegardner, Mark. *Prophet of the Sandlots*. New York: The Atlantic Monthly Press, 1990.

Anthologies

Baldassaro, Lawrence, ed. *The Ted Williams Reader*. New York: Simon & Schuster/Fireside, 1991.

Cooke, Bob, ed. *Wake up the Echoes: From the Sports Pages of the* New York Herald Tribune. Garden City, N.Y.: Hanover House, 1956.

Danzig, Allison, and Peter Brandwein, eds. *The Greatest Sports Stories from the* New York Times. New York: A. S. Barnes & Co., 1951.

Ehre, Edward, and the editors of the *Sporting News*, eds. *Best Sports Stories: 1982 Edition*. New York: E. P. Dutton, 1982.

Einstein, Charles, ed. *The Fireside Book of Baseball*. New York: Simon & Schuster, 1956.

———. *The Second Fireside Book of Baseball*. New York: Simon & Schuster, 1958.

———. *The Third Fireside Book of Baseball*. New York: Simon & Schuster, 1968.

———. *The Fireside Book of Baseball*. Vol. 4. New York: Simon & Schuster, 1987.

Fimrite, Ron, ed. *Birth of a Fan*. New York: Macmillan, 1993.

Frank, Stanley, ed. *Sports Extra*. New York: A. S. Barnes, 1944.

Fulk, David, and Dan Riley, eds. *The Cubs Reader*. Boston: Houghton Mifflin, 1991.

Gallen, David, ed. *The Baseball Chronicles*. New York: Carroll & Graf, 1991.

Grossinger, Richard, and Kevin Kerrane, eds. *Into the Temple of Baseball*. Berkeley, Calif.: Celestial Arts, 1990. Includes selections from all three editions of Grossinger and Kerrane's three previous anthologies, as well as a considerable amount of new work, covering through the 1989 World Series.

Kirschner, Allen, ed. *Great Sports Reporting*. New York: Dell, 1969.

Klinkowitz, Jerry, ed. *Writing Baseball*. Urbana and Chicago: University of Illinois Press, 1991.

Marsh, Irving T., and Edward Ehre, eds. *Best Sports Stories*. 37 vols. New York: E. P. Dutton, 1944–80.

———. *Thirty Years of Best Sports Stories*. New York: E. P. Dutton, 1975.

Meany, Tom, ed. Collier's *Greatest Sports Stories*. New York: A. S. Barnes, 1955.

Murray, Tom, ed. Sport *Magazine's All-Time All-Stars*. New York: Atheneum, 1977.

Okrent, Daniel, and Harris Lewine, eds. *The Ultimate Baseball Book*. Boston: Houghton Mifflin, 1979.

Reisler, Jim. *Black Writers/Black Baseball: An Anthology of Articles from Black Sportswriters Who Covered the Negro Leagues*. Jefferson, N.C.: McFarland & Co., 1994.

Rice, Grantland, and Harford Powel, eds. *The Omnibus of Sport*. New York: Harper Brothers, 1932.

Riley, Dan, ed. *The Dodgers Reader*. Boston: Houghton Mifflin, 1992.

————. *The Red Sox Reader*. Boston: Houghton Mifflin, 1991.

Ruscoe, Michael, ed. *Baseball: A Treasury of Art and Literature*. New York: Hugh Lauter Levin Associates, 1992.

Silverman, Al, ed. *The Best of* Sport, *1946–1971*. New York: Viking, 1972.

Silverman, Al, and Brian Silverman, eds. *The Twentieth Century Treasury of Sports*. New York: Viking, 1992.

Sports Illustrated Baseball. Birmingham: Oxmoor House, 1993.

Thorn, John, ed. *The Armchair Book of Baseball*. New York: Scribner's, 1985.

————. *The Armchair Book of Baseball II*. New York: Scribner's, 1987.

Wallace, Joseph, ed. *The Baseball Anthology*. New York: Harry N. Abrams, 1994.

Ward, Arch, ed. *The Greatest Sports Stories from the* Chicago Tribune. New York: A. S. Barnes, 1953.

Weinberger, Miro, and Dan Riley, eds. *The Yankees Reader*. Boston: Houghton Mifflin, 1991.

Other Important Books

Allen, Lee. *The Hot Stove League*. New York: A. S. Barnes, 1955. Allen, the one-time *Sporting News* columnist and historian at the National Baseball Library of the Hall of Fame in Cooperstown, goes to the roots of many historical anecdotes. Written in the light, *Saturday Evening Post* style of the day.

Asinof, Eliot. *Eight Men Out*. New York: Holt, Rinehart, and Winston, 1963. Reprint, New York: Pocket Books, 1979. Asinof pieced together all of the fragmentary accounts of the 1919 Black Sox scandal in a fine work of investigative journalism.

Cobb, Ty, with Al Stump. *My Life in Baseball: The True Record*. New York: Doubleday, 1961. Reprint, Lincoln: University of Nebraska Press, 1993. According to Jim Brosnan, "His book, sympathetically transcribed . . . is written in the Gee Whiz style of the early Nineteen-Twenties sport page, and no doubt pleased Cobb's conception of how he should sound."

Cohen, Marvin. *Baseball the Beautiful: Decoding the Diamond*. New York: Links Books, 1974. Deep philosophical works on baseball like this one come along every 20 years or so. Overwritten and outmoded, the book nonetheless reiterates the baseball myths ("every summer is played the same eternal baseball game") while acknowledging that we now "know too much, . . . have too much information about what's going on, leaving no room for fantasy to rove and spin its thrilling emotional web."

Cramer, Richard Ben. *The Seasons of the Kid*. New York: Prentice Hall Press, 1991. According to Daniel Okrent, "It merges Updike's awe-struck regard with Linn's piercing iconoclasm, largely by letting some air out of the former and shelving the prejudgment of the latter."

Creamer, Robert W. *Babe: The Legend Comes to Life*. New York: Simon & Schuster, 1974. Still the best biography of the famous star.

————. *Stengel: His Life and Times*. New York: Simon & Schuster, 1984. Acknowledges Stengel's familiar role as a baseball clown but sees him in a more complex light—as a man "always serious about the game of baseball, about how it should be played, and particularly about his role as manager."

————. *Baseball in '41*. New York: Viking, 1991. Baseball's last great season before the war. A personal reminiscence filled with mythic overtones and the author's great command of baseball history.

Einstein, Charles. *Willie's Time: A Memoir of Another America*. Philadelphia: Lippincott, 1979. Pulitzer Prize nominee in biography. In the assessment of the *New York Times* (17 June 1979), "Mr. Einstein uses history and Willie Mays interchangeably, and it works."

Flood, Curt, and Richard Carter. *The Way It Is*. New York: Trident Press, 1970. Flood's famous challenge to baseball's reserve clause, which "violated the logic and integrity of my existence. I was not a consignment of goods. I was a man, the rightful proprietor of my own person and my own talents."

Giamatti, A. Bartlett. *Take Time for Paradise: Americans and Their Games*. New York: Summit Books, 1989. Baseball is America's Homeric *Odyssey*, "the story of going home after having left home."

Hall, Donald. *Principal Products of Portugal: Prose Pieces*. Boston: Beacon Press, 1995. Collects several of Hall's baseball essays from the late eighties, including his splendid dissertation on "Casey at the Bat" ("Ballad of the Republic"). Casey's strikeout celebrates failure ("a mothering nurturing common humanity") and mocks the myth of heroes ("dangerous . . . in a democracy if we will remain democratic").

Heinz, W. C. *Once They Heard the Cheers*. New York: Doubleday, 1979. Heinz catches up with retired sports figures he has known and written about. Includes two wonderful baseball essays on Joe Page and Pete Reiser.

Higgins, George V. *The Progress of the Seasons: Forty Years of Baseball in Our Town*. New York: Holt, 1989. Not a particularly good book, but one by a well-known American author, who milks the theme of fathers and sons and Red Sox lore. Baseball, like the Thorton Wilder play of the subtitle, is "something large enough and sufficiently exciting to engage the mind initially and keep it entertained while the process of learning proceeds."

Hill, Art. *I Don't Care If I Never Come Back: A Baseball Fan and His Game*. New York: Simon & Schuster, 1980. Early example of baseball as palliative—in Hill's case, as a refuge from alcoholism. Donald Hall observed, "For Art Hill and for many others, baseball is a clean well-lighted place that keeps terrors away until dawn."

Kuklick, Bruce. *To Every Thing a Season: Shibe Park and Urban Philadelphia, 1909–1976*. Princeton, N.J.: Princeton University Press, 1991. The familiar baseball myths appear unobtrusively in a lively and entertaining scholarly work.

Lamb, David. *The Stolen Season: A Journey Through America and Baseball's Minor Leagues*. New York: Random House, 1991. Excellent baseball travelogue and detailed account of the recently rejuvenated minor leagues.

Lieb, Fred. *Baseball as I Have Known It*. New York: Coward, McCann & Geoghegan, 1977. Lieb, a member of the "foremost freshman class that ever broke into a New York press box," covers over 60 years of baseball history. "This is the way it was. I was there."

Meany, Tom. *Mostly Baseball*. New York: A. S. Barnes, 1958. Collection of articles from *Collier's* and other magazines by one of the country's most perspicacious sportswriters.

Okrent, Daniel. *Nine Innings*. New York: McGraw-Hill, 1983. Self-proclaimed "anatomy of baseball as seen through the playing of a single game." Too caught up in its own sense of self-importance, and the style is affected: Baseball is "25 men . . . attempting to touch their feet safely on a pentagonal piece of rubber more times than their opponents."

Piersall, Jimmy, and Al Hirshberg. *Fear Strikes Out: The Jimmy Piersall Story*. Boston: Atlantic/Little, Brown, 1955. One of the first "adult" baseball books recounts Piersall's nervous breakdown and recovery. "Uplifting" in a sentimental way; at times the narrative, filled with stream-of-consciousness techniques, reads like a French new novel.

Ritter, Lawrence. *The Glory of Their Times*. New York: Macmillan, 1966. Revised edition, New York: William Morrow, 1984. Four interviews were added to the revised edition. The first and best book in a long string of baseball oral histories.

Seidel, Michael. *Streak: Joe DiMaggio and the Summer of '41*. New York: McGraw-Hill, 1988. The best account of DiMaggio's rise as a national hero.

Tygiel, Jules. *Baseball's Great Experiment: Jackie Robinson and His Legacy*. New York: Oxford University Press, 1983. The most precise account of baseball's slow move toward integration and the inevitable collapse of the Negro leagues. Also notes the contributions of black sportswriters like Wendell Smith and Sam Lacy.

Williams, Joe. *The Joe Williams Baseball Reader*. Edited by Peter Williams. Chapel Hill, N.C.: Algonquin Books of Chapel Hill, 1989. Collection of Williams's New York *World-Telegram* columns. Contains a worthwhile essay by the editor, his son Peter Williams, on "Baseball in '47: Racism and Scapegoats."

Zinsser, William. *Spring Training*. New York: Harper & Row, 1989. Zinsser follows his own advice from *On Writing Well* on the subject of sportswriting: "Hang around the . . . stadium. . . . Observe closely. Interview in depth. Listen to old-timers. Ponder the changes. Write well."

Articles and Parts of Books

Barthelme, Donald. "The Art of Baseball." In *The Spirit of Sport*, edited by Constance Sullivan, 43–53. Boston: Little, Brown/New York Graphics Society, 1985.

Farrell, James T. "Baseball: A Fan's Notes." *American Scholar* (Summer 1979): "Long before I possessed any capacity to examine myself or the reason for the game's appeal to me, I loved it."

Goodwin, Doris Kearns. "From Father, With Love." *Boston Globe*, 6 October 1986.

Gould, Stephen Jay. "Good Sports and Bad." *New York Review of Books*, 2 March 1995, 20–24.

Kagan, Donald. "George Will's Baseball—A Conservative Critique." *The Public Interest* 101 (Fall 1990): 3–20.

Lipsyte, Robert. "The Dying Game." *Esquire*, April 1993, 101–5.

Moore, Marianne. "One Poet's Pitch for the Cardinals to Win the Series." *New York Times*, 28 September 1968.

———. "Ten Answers: Letter from an October Afternoon, Part II." *Harper's*, November 1964, 94–98.

Novak, Michael. "The Rural Anglo-American Myth." In *The Joy of Sports: End Zones, Bases, Baskets, Balls, and the Consecration of the American Spirit*, 56–69. New York: Basic Books, 1976.

Okrent, Daniel. "Endless Summer." In *Summer*, edited by Alice Gordon and Vincent Vega, 39–45. Reading, Mass.: Addison-Wesley, 1990.

Plimpton, George. "Letter from an October Afternoon." *Harper's*, October 1964, 50–58.

Roth, Philip. "My Baseball Years." *New York Times*, 2 April 1973.

Runyon, Damon. "The Main Event." In *A Treasury of Damon Runyon*, edited by Clark Kinnaird, 415–18. New York: Modern Library, 1958.

Skloot, Floyd. "Trivia Tea: Baseball as Balm." In *The Best American Essays 1993*, edited by Joseph Epstein, 326–40. New York: Ticknor & Fields, 1993.

Will, George. "The Romantic Fallacy in Baseball—A Reply." *The Public Interest* 101 (Fall 1990): 21–27.

Secondary Works

Alexander, Charles. *Our Game*. New York: Henry Holt, 1991. A single-volume history that provides an effective overview and a bibliographic essay.

Angell, Roger. [Review of *Ball Four*]. *New Yorker*, 25 July 1970, 79. "The success here is Mr. Bouton himself as a day-to day observer, hard thinker, marvelous listener, comical critic, angry victim, and unabashed lover of a sport."

The Baseball Encyclopedia. 9th ed. New York: Macmillan, 1993. Indispensable, even when writing about baseball literature.

Berger, Darrell. "Revealing a Larger Truth." *SABR Review of Books* ([premier issue] 1986): 73–75. Essay-review of *A False Spring* sees Pat Jordan as baseball's Jack Kerouac.

Bjarkman, Peter C., ed. *Baseball and the Game of Ideas: Essays for the Serious Fan.* Delhi, N.Y.: Birch Brook Press, 1993. Though the works in this anthology are too academic and esoteric, Bjarkman's introduction is of interest, particularly given his preference for "resounding metaphors for the meaning of life" and his categorization of baseball essays under the headings "humanism," "mathematical aura," "memory," and "narrative structure."

Breslin, Jimmy. *A Life of Damon Runyon.* New York: Ticknor & Fields, 1991. Idiosyncratic biography of Runyon by one of his literary "heirs." Includes some Runyon material not anthologized elsewhere.

Broun, Heywood Hale. "Brooks, Bums, Dodgers, Men." [Review of *The Boys of Summer*]. *Chicago Tribune Bookworld*, 27 February 1972, 4. "He takes a *Carnet de Bal* trip around the country to visit old Dodgers, and finds tragedy but not unhappiness, disaster but not defeat, and some notable victories of the human spirit."

———. *Whose Little Boy Are You? A Memoir of the Broun Family.* New York: St. Martin's Press/Marek, 1983. Offers a little background on the elder Broun's baseball writing days.

Clark, Tom. *The World of Damon Runyon.* New York: Harper & Row, 1978. This Runyon biography contains additional information on writers of the era before Babe Ruth, as well as some hard-to-find Runyon journalism. Clark, better known for his baseball poetry, writes frequently about the game's eccentrics and iconoclasts.

Coffin, Tristram P. *The Old Ball Game: Baseball in Folklore and Fiction.* New York: Herder and Herder, 1971. The best study of baseball literature in American popular culture, with two key chapters on baseball talk and dime novels.

Dickson, Paul. *Baseball's Greatest Quotations.* New York: HarperCollins, 1991. Provides many leads and excerpts from significant works of baseball prose.

———. *The Dickson Baseball Dictionary.* New York: Facts on File, 1989. Helpful source for clarifying many baseball terms, but not nearly comprehensive.

Elder, Donald. *Ring Lardner.* Garden City, N.Y.: Doubleday, 1956. Best written of the Lardner biographies. Creates a strong feel for Lardner's early baseball writing years in Chicago.

"The Essential Baseball Library." Compiled by Paul D. Adomites. *SABR Review of Books* 2, no. 1 (1987): 9–19. Listing of favorite and most influential baseball books in all fields by 22 *SABR* notables.

Fountain, Charles. *Sportswriter: The Life and Times of Grantland Rice.* New York: Oxford University Press, 1993. Superb biography of Grantland Rice.

Fullerton, Hugh. "The Fellows Who Made the Game." *Saturday Evening Post*, 21 April 1928, 18–19, 184–86, 188. The earliest authoritative account of writers of the Chicago school.

Gould, Steven Jay. "The Virtues of Nakedness." [Review of *Men at Work*]. *New York Review of Books*, 11 October 1990, 3–4, 6–7. "I do quarrel with the premise that major league baseball, as a totality, represents an island of self-motivated excellence that could save us by extensive emulation."

Hall, Donald. "Mother Could Hit a Curve Ball." [Review of *A Season in the Sun*]. *New York Times Book Review*, 3 July 1977, 5, 17. "For baseball's characteristic stories—anecdotes and the lore the game is rich with— Roger Kahn is best of all, with his sweet ear for the cadence of baseball talk."

Hano, Arnold. "A View from the Field." [Review of *Pennant Race*]. *New York Times Book Review*, 10 June 1962, 24. "[Brosnan's] book is beautifully constructed, helped no end by the essential unity and chronology of a baseball season, and strengthened by a central theme: the increasing possibility that the Reds will win the pennant."

Harris, Mark. "Between Pitches, There Was a Lot to Think About." [Review of *The Long Season*]. *New York Times Book Review*, 10 July 1960, 7. "A fine, frank volume infinitely more valuable than the several tons of articles 'as told to' with which we are annually forced to contend."

———. "Playing the Game." [Review of *Late Innings*]. *New York Times Book Review*, 23 May 1982, 3, 18. "Mr. Angell respects the game these people play, and because he cares for his own style and is rather a genius at writing well without seeming to press . . . he feels or understands the meaning of being excellent at the work one does."

Hoagland, Edward. "A Fan's Notes." [Review of *Five Seasons*]. *Harper's*, July 1977, 76, 78. "So jammed with glee and eagerness and lore and exact fact that they all do manage to meld together."

Holtzman, Jerome. *No Cheering in the Press Box*. New York: Holt, Rinehart, & Winston, 1974. A collection of 18 interviews with American sportswriters of the first half of the twentieth century, including Kieran, Gallico, Smith, and Cannon. A major work of oral biography and sports history. Revised edition (Holt, 1995) added six new interviews.

James, Bill. *The Bill James Historical Baseball Abstract*. New York: Villard Books, 1986; revised edition, 1988. Information on books and authors in each decade of baseball briefly discussed. The quintessential hot-stove book.

Johnson, Dick. "A Conversation with Roger Angell." *SABR Review of Books* 3 (1988): 43–52. One of the very few interviews Angell has given.

Lang, Jack. "Baseball Reporting." In *Total Baseball*, 2d ed., edited by John Thorn and Peter Palmer, 648–53. New York: Warner Books, 1991. Short overview of the history, especially the Chicago school, but too much emphasis on the Baseball Writers Association of America, of which Lang has been a longtime member and president.

Lardner, Rex. [Review of *Ball Four*]. *New York Times Book Review*, 26 July 1970, 8. "Bouton has written the funniest, frankest book yet about the species *ballplayer satyriaticus*."

Lichtenstein, Grace. "The Last Days of the Daffy Brooklyn Dodgers." [Review of *The Boys of Summer*]. *New York Times Book Review*, 5 March 1972, 32. "What counts is that Roger Kahn has composed a very stylish piece of fifties nostalgia that puts us back in touch with our heroes without either cosmetizing or demeaning them."

Lipsyte, Robert. [Review of *Ball Four*]. *New York Times*, 22 June 1970. Lipsyte viewed the book's sensationalism sympathetically in relation to the nature of ballplayers, who "keep circling the country to play before fans who do not understand their problems or their work, and who use them as symbols for their own fantasies."

McDowell, Edwin. "The Literati's Appreciation for Baseball." *New York Times*, 8 April 1981. "It is generally conceded that baseball is far and away the preferred sport among America's best writers."

Moore, Marianne. "A Poet on the Mound." [Review of *Out of My League*]. *New York Herald Tribune Lively Arts*, 23 April 1961. "*Out of My League* copes with the problems of the imaginary nightmare of walking every batter and the glittering triumph [the shutout] of striking them out one after another."

Nawrocki, Tom. "The Chicago School of Baseball Writing." *The National Pastime* 13 (1993): 84–86. Fills in some of the gaps in Fullerton's "The Fellows Who Made the Game."

Reynolds, Quentin. *By Quentin Reynolds*. New York: McGraw-Hill, 1963. Includes chapter of reminiscences about the baseball beat in the 1930s. "Probably one of the pleasantest assignments anyone could hand a young sports writer in the depression spring of 1931 was that of covering a baseball team for a metropolitan newspaper."

Salisbury, Luke. "On Baseball Books." *Cooperstown Review* ([premier issue] 1993): 96–104. Personal memoir on the passion of collecting baseball books, with a few insights into the better ones.

Sanders, David. "The Field of Play." *The National Pastime* ([premier issue] 1982): 13–14. "More than any other game, [baseball] is a world in itself, and so it draws writers, whose occupation it is to create other worlds."

———. "Farrell as Fan." *The National Pastime* 4 (Spring 1985): 85–86. "James T. Farrell was unquestionably the most devoted baseball fan among America's significant writers."

Seymour, Harold. *Baseball: The Early Years*. New York: Oxford University Press, 1960; revised edition, 1989. Plentiful information on baseball prose in the late nineteenth century.

———. *Baseball: The People's Game*. New York: Oxford University Press, 1990. Third volume of Seymour's seminal history work. Covers baseball on all the peripheries of the professional level.

Shannon, Mike. *Diamond Classics: Essays on 100 of the Best Baseball Books Ever Published*. Jefferson, N.C.: McFarland & Co., 1989. Many excellent critiques of all sorts of baseball books (including pictorials and Charles Schultz's *Sandlot Peanuts*). One of the first baseball writers to establish literary criteria with the average reader in mind.

———. *Baseball: The Writers' Game*. South Bend, Ind.: Diamond Communications, 1992. Oral histories by 15 contemporary baseball writers, including Kahn, Jordan, Einstein, and Brosnan.

Solotaroff, Ted. "Green and Spacious, Played in Clockless Time." [Review of *The Summer Game*]. *New York Times Book Review*, 11 June 1972, 1, 14, 16, 18. "His genuine enthusiasm and empathy can tail off into the habitual amiability and coyness of the 'Talk of the Town' [but] Angell's point of view fits into and is sustained by its dominant editorial purpose: the conservation of traditions."

Voigt, David Quentin. *American Baseball: From the Commissioners to Continental Expansion*. Vol. 2. University Park: Pennsylvania State University Press, 1983. Good study of baseball's silver and golden ages. Pages 94–101 deal with early sportswriting, which Voigt terms "Baseball's Second Dimension."

Walker, Stanley. [Review of *Farewell to Sport*]. *Books*, 17 April 1938, 9. "The book is marred by many inaccuracies in facts and names . . . but they are not serious [enough] to mar . . . the essential soundness of a highly readable work."

Will, George. *Suddenly: The American Idea Abroad and at Home: 1986–1990*. New York: Free Press, 1990.

Yardley, Jonathan. "The Diamond's Best Friend." [Review of *Five Seasons*]. *Washington Post Book World*, 5 June 1977, G1–G2. "*Five Seasons* makes abundantly clear that Angell has been altering the focus of his writing rather than trading on past glories, and that he has become a ferocious and devastating critic of the game's commercialization and debasement."

———. *Ring: A Biography of Ring Lardner*. New York: Random House, 1977. Updates all previous Lardner biographies and includes plentiful examples of Lardner's baseball journalism.

Zoss, Joel, and John Bowman. *Diamonds in the Rough: The Untold History of Baseball*. New York: Macmillan, 1989. Informative section on baseball literature from Whitman and Crane to contemporary authors.

Other Baseball Sources

Aaron, Henry, and Lonnie Wheeler. *I Had a Hammer: The Hank Aaron Story*. New York: HarperCollins, 1991.

Alexander, Charles C. *Ty Cobb*. New York: Oxford University Press, 1984.

———. *John McGraw*. New York: Viking, 1988.

Allen, Maury, with Bo Belinsky. *Bo: Pitching and Wooing*. New York: Dial Press, 1973.

Bouton, Jim, and Neil Offen, eds. *I Managed Good, but Boy Did They Play Bad*. New York: Playboy Press, 1973.

Brock, Darryl. "Mark Twain and the Great Base Ball Match." *The National Pastime* 14 (1994): 55–58.

Brown, Warren. *The Chicago Cubs*. New York: Putnam, 1946.

———. *The Chicago White Sox*. New York: Putnam, 1952.

Daley, Arthur. *Times at Bat: A Half Century of Baseball*. New York: Random House, 1950.

Dawidoff, Nicholas. *The Catcher Was a Spy: The Mysterious Life of Moe Berg*. New York: Pantheon Books, 1994.

Durocher, Leo, with Ed Linn. *Nice Guys Finish Last*. New York: Simon & Schuster, 1975.

Fleming, G. H. *The Unforgettable Season*. New York: Holt, Rinehart, Winston, 1981. Story of the 1908 pennant race between Cubs, Pirates, and Giants, pieced together from contemporaneous accounts in newspapers and baseball journals.

———. *The Dizziest Season: The Gashouse Gang Chases the Pennant*. New York: Morrow, 1984. Writings about the 1934 season by Runyon, Rice, Pegler, Gallico, John Lardner, and others.

Gammons, Peter. *Beyond the Sixth Game: What's Happened to Baseball since the Greatest Game in World Series History*. Boston: Houghton Mifflin, 1985.

Gibson, Bob, with Lonnie Wheeler. *Stranger to the Game: The Autobiography of Bob Gibson*. New York: Viking Press, 1994.

Gordon, Allison. *Foul Ball! Five Years in the American League*. New York: Dodd, Mead, 1984.

Graham, Frank. *Lou Gehrig: A Quiet Hero*. New York: Putnam, 1942.

Hall, Donald, with Dock Ellis. *Dock Ellis in the Country of Baseball*. New York: Coward, McCann & Geoghegan, 1976.

Harris, Mark. *The Southpaw*. New York: Bobbs-Merrill, 1953.

Holway, John B. *Voices from the Great Black Baseball Leagues*. New York: Dodd, Mead, 1975.

Honig, Donald. *Baseball America: The Heroes of the Game and the Times of Their Glory*. New York: Macmillan, 1985.

———. *The Donald Honig Reader*. New York: Simon & Schuster, 1988.

Kaese, Harold, and R. G. Lynch. *The Milwaukee Braves*. New York: Putnam, 1954.

Krauthammer, Charles. "A Bad Year for Baseball." *Philadelphia Inquirer*, 8 October 1994.

McCue, Andy. *Baseball by the Books*. Dubuque: William C. Brown, 1991.

Paige, Leroy "Satchel," with David Lipman. *Maybe I'll Pitch Forever*. Garden City, N.Y.: Doubleday, 1962. Reprint, Lincoln: University of Nebraska Press, 1993.

Peterson, Robert. *Only the Ball Was White: A History of Legendary Black Players and All-Black Professional Teams*. New York: Prentice-Hall, 1970.

Plaut, David. *Speaking of Baseball*. Philadelphia: Running Press, 1993.

Plimpton, George, ed. *The Norton Book of Sports*. New York: W. W. Norton, 1992.

Povich, Shirley. *The Washington Senators: An Informal History*. New York: Putnam, 1954.

Ruth, George Herman. *Babe Ruth's Own Book of Baseball*. New York: Putnam, 1928.

Smelser, Marshall. *The Life That Ruth Built*. New York: Quadrangle/New York Times Book Co., 1975. Reprint, Lincoln: University of Nebraska Press, 1993.

Smith, Curt. "Where Have All the Children Gone." *Reader's Digest*, October 1993, 61–63.

Smith, Ira. L., and H. Allen Smith. *Low and Inside*. Garden City, N.Y.: Doubleday, 1949.

Sowell, Mike. *One Pitch Away: The Players' Stories of the 1986 League Championships and World Series*. New York: Macmillan, 1995.

Torrez, Danielle Gagnon, and Ken Lizotte. *High Inside: Memoirs of a Baseball Wife*. New York: Putnam, 1983.

Veeck, Bill, with Ed Linn. *Veeck as in Wreck*. New York: Putnam, 1962.

Wheeler, Lonnie. *Bleachers: A Summer in Wrigley Field*. Chicago: Contemporary Books, 1988.

Will, George. "Baseball's Woes—and Ours." *Newsweek*, 21 September 1992, 92.

Williams, Ted, with John Underwood. *My Turn at Bat*. New York: Simon & Schuster, 1969.

Non-Baseball Works

Krim, Seymour. *Shake It for the World, Smartass*. New York: Delta, 1970. Krim's "The Newspaper as Literature/Literature as Leadership" remains one of the best single essays on new journalism.

Oriard, Michael. *Reading Football: How the Popular Press Created an American Spectacle*. Chapel Hill: University of North Carolina Press, 1993. Gives valuable information on the early days of sports pages in American newspapers.

Walker, Stanley. *City Editor*. New York: Frederick A. Stokes, 1934. Contains a major chapter on sportswriters by the former *New York Herald Tribune* editor, who knew most of them personally.

Wolfe, Tom, and E. W. Johnson, eds. *The New Journalism*. New York: Harper & Row, 1973. Focuses on changes in American writing and journalism since the early 1960s.

Woodward, Stanley. *Sports Page*. New York: Simon & Schuster, 1949. Ostensibly a work on writing sports journalism, the book includes Woodward's opinions on writing styles and key authors.

Woodward, Stanley, and Frank Graham, Jr. *Sportswriter*. Garden City, N.Y.: Doubleday, 1967. Update of *Sports Page*.

Zinsser, William. *On Writing Well*. 4th ed. New York: Harper Perennial, 1990. A great chapter on writing sports includes a brief analysis of Updike's "Hub Fans Bid Kid Adieu."

Memoirs and Other Books

Barzun, Jacques. *God's Country and Mine*. Boston: Atlantic/Little, Brown, 1954.

Dillard, Annie. *An American Childhood*. New York: Harper & Row, 1987.

Hall, Donald. *Life Work*. Boston: Beacon Press, 1993.

Hugo, Richard. *The Real West Marginal Way*. New York: W. W. Norton, 1986.

Jackson, Shirley. *Raising Demons* in *The Magic of Shirley Jackson*. Edited by Stanley Edgar Hyman. New York: Farrar, Straus, and Giroux, 1966, 531–753.

King, Florence. *With Charity Toward None: A Fond Look at Misanthropy*. New York: St. Martin's Press, 1992.

Morris, Willie. *North Toward Home*. Boston: Houghton Mifflin, 1970.

Updike, John. *Assorted Prose*. New York: Alfred A. Knopf, 1965.

Index

Entries on ballplayers are limited to those who are subjects of major works of baseball prose or are otherwise influential to the game or to its literature.

The Author

Richard Orodenker received his M.A. from the Johns Hopkins Writing Seminars in 1976 and taught English and humanities at Peirce College in Philadelphia, Pennsylvania, from 1976 to 1992. He now teaches English and American Studies at Pennsylvania State University (Ogontz). He resides with his wife and two children in the Philadelphia suburbs.

The Editor

Frank Day is a professor of English and head of the English Department at Clemson University. He is the author of *Sir William Empson: An Annotated Bibliography* (1984) and *Arthur Koestler: A Guide to Research* (1985). He was a Fulbright lecturer in American literature in Romania (1980–81) and in Bangladesh (1986–87).